The pocket companion to

Shakespeare's Plays

J.C. Trewin

with a foreword by

John Houseman

Simon and Schuster/New York

The author

J.C. Trewin, stage historian and since 1934 a London drama critic, is a Cornishman, author of fifty books and editor of fifty, and a former literary editor of the *Observer*. He has lectured on Shakespeare (in whose stage history he has specialized), and on other theatre subjects, in Britain, Central Europe, and Canada. Holding an honorary degree from Birmingham University, he is a Fellow of the Royal Society of Literature and a former President of the Shakespeare Club of Stratford-upon-Avon.

Author's Note

Shakespeare, an actor himself, wrote his plays to be acted, and no dramatist in the history of the world has been performed more often and in more languages. Though the book's emphasis is upon the theatre, it does also, I hope, answer concisely many of the questions about Shakespeare himself, the origin and history of his work, and of the characters he created. I am most grateful to Wendy, my wife, for her watchfulness, and to Susannah Read, Ken Hewis, Halina Tunikowska and Keith Spence for their great help and care in editing.   J.C.T.

for Wendy
Love's Labour's Lost, IV.3, 340–1

Abbreviations and star ratings

★(★★) Indicates a good, very good or exceptional performance. For reasons of space and to avoid repetition, the names of the plays are not always given when characters are mentioned in the Biographies (pp 134–169). There is a list of the plays in which they appear on p. 170 and a list of abbreviations used for the plays on p. 171.

Edited and designed by
Mitchell Beazley Publishers
87–89 Shaftesbury Avenue, London W1V 7AD
© Mitchell Beazley Publishers 1981
All rights reserved, including the right of
reproduction in whole or in part in any form
Printed and bound in Hong Kong by
Mandarin Offset International Ltd.

A Fireside Book
Published by Simon and Schuster
A Division of Gulf & Western Corporation
Simon and Schuster Building
Rockefeller Center
1230 Avenue of the Americas
New York, New York 10020

Library of Congress Cataloging in
Publication Data
Trewin, John Courtenay
The Pocket Companion to Shakespeare's Plays
1. William Shakespeare
2. William Shakespeare—Life and Works
1. Title
80–5765
ISBN 0–671–42006–2

Designer Ray Smithwhite **Executive Art Editor** Douglas Wilson
Production Sarah Goodden

CONTENTS

Foreword 4

William Shakespeare: 1564–1616 5

The Plays

Henry VI, Part 1 11
Henry VI, Part 2 14
Henry VI, Part 3 16
Richard III 18
Titus Andronicus 23
The Comedy of Errors 26
The Taming of the Shrew 29
The Two Gentlemen of
  Verona 33
Love's Labour's Lost 35
King John 38
Richard II 42
Romeo and Juliet 46
A Midsummer Night's
  Dream 49
The Merchant of Venice 53
Henry IV, Part 1 57
Henry IV, Part 2 60
The Merry Wives of
  Windsor 63
Much Ado About Nothing 66
As You Like It 69

Henry V 72
Julius Caesar 75
Twelfth Night; or What You
  Will 78
Hamlet, Prince of
  Denmark 81
Troilus and Cressida 85
All's Well That Ends Well 88
Measure for Measure 90
Othello, the Moor of
  Venice 93
King Lear 97
Macbeth 100
Antony and Cleopatra 104
Timon of Athens 107
Coriolanus 109
Pericles, Prince of Tyre 112
Cymbeline 115
The Winter's Tale 118
The Tempest 121
Henry VIII 124
The Two Noble Kinsmen 126

The Poems and Sonnets 128

The Apocrypha 133

Biographies 134

Shakespeare Theatres 171

Shakespeare Festivals in the United States 179

Select Glossary of Shakespeare's English 181

Genealogical Tree of The Histories 190

Some Books 192

FOREWORD

For four years, as artistic director of the American Shakespeare Festival Theatre at Stratford, Connecticut, I watched the crowds (close to a quarter million a year, including schoolchildren) react to Shakespeare's plays as they were performed on our stage. No detailed statistics were gathered in those early days, but it was our impression that for half of our audiences this was the only live theatrical production they had seen in recent months and that, for three-quarters of them, ours was the first professional performance of a Shakespearean play they had ever attended.

Without question many of them were confused. Much of what went on on that stage – some of it in unfamiliar style and idiom – was obscure, if not downright incomprehensible. Yet, surprisingly, after the first few bewildering minutes, those audiences did not seem to be bored. And when the play was over and they walked out toward their buses or cars, they left the theater richer than when they entered. For more than two hours they had been exposed to language which, even if they understood only part of it, could not fail to impress them with its power and beauty; they had met striking (and sometimes recognizable) characters engaged in conflicts that were no less violent and relationships that were no less moving, and often just as empathic, as those they were used to seeing in their local movie theaters or on the screens of their recently acquired television sets. The comedy routines, in particular, were accessible and enjoyable.

The plain truth is that what they had seen and heard in those two hours was more dramatic, more variegated and far more imaginative than the entertainment to which they were habitually exposed: love, death, ambition, politics, romance, fights, dance, music, colorful costumes, moral judgments, poetry, and even, occasionally, philosophy – all these elements were being presented to them as part of an exciting dramatic action. And even if all this was not entirely or immediately comprehensible, I like to think that many of them went out into the world with the vaguely exhilarating sense, when the show was over, of having been brushed, ever so lightly, by genius.

Festivals have proliferated since then and productions of Shakespeare's plays are becoming part of the standard repertory in the numerous regional theaters that have become such an essential part of our cultural life. With our brief national history of violent change and our ethnic complexity, it is unlikely that Americans will ever come to share the deep sense of national heritage that the British have long felt for Shakespeare and his works. But as we become increasingly exposed to the performance of his plays, the sense of strangeness (not to mention the outright hostility engendered by so many years of inadequate teaching) is gradually disappearing – to be replaced by a real sense of theatrical kinship with the world's greatest English-speaking playwright.

This book is aimed at those who are beginning to feel this kinship. Scholars and theater professionals may feel it necessary to turn to the numerous, more or less elaborate editions of the plays. But for the rest, this Shakespearean almanac – with its general, historical information and its condensed biographical and theatrical material, should prove of substantial value.

—John Houseman

WILLIAM SHAKESPEARE
1564–1616

A brief walk through the market town of Stratford-upon-Avon in the south of Warwickshire can suggest a diagram of William Shakespeare's life. The substantial house known as the Birthplace stands in Henley Street. There, in its western end, and probably on April 23, 1564, it is presumed that William was born, the eldest son and third surviving child of John Shakespeare, a glover and dealer in various commodities such as leather and wool, and his wife Mary, who was the youngest daughter of Robert Arden of Wilmcote. Ten minutes from the Birthplace is the great modern theatre (1932) on a meadow by the Avon, where the plays of Shakespeare are now acted practically throughout the year.

Five minutes from this, and approached by an avenue of lime trees is the Collegiate Church of the Holy Trinity where the boy William was baptized (the Latin entry in the register for April 26, 1564 is *Gulielmus filius Johannes Shakspere*). Fifty-two years later, on April 25, 1616, William Shakespeare, who had died two days before, was buried within the chancel at the eastern end of the church. Here, looking down from the north wall, is the monument that was very likely placed there in 1622, a half-length, bare-headed figure carved in Cotswold limestone and set in an arched recess. There is a quill pen in Shakespeare's hand. The hair and beard are auburn; the eyes are hazel, darkened by time.

In 1564 Stratford, remote among its water-meadows, had a population of about two thousand. John Shakespeare, the son of a farmer in the hill village of Snitterfield near Stratford, became a glover and "whittawer" (dresser of white leather) and an important man in the little town. His wife was a rich farmer's daughter – Arden is an ancient name in Warwickshire – from the hamlet of Wilmcote, about three miles north-west of Stratford. They had eight children, of whom the first and second, both daughters, Joan and Margaret, died in infancy. Then William was born; we have only the christening date, but April 23 (coinciding with the festival of St George, the patron saint of England) is a plausible assumption. Of the Shakespeares' other five children, only one, a second Joan (1569–1646), who married William Hart, a Stratford hatter, survived her famous brother. The others were Gilbert (1566–1612), Anne (1571–9), Richard (1574–1613) and Edmund, the youngest (1580–1607), a "player" who was buried in the chancel of the London church of St Saviour's at Southwark.

John Shakespeare, the poet's father, had several years of prosperity. He was an alderman of Stratford in 1565, its high bailiff (or mayor) and a justice of the peace in 1568, and in 1571 an alderman again. A period of adversity followed: one of money difficulties when he incurred debts and had to sell or mortgage property, and of local troubles in Stratford when he ceased to go to council meetings and was replaced in 1586 by another alderman. But his final years were happy. In 1596, thanks possibly to his son's influence, he received a grant of a coat-of-arms as a "gentleman" from the College of Heralds, something he was entitled to anyway as a former high bailiff of Stratford. In 1601 he returned to the borough council. That autumn he died and was buried on September 8; his wife Mary died in 1623.

At his father's death William was one of the best-reputed English dramatists. As a boy he had almost certainly gone to the local grammar school, the King's New School of Stratford-upon-Avon (which as the King Edward VI Grammar School still flourishes). After this he may have been apprenticed in his father's shop. We know that in November 1582, when he was eighteen, he married Anne Hathaway, probably the eldest daughter of a farmer with a large family who lived in an impressive thatched house in Shottery, a mile west of Stratford. Then known as Hewlands Farm, it is today Anne Hathaway's Cottage. Anne (or Agnes) was seven or eight years William's senior. They had three children, a daughter Susanna (1583–1649) and twins, Hamnet (1585–96) and Judith (1585–1662).

Between 1585, when the twins were born, and 1592, when his name reappears, lie the conjectural "lost years", prodigal in legends. Dr Gareth Lloyd Evans, a consistently wise Shakespeare scholar, has replied cogently to those who ask why we know so little of Shakespeare's youth: "Why should we? No one knew he was to become famous and there was no tradition of biography. The documentation of evidence was haphazard."

During the lost years, if we are to credit every suggestion, Shakespeare might have been practically anything: soldier, sailor, lawyer's clerk, schoolmaster. It is no longer fashionable to drag into the story the Elizabethan mansion of Charlecote, four miles east of Stratford, where – so the unfounded legend goes – Shakespeare poached the deer of Sir Thomas Lucy and had to leave home because of his escapade. Maybe the most tenable surmise is that sometime after 1585 he joined one of the acting companies (conceivably Queen Elizabeth's Men) which came to Stratford at irregular intervals. If this were so, Shakespeare would have been before long at the centre of the fast-developing world of the London stage.

Groups of players had until then acted in various inn yards; but during 1576 James Burbage, a joiner turned actor, had put up the first purpose-built theatre in England (in Shoreditch, north of the Thames), which was called simply The Theatre. The Curtain, not far away, taking its name from its site, Curtain Close, was erected a year later. Then came the theatre at Newington Butts, about a mile to the south-west of London Bridge, and later, on the south bank of the Thames, such buildings – still new in Shakespeare's flowering years as a dramatist – as the Rose (1587), famous for the actor Edward Alleyn, who led the company of the Admiral's Men, the Swan (1595) and the splendid Globe, erected in 1598–9 from the timbers of James Burbage's old Theatre in Shoreditch. There were no women on Shakespeare's stage. Boys played the female parts – we gather, expertly – and actresses do not appear on record until 1660.

Shakespeare would have reached London at an exciting time. The late Elizabethan era was passionate and adventurous. Maps were expanding; seamen brought news from afar. In the summer of 1588 an English fleet scattered the invading Spanish Armada. Drama in this English renaissance had to be larger than life-size. The young Shakespeare, aspiring actor and dramatist, had before him the example of Christopher Marlowe (1564–93), poet of "brave translunary things", in whose hand the ten-syllabled unrhymed blank verse line became a remarkable instrument. Players were in full cry in the new theatres. There a wide stage, covered partly by a roof supported on pillars, jutted into the centre of an open courtyard filled with spectators and overlooked on three sides by three tiered galleries for the more opulent.

Shakespeare must have spent these years in learning his trade

and much else that would fortify him in time ahead. After the long gap, the name reappears in an attack written upon his death-bed by the gifted and dissolute Robert Greene (1558–92). In his pamphlet Greene, who was himself a dramatist, spoke of "an upstart crow, beautified with our feathers, that with his *Tygers hart wrapt in a Players hyde*, supposes he is as well able to bombast out a blanke verse as the best of you; and beeing an absolute *Johannes factotum*, is in his own conceit the onely Shake-scene in a countrey." The "tiger's heart" parodies a line in *Henry VI, Part 3 (I.4)*, "O, tiger's heart wrapp'd in a woman's hide!"

By the time of this outburst of jealousy, Shakespeare, clearly a versatile jack-of-all-trades in the theatre, had begun as a chronicle-dramatist (see Plays, p. 12); and thereafter his name was progressively prominent among London writers. They included the courtly and fashionable John Lyly (c.1554–1606); Thomas Kyd (1558–94), author of *The Spanish Tragedy* (c.1589), the period's popular "revenge" melodrama; George Peele (c.1557–96), like Lyly and Greene a "University wit", and a writer of melodious theatrical verse; Henry Chettle (c.1560–1607), painter turned dramatist; the prolific Thomas Heywood (1573–1641); and Thomas Dekker (c.1572–c.1632), another copious dramatist and author of the London apprentices' comedy, *The Shoemaker's Holiday* (1599).

Throughout the 1590s we find references to the various performances and publications of Shakespeare's plays and poems (see Poems, p. 128). He had private griefs, such as the death of his young son Hamnet at Stratford in 1596, but in his public work and reputation he was already a prominent member of the Lord Chamberlain's company, which acted at The Theatre. During 1597 he was wealthy enough to buy the big three-storeyed Stratford house called New Place, at the corner of Chapel Street and Chapel Lane, the second largest house in the town.

By 1598 Francis Meres, a parson and schoolmaster, in his book, *Palladis Tamia: Wit's Treasury*, was praising Shakespeare as a "mellifluous and honey-tongued" poet and as "the most excellent" on the stage for comedy and tragedy. "I say," he wrote, "that the Muses would speak with Shakespeare's fine filed phrase if they would speak English." In 1599 Shakespeare was named, with others in a syndicate, as a shareholder in the land where the Globe Theatre, most easterly of those on Bankside, was built. By then he had been active for some years in the company of the Lord Chamberlain's Men – as its dramatist, as a shareholder (or "housekeeper") and as an actor. Obviously he was not primarily an actor: it has been suggested that he played, among other parts, the Ghost in *Hamlet*, Adam (*As You Like It*) and Duncan (*Macbeth*).

Queen Elizabeth, who had reigned for forty-five years, died in the spring of 1603, ending the Tudor dynasty on the English throne. King James VI of Scotland succeeded her as King James I of England (the beginning of the House of Stuart), and in due time the acting company of the Lord Chamberlain's Men

> theise our servauntes Laurence ffletcher William
> Shakespeare Richard Burbage Augustyne Phillips
> John Heminges henrie Condell William Sly Robert
> Armyn Richard Cowly and the rest of their
> Assosiates ...

became the King's Men, each entitled as a Groom of the Chamber to 4½ yards of scarlet-red cloth as livery. Between then and 1616, when Shakespeare died, the company acted more than a hundred times before the King.

The period had many other valuable dramatists. Chief among

them was Benjamin (Ben) Jonson (1572–1637) who besides his major comedies, wrote humorous masques, or court entertainments. A rival of Shakespeare, he could be shrewdly sarcastic; but we owe to him the great tribute in the First Folio (pp. 9–10). Among other writers were the collaborators, John Fletcher (1579–1625) – probably Shakespeare's partner in *Henry VIII* (see p. 124) and *The Two Noble Kinsmen* (p. 127) – and Francis Beaumont (*c.*1584–1616), the most generally fashionable dramatists of their day; George Chapman (1559–1634), who could achieve a sombre power; John Marston (*c.*1575–1634), the Warwickshire man who joined Jonson and Chapman in *Eastward Ho!*; Thomas Middleton (*c.*1570–1627), remembered for an uneven tragedy, *The Changeling*; Cyril Tourneur (d. 1626), who wrote *The Revenger's Tragedy*, an extraordinary flare of the imagination; and John Webster (d. 1634), a dramatist called by a modern critic the First Gravedigger of his time. His private life is obscure, but he lives because of a pair of tragedies, *The White Devil* and *The Duchess of Malfi*, which mingle startling poetry with their vehemence.

Shakespeare, who surpassed them all, remained in London until about 1610. Through several business transactions he had kept closely in touch with Stratford (something Marlowe never did with Canterbury). In 1608 the King's Men took, not far from St Paul's Cathedral, the enclosed Blackfriars Theatre, an intimate, candle-lit place, more fashionable, sophisticated and expensive than the Globe. It had been the home of the applauded children's company – the "eyrie of children" mentioned in *Hamlet*, II.2 – that for a time rivalled the adult players and went under such names as the Children of the Chapel and Children of the Queen's Revels. From 1609 the King's Man probably used the theatre during the winter months and crossed to Bankside in the spring. In 1613 Shakespeare bought a house at Puddle Dock, near Blackfriars, doubtless as a speculation. By then he was established at Stratford, though he could have been in London when the Globe was destroyed by fire in June 1613 during a performance of *Henry VIII*; within twelve months a new theatre had risen on the site.

During his last few years all references to Shakespeare are involved with Stratford matters, local transactions. In retirement he could look back over nearly a quarter of a century of playwriting – first (see Plays, pp. 11–127), the historical chronicles and the comedies, then in the early 1600s the "dark" comedies, the supreme tragedies, the Roman plays and the ultimate romances. It was ironical that in puritan Stratford the acting companies were now banned: plays, the council insisted, were unlawful and "the sufferance of them is againste the orders heartofore made, and againste the examples of other well-goouerned citties and burrowes."

Susanna Shakespeare, William's eldest child ("witty above her sex" according to her epitaph in 1649), was married as early as June 1607 to a prosperous Stratford physician, John Hall (1575–1635); they lived in the street called Old Town and one day would profit greatly by Shakespeare's will. Judith, the second and longer-lived daughter, had a less fortunate marriage, in February 1616, to a local vintner of dubious morals, Thomas Quiney. Two months afterwards William Shakespeare died at New Place, leaving the bulk of his property to the Halls. Among the bequests in his will, which he had signed a month earlier, was one of "my second best bed" with its linen, hangings and so forth, to his wife Anne. Some have taken this as a sign of derision, but it is clear enough that it was an affectionate gift. Anne was entitled by law to the income from one-third of the estate during the rest of her

life, which she would spend at New Place with the Halls; the second-best bed was the marriage bed and would have had special associations.

We do not know from what cause Shakespeare died in late April 1616; there is an unsupported legend that he, Ben Jonson and the poet Michael Drayton had a "merry meeting" from which he contracted a fever. On his chancel-tomb in Holy Trinity Church (where he was buried on April 25) a doggerel quatrain ends with a warning to any intrusive sexton, "Curst be he that moves my bones" (there was a charnel-house hard by).

Probably in 1622 a monument was erected, the work of Gerard Johnson (anglicized name of Gheerart Janssen), a Southwark stonemason of Dutch ancestry. Opinions of the bust have always been conflicting. Thus Thomas Gainsborough, the eighteenth-century painter, said: "A silly, smiling thing." Professor Dover Wilson, the twentieth-century critic, thought of "an affluent and retired pork butcher"; but in 1963 John Masefield, then Poet Laureate, saw a man "with much vitality of mind ... an alert and sunny man, energetic and effective." Whatever we think of it, it is one of the only presumably authentic likenesses of Shakespeare, whom the gossip John Aubrey, towards the end of the seventeenth-century, described as "a handsome well-shaped man." The bust would have been approved by Anne Shakespeare and by members of the King's Men who came to Stratford in 1622, possibly to see the monument. The local council hastily forbade them to perform, but remembered at the same time that they were the King's players, with special licence "freely to use and exercise the arte and facultie of playing Comedies, Tragedies, Histories, Enterludes, Moralls, Pastorelles, stage-plaies ... and such other like." Hence a serio-comic entry in the accounts of the borough chamberlain of Stratford. It reads simply, 'To the King's Players for not playing in the Hall, 6/–.'

The other accepted likeness of Shakespeare, an awkwardly engraved portrait by young Martin Droeshout (1601–50), from an Anglo-Flemish family, appeared at the end of 1623 on the title page of a massive volume, the First Folio★ of "Mr William Shakespeare's Comedies, Histories, and Tragedies. Published according to the True Originall Copies." It was edited by two of Shakespeare's old colleagues in the King's Company, John Heminges and William Condell. The noblest memorial to their friend, it contained thirty-six plays, of which sixteen had not been published before and two only in doubtful texts. There were also better texts of some of the other plays which had appeared in Quarto editions most uneven in quality; these had been printed either honestly from manuscripts owned by the acting company (the proprietors), or surreptitiously from a mosaic of uncertain memories.

The Folio, in an edition of a thousand copies, was dedicated to the Lord Chamberlain, who was William Herbert, third Earl of Pembroke, and his younger brother, Philip, first Earl of Montgomery. Its prefatory eulogies include Ben Jonson's famous poem which in spite of some critical debate it is right to accept as an honest tribute "to the memory of my beloved, the author Mr William Shakespeare: and what he hath left us." After a long panegyric, with the phrases, "The applause! delight! the wonder of our Stage!" and "He was not of an age, but for all time", the poem ends with this apostrophe:

★A folio is a large-sized book made of sheets of paper folded only once; in a quarto each sheet, folded twice, makes eight pages (four leaves).

Sweet Swan of Avon! What a sight it were
　　To see thee in our waters yet appeare,
And make those flights upon the bankes of Thames,
　　That so did take Eliza, and our James!
But stay, I see thee in the Hemisphere
　　Advanced, and made a Constellation there!
Shine forth, thou Starre of Poets, and with rage,
　　Or influence, chide, or cheere the drooping Stage;
Which, since thy flight from hence, hath mourn'd like night,
　　And despaires day, but for thy Volumes light.

In spite of misreadings and misprints that have created so many textual problems, the Folio was a grand achievement. A Second Folio, a reprint of the first, appeared in 1632, a Third in 1663, and a second impression of this, with fresh plays added (see Apocrypha, p. 133) in 1664. The Fourth Folio, again with the spurious plays, arrived in 1685, fifteen years after William Shakespeare's direct line had become extinct with the death of his granddaughter Elizabeth (Susanna's child).

The Works have appeared in innumerable editions prepared with various degrees of scholarship. Among eighteenth-century editors alone were such men as Nicholas Rowe, Alexander Pope the poet, Lewis Theobald, Thomas Hanmer, William Warburton, Samuel Johnson the lexicographer, Edward Capell, George Steevens and Edmund Malone. Since then fresh editions have proliferated, and they continue to do so. Among the best today are Peter Alexander's complete edition in one volume (London, 1951), and – with a fresh volume for each play – the New Cambridge (1921–66), edited at first by J. Dover Wilson, with introductions by Sir Arthur Quiller-Couch, and from 1944 under Wilson's general guidance; the New Penguin (begun in 1967 and still in progress); and the New Arden (in progress since 1951). A notable American edition, complete in a single volume, is the Riverside, under G. Blakemore Evans and others (Boston, 1974).

Numerous earnest groups have sought to make a mystery of the authorship. Shakespeare, the argument runs, was a crude countryman about whose life little is known (this is demonstrably nonsensical). Therefore he could not have written plays so astonishing in range; therefore, and illogically, we should look for the author in the peerage. Indeed, the general epigraph might be W.S. Gilbert's line: "With all our faults we love our House of Peers." All the theories have been refuted in a number of books, of which R.C. Churchill's *Shakespeare and His Betters* (London, 1958) is as precise as any. For the record, principal faction-fighters have been the Baconians, who are obsessed with "cipher messages" and who support Francis Bacon, Lord Verulam (1561–1626); the Oxfordians, supporting Edward de Vere, seventeenth Earl of Oxford (1550–1604); and among eighty or so pretenders, adherents of William Stanley, Earl of Derby.

The noisy theorists forget that genius makes its own rules. Denial of Shakespeare's authorship has become a dull and complicated pastime with no kind of genius behind it, merely obstinate misguided ingenuity and a confusion of ciphers: an example of man's delight in hunting for a conspiracy where none exists. John Masefield said of Shakespeare: "Imagination, being much neglected in the modern world, is little understood." Certainly it is beyond pedantries and sophistries. Nothing has begun to diminish William Shakespeare of Stratford, the "dear son of memory, great heir of fame", of whom (fourteen years after his death) the young John Milton wrote:

　　Thou in our wonder and astonishment
　　Hast built thyself a livelong monument.

HENRY VI
PART 1
1589–90

King Henry the Sixth	*Mayor of London*
Duke of Gloucester, uncle to the King, and Lord Protector	*Woodville*, Lieutenant of the Tower
Duke of Bedford, uncle to the King, and Regent of France	*Vernon*, of the White Rose or York faction
Thomas Beaufort, Duke of Exeter, great-uncle to the King	*Basset*, of the Red Rose or Lancaster faction
Henry Beaufort, Bishop of Winchester, afterwards Cardinal, great-uncle to the King	*Charles*, Dauphin, and later King of France
	Reignier, Duke of Anjou, and titular King of Naples
John Beaufort, Earl (afterwards Duke) of Somerset	*Duke of Burgundy*
Richard Plantagenet, son of Richard, late Earl of Cambridge; afterwards Duke of York	*Duke of Alençon*
	Bastard of Orleans
	Governor of Paris
	Master Gunner of Orleans; and his Son
Earl of Suffolk	*General* of the French forces in Bordeaux
Richard Beauchamp, Earl of Warwick	*An old shepherd*, Joan's father
Earl of Salisbury	*Margaret*, daughter to Reignier
Lord Talbot, afterwards Earl of Shrewsbury	*Countess of Auvergne*
John Talbot, his son	*Joan la Pucelle*, commonly called Joan of Arc
Edmund Mortimer, Earl of March	A Lawyer, Legate, Warders of the
Sir John Fastolfe, a cowardly knight	Tower, Herald, Officers, Soldiers, Messengers, a Porter,
Sir William Lucy	English and French Attendants,
Sir William Glansdale	Watch, Servants, Fiends
Sir Thomas Gargrave	appearing to La Pucelle

Scene: England and France

Synopsis

This is a play of battles in France (where the English try vainly to hold their possessions) and of a perilous breakdown of order in England. Internal dissension, fatal to a campaign abroad, presages civil war.

At the Westminster Abbey funeral of Henry V news arrives ("Sad tidings bring I to you out of France") that the French have beaten back the English; Talbot, the valiant general, has been captured, and the Dauphin crowned. At home Gloucester (Lord Protector, the gentle young Henry VI's uncle) and Beaufort, Bishop of Winchester and later Cardinal (Henry's great-uncle), are dangerously at odds. In France Joan La Pucelle, seen here not as the saintly Joan of Arc but as a harlot and witch in league with the powers of darkness, raises the siege of Orleans. Talbot (Act II) regains the city.

In London a feud between the ambitious Richard Plantagenet, claimant to the crown, and the Earl (later Duke) of Somerset, moves to the symbolic plucking of the roses in Temple Gardens:

a white rose for Plantagenet, a red for Somerset. King Henry (Act III) makes Plantagenet Duke of York and goes to be crowned King of France in Paris. La Pucelle captures, then loses, Rouen, but wins the support of the Duke of Burgundy.

Henry, seeking to make peace among the English factions (Act IV), puts on a red rose, saying:

> I see no reason, if I wear this rose,
> That anyone should therefore be suspicious
> I more incline to Somerset than York.

Talbot dies, beleaguered with his son outside Bordeaux where no reinforcement has reached him from the quarrelling nobles. But (Act V) La Pucelle is taken prisoner before Angers, deserted by her familiar spirits, and sent to the stake. A "solemn peace" is patched up between France and England. The unscrupulous Earl of Suffolk, entranced by his captive, Margaret, beautiful daughter of Reignier, the Duke of Anjou, plans for his own benefit to have her married to the King; Henry, influenced by a "wondrous rare description", breaks a previous diplomatic betrothal and orders Suffolk to bring back Margaret as his Queen.

In performance

Probably acted at, appropriately, the Rose on Bankside, and manipulated, in many short scenes, from the history by Edward Halle, *Henry VI, Part 1* has divided scholars. Though assigned to a variety of candidates, even to a syndicate, most of it is likely to be Shakespeare's apprentice work. In general, its characters all use the same kind of serviceable blank-verse grandiloquence and good mixed invective. Highly popular in its time, this beginning of the medieval tournament had no real restoration until the twentieth century, though there had been various muddled conflations of the *Henry VI* plays in which Part 1 had little share. It did have a single performance (Covent Garden, 1738) for some unspecified "Ladies of Quality".

Curiously, Osmond Tearle chose Part 1 for revival at the old Stratford Memorial Theatre in 1889, maybe 300 years after the play was written. It was left to Frank Benson, whose Talbot was "a rugged dog of war", to stage the entire trilogy (Stratford, 1906). Robert Atkins, a Talbot among directors, did Part 1 (also with copious cuts) at the Old Vic in 1923, the First Folio tercentenary year; his enterprise had surprisingly little critical response. At last, in the early 1950s, the Birmingham Repertory under Barry Jackson, with Douglas Seale as director, presented the three plays superbly, opening with Part 2 (1951) and ending with Part 1 (1953): Jackson joined it to Shakespeare's earlier chronicles by opening with the final Chorus of *Henry V* ("Henry the Sixth, in infant bands crowned king"). The trilogy was later done in chronological order at the Old Vic in the summer of 1953, and Seale revived it in 1957.

The next adventure was *The Wars of the Roses* at Stratford (1963). Here John Barton, cutting, rearranging and vigorously adapting the text – far more than most people realized – provided a new trilogy: *Henry VI*, *Edward IV* and *Richard III*. The opening play covered Part 1 and the first half of Part 2. Barton's apt pastiche could go like this (the Duke of Bedford speaking):

> The honourable spleen which thou dost spend
> Upon the French is not one half so sharp
> As that our peers now spend on one another.

Ultimately, returning to the original text, Terry Hands directed the trilogy, practically uncut, on consecutive nights at Stratford (1977; Aldwych, London, 1978). He included the hitherto seldom-played scene (II.3), poor enough in quality, where the Countess of Auvergne – subtly acted by Yvonne Coulette – seeks to entrap Talbot.

In the United States the play had probably its first American performances during the summer of 1935, at the Pasadena Community Playhouse, where all ten histories were done consecutively under the direction of Gilmor Browne.

In other terms

The trilogy was included in Peter Dews's television sequence, *An Age of Kings*, for the BBC (1961), which spanned the histories from *Richard II* to (and including) *Richard III*.

Chief characters

Henry VI Very young, gentle, and unequal to the demands of kingship. Acted by such players as Jack May (Birmingham and Old Vic, 1953), David Warner (Stratford/Aldwych, 1963–4), and Alan Howard (Stratford/Aldwych, 1977–8).

Richard Plantagenet, Duke of York Self-centred, ambitious, and a sensualist. Emrys James** (Stratford/Aldwych, 1977–8).

Lord Talbot (later Earl of Shrewsbury). A gallant soldier betrayed. The longest part in the play. We recognise the voice of Shakespeare in Talbot's elegiac couplet over his son "Poor boy! He smiles, methinks, as who should say, 'Had Death been French, then Death had died today.'" Thomas Nashe wrote in his *Pierce Pennilesse* (1592): "How would it have joyed brave Talbot (the terror of the French) to think that after he had lain two hundred years in his tomb, he should triumph again on the stage, and have his bones new embalmed with the tears of ten thousand spectators at least (at several times) who, in the tragedian that represents his person, imagine they behold him fresh bleeding?" (An odd figure in Part 1 is Sir John Fastolfe, who flies shamefully from the battle before Rouen, and from whose "craven's leg" Talbot later tears the Garter (IV.1). The kernel of the later Falstaff is here, but Shakespeare's use of the name is an unprofitable complexity.)

Duke of Somerset There are three in the *Henry VI* trilogy. In Part 1 it is the third Earl, and later first Duke, John Beaufort; in Part 2 it is the second Duke, Edmund Beaufort, John's younger brother; and in Part 3 it is the fourth Duke, another Edmund.

Earl of Suffolk Woos Margaret for the King, and for himself. He has the play's final lines: "Margaret shall now be Queen, and rule the King;/But I will rule both her, the King and realm."

Duke of Gloucester The Lord Protector, a man free from all cunning, whose last line is ominous: "Ay, grief, I fear me, both at first and last."

Joan la Pucelle After an opening (I.2) in the heroic manner, her treatment – derived from the Elizabethan historian Raphael Holinshed – is scurrilously anti-French, the Tudor idea of Joan as a harlot and witch, aided by the powers of darkness. Even so, in her first scene (I.2) she has three of the most quoted lines. Joan's part is the second largest, 260 lines. Best performances: Nancie Jackson* (Birmingham and Old Vic, 1953); Charlotte Cornwell* (Stratford/Aldwych, 1977–8), who had a notable early moment when she recoiled prophetically at the sight of a torch held by a soldier.

Margaret A single scene (V.3) for the wilful and alluring princess who develops into the tigress-Queen, one of Shakespeare's great full-length portraits.

13

HENRY VI
PART 2
1590–1

<table>
<tr><td>King Henry the Sixth</td><td>Thomas Horner, an armourer</td></tr>
<tr><td>Humphrey, Duke of Gloucester, his
uncle, Lord Protector</td><td>Peter, Horner's man
Clerk of Chatham</td></tr>
<tr><td>Cardinal Beaufort, Bishop of
Winchester, great-uncle to the
King</td><td>Mayor of St Albans
Saunders Simpcox, an impostor
Alexander Iden, a Kentish
gentleman</td></tr>
<tr><td>Richard Plantagenet, Duke of York</td><td></td></tr>
<tr><td>Edward and Richard, his sons</td><td>Jack Cade, a rebel</td></tr>
<tr><td>Duke of Somerset</td><td>George Bevis, John Holland, Dick</td></tr>
<tr><td>Duke of Suffolk</td><td>the butcher, Smith the weaver,</td></tr>
<tr><td>Duke of Buckingham</td><td>Michael, &c., followers of Cade</td></tr>
<tr><td>Lord Clifford</td><td>Margaret, Queen to King Henry</td></tr>
<tr><td>Young Clifford, his son</td><td>Eleanor, Duchess of Gloucester</td></tr>
<tr><td>Earl of Salisbury</td><td>Margery Jourdain, a witch</td></tr>
<tr><td>Richard Neville, Earl of Warwick,
son of the Earl of Salisbury</td><td>Wife to Simpcox
Lords, Ladies, and Attendants;</td></tr>
<tr><td>Lord Scales</td><td>Petitioners, Aldermen, a Herald, a</td></tr>
<tr><td>Lord Say</td><td>Beadle, a Sheriff, a Lieutenant, a</td></tr>
<tr><td>Sir Humphrey Stafford</td><td>Shipmaster, a Master's Mate, two</td></tr>
<tr><td>William Stafford, his brother</td><td>Gentlemen (prisoners with</td></tr>
<tr><td>Sir John Stanley</td><td>Suffolk), Matthew Goffe ("is</td></tr>
<tr><td>Sir William Vaux</td><td>slain": IV.7), a Spirit raised by</td></tr>
<tr><td>Walter Whitmore, a pirate</td><td>Bolingbroke, Officers, Citizens,</td></tr>
<tr><td>John Hume and John Southwell,
two priests</td><td>Prentices, Falconers, Guards,
Soldiers, Messengers</td></tr>
<tr><td>Roger Bolingbroke, a conjuror</td><td></td></tr>
</table>

Scene: England

Synopsis

Here the main theme is York's gradual rise to power; in the middle is Jack Cade's mob-law rebellion. The Quarto of 1594 puts it all in the title: "The First Part of the Contention betwixt the two famous Houses of Yorke and Lancaster, with the death of the good Duke Humphrey: And the banishment and death of the Duke of Suffolke, and the Tragicall end of the proud Cardinall of Winchester, with the notable Rebellion of Jacke Cade: And the Duke of Yorkes first claime vnto the Crowne."

York (Act I), in the speech beginning "Anjou and Maine are given to the French", vows "when I spy advantage" to claim the crown. The peers have split into their factions. The Duchess of Gloucester, the Lord Protector's thrusting wife, attempts to learn the future from a "conjuror" and a witch and is arrested for treason. She is banished (Act II) to the Isle of Man after doing penance through London, barefoot and in a white sheet, and warning her honest husband of his enemies. The King, though believing the heavily assailed Gloucester to be honest, removes him from the Protectorship; he, too, is arrested (Act III) – York manages to implicate him in what is now the complete loss of France – and later he is murdered through the agency of Suffolk and of Cardinal Beaufort, who dies while confessing it.

York has gone to quell an Irish rising, leaving the ruffianly Jack Cade of Ashford (claiming to be John Mortimer, Richard II's heir) to begin a rebellion in and around London: this (Act IV) ends with a pardon to those who forsake Cade, and Cade's death in combat with Alexander Iden in a Kentish garden. Pirates, meanwhile, have murdered Suffolk who in spite of Margaret has been banished.

When York returns with his army (Act V) the Wars of the Roses open in earnest: Henry, Margaret, Somerset and old Clifford for Lancaster; Warwick and Salisbury for York and his sons. York, demanding the crown, wins the battle of St Albans where Clifford and Somerset are slain. "Sound drum and trumpets", cries Warwick, "and to London all;/And more such days as these to us befall!"

In performance

Henry VI, Part 2, the best of the plays, was rather more fortunate than its predecessor – not that this says much, as the adaptations and compressions were so mutilated. Edmund Kean (1817) had one of his less acclaimed nights as York in a version of the trilogy resting heavily on Part 2, entitled *Richard, Duke of York; or, The Contentions of York and Lancaster,* and obviously a frightful mess. Frank Benson did the play by itself at Stratford (1899), again in 1901, and at length – as part of the trilogy – in 1906. W.B. Yeats, writing about the so-called Stratford "Week of Kings" in 1901, called the chronicles (including Part 2) "a strange procession of kings and queens, of warring nobles, of insurgent crowds, of courtiers, and of people of the gutter."

For other major productions, see Part 1, "In Performance" (p. 12). The mingling of the second half of Part 2 with Part 3 in the Barton trilogy was labelled *Edward IV.*

Chief characters

Henry VI Mature by now but better fitted to be a monk than to rule what Hazlitt described as "the bear-garden in uproar" of his England.

Richard Plantagenet, Duke of York The longest part in the play (380 lines): "Dogged York that reaches at the moon."

Humphrey, Duke of Gloucester, fourth son of Henry IV, the dismissed Lord Protector, the King's true friend.

Earl of Salisbury York says of him after St Albans: "That winter lion, who in rage forgets/Aged contusions and all brush of time" (V.3).

Earl of Warwick Richard Neville, a great landowner known to history as "Warwick the Kingmaker'. Son of the Earl of Salisbury and husband of Anne Beauchamp, daughter of Richard Beauchamp, Earl of Warwick, to whose title he succeeded.

Duke of Suffolk A study in relentless arrogance.

Cardinal Beaufort "As stout and proud as if he were lord of all", but he has a frenzied death scene (III.3).

Jack Cade of Ashford. Brutal Kentish rebel of an attempted civil war. "There shall be in England seven halfpenny loaves sold for a penny; the three-hoop'd pot shall have ten hoops, and I will make it felony to drink small beer" (IV.2). Oscar Asche* (Stratford, 1899); James Laurenson* (Stratford/Aldwych, 1977–8).

Queen Margaret The tigress testing her claws for the years ahead. Her line, "I stood upon the hatches in the storm" (III.2), might be an epigraph for the trilogy. One of Peggy Ashcroft's*** most sustained performances (Stratford/Aldwych, 1963–4).

15

HENRY VI
PART 3

1590–1

King Henry the Sixth	Lord Hastings
Edward, Prince of Wales, his son	Lord Stafford
Louis XI, King of France	Sir John Mortimer and Sir Hugh
Duke of Somerset	Mortimer, uncles to the Duke of
Duke of Exeter	York
Earl of Oxford	Henry, Earl of Richmond, a youth
Earl of Northumberland	Lord Rivers, brother to Lady Grey
Earl of Westmoreland	Sir William Stanley
Lord Clifford	Sir John Montgomery
Richard Plantagenet, Duke of York	Sir John Somerville
Edward, Earl of March, afterwards	A Son that has killed his father
King Edward IV	A Father that has killed his son
Edmund, Earl of Rutland	Queen Margaret
George, later *Duke of Clarence*	Lady Grey, later Queen to Edward
Richard, later *Duke of Gloucester*	IV
(the four sons to Richard	Bona, sister to the French Queen
Plantagenet)	Tutor (to Rutland), Mayor of
Duke of Norfolk	York, Lieutenant of the Tower, a
Marquess of Montague	Nobleman, Two Keepers, a
Earl of Warwick	Huntsman, Soldiers, Attendants,
Earl of Pembroke	Messengers, Watchmen, etc.

Scene: England and, briefly, France

Synopsis

Early in this masque of kings, Henry makes York his heir if he himself is allowed to reign undisturbed during his life, a hopeless provision. Queen Margaret, aided by young Lord Clifford, continues to fight on behalf of her son, Edward, Prince of Wales. At the Battle of Wakefield, Clifford kills York's youngest son, Rutland; York himself is taken prisoner, humiliated and stabbed to death by Clifford and the devilishly mocking Margaret. Avenging him, his three other sons defeat the Lancastrians at Towton (Act III) where Clifford dies. King Henry, away from the battle and soliloquizing about the peace of country life as a shepherd ("O God, methinks it were a happy life/To be no better than a homely swain"), listens to the terrors of civil war symbolized in the laments of a son who has killed his father and a father who has killed his son (II.5).

The King escapes to the North; Edward, having ennobled his brothers as the Dukes of Clarence and Gloucester, makes for London and the crown. Henry is captured (Act III) and sent to the Tower; Warwick, angered by Edward's decision to marry Lady Grey, joins Margaret, and (Act IV) releases and reinstates Henry and captures Edward. Promptly Edward escapes in his turn and Henry is sent back to imprisonment. Ultimately (Act V), Warwick is defeated and killed at Barnet; and Margaret, who has brought reinforcements from France ("Great lords, wise men ne'er sit and wail their loss"") is taken at Tewkesbury, where York's sons stab the Prince of Wales to death. Richard, on his sanguinary way to the throne, kills Henry in the Tower ("He's sudden if a thing comes in his head," says Edward). Margaret is banished to France, and Edward IV has the last words.

In performance

This is the whole fury of civil war, a record of revenge. Part 3 (see "In performance", p. 12) has had full recognition only in the present century; the productions have shown how unwise it is to toss a play into the discard because it may not flash in the study. The Irish dramatist, Sean O'Casey, described the trilogy in his memoirs: "Battles, castles, and marching armies; kings, queens, knights and esquires in robes today and in armour tomorrow, shouting their soldiers to the attack, or saying a last lone word before poor life gave out; of mighty men of valour joining this king and ravaging that one; of a king gaining a crown and a king losing it; of kings and knights rushing on their foes and of kings and captains flying from them."

"Here, I hope, begins our lasting joy" are Edward's last words. As they ceased in the Birmingham Repertory production of 1952, the sardonic Richard of Gloucester swept into the first soliloquy of *Richard III*, "Now is the winter of our discontent/Made glorious summer by this sun of York." He had spoken barely half a dozen lines when the offstage noises of bells and cheering blurred his words, the lights dimmed and upon darkness the curtain fell.

The child Henry, Earl of Richmond, who appears for a moment (IV.6) in a non-speaking part, is the future Henry VII who will conquer Richard at Bosworth Field.

Chief characters

Henry VI A wise man in the wrong place. Harried across his realm during the alarums of the war, he is finally killed by Richard in the Tower ("O, God forgive my sins and pardon thee!"). Alone on the molehill by the field of Towton (II.5) he has his wistful speech of longing for a shepherd's life. Major performances: Jack May** (Birmingham, 1952; Old Vic, 1953); David Warner* (Stratford/Aldwych, 1963–4); Alan Howard** (Stratford/Aldwych, 1977–8).

Richard, Duke of York Captured at last at Wakefield and stabbed to death after being reviled by Margaret, who gives him a cloth dipped in his young son's blood. Donald Sinden** (Stratford/Aldwych, 1963–4); Emrys James** (Stratford/Aldwych, 1977–8).

Edward IV, York's eldest son, the former Earl of March. "The wanton Edward", says Margaret (I.4).

Richard, York's son, who becomes Duke of Gloucester and will soon be King Richard III. A hunchback with a withered arm, who declares himself in III.2:

> I can add colours to the chameleon,
> Change shapes with Protheus for advantages,
> And set the murderous Machiavel to school.

Earl of Warwick Margaret calls him "proud setter up and puller down of kings" (III.3). The longest part, 443 lines. Julian Glover** (Stratford/Aldwych, 1977–8).

Lord Clifford The "Young Clifford" of Part 2. He kills York's son, Rutland (I.3), "Thy father slew my father; therefore, die"; mocks and stabs the helpless York, crowned by Margaret with paper (I.4); and dies at Towton (II.6), "Here burns my candle out; ay, here it dies,/Which, whiles it lasted, gave King Henry light".

Queen Margaret The brave but pitiless woman for whom York, in his extremity (I.4), cannot find curses enough. "She-wolf of France, but worse than wolves of France", he cries to her. And again: "O tiger's heart wrapp'd in a woman's hide", a phrase that the dramatist Robert Greene, who attacked Shakespeare (1592) in a work written on his death-bed, parodied as "Tiger's heart wrapt in a Player's hide". Finest performance of Margaret: Peggy Ashcroft*** (Stratford/Aldwych, 1963–4).

RICHARD III

1592–3

King Edward the Fourth	*Sir Richard Ratcliff*
Edward, Prince of Wales, son to the King, afterwards King Edward V	*Sir William Catesby*
	Sir James Tyrrel
	Sir James Blount
Richard, Duke of York, son to the King	*Sir Walter Herbert*
	Sir Robert Brakenbury, Lieutenant of the Tower
George, Duke of Clarence, brother to the King	*Sir William Brandon*
Richard, Duke of Gloucester, afterwards King Richard III, brother to the King	*Christopher Urswick*, a priest
	Lord Mayor of London
	Sheriff of Wiltshire
A young son of Clarence (Edward, Earl of Warwick)	*Hastings*, a pursuivant
	Tressel and *Berkeley*, gentlemen attending on Lady Anne
Henry, Earl of Richmond, afterwards King Henry VII	*Elizabeth*, Queen to King Edward IV
Cardinal Bourchier, Archbishop of Canterbury	*Margaret*, widow of King Henry VI
Thomas Rotherham, Archbishop of York	*Duchess of York*, mother to King Edward IV, Clarence and Gloucester
John Morton, Bishop of Ely	
Duke of Buckingham	*Lady Anne*, widow of Edward, Prince of Wales (son to King Henry VI), afterwards married to Duke of Gloucester
Duke of Norfolk	
Earl of Surrey, his son	
Anthony Woodville, Earl Rivers, brother to King Edward's Queen Elizabeth	*A young daughter of Clarence* (Margaret Plantagenet, Countess of Salisbury)
Marquis of Dorset and *Lord Grey*, the Queen's sons	
Earl of Oxford	Ghosts of Richard's victims;
William, Lord Hastings	Lords, Gentlemen, and
Lord Stanley, called also Earl of Derby	Attendants; Priest, Scrivener, Page, Bishops, Aldermen,
Lord Lovel	Citizens, Soldiers, Messengers,
Sir Thomas Vaughan	Murderers, Keeper

Scene: England

Synopsis

The First Quarto (1597) summarizes the play: "The Tragedy of King Richard the Third, Containing, His treacherous Plots against his brother Clarence: the pittifull murther of his innocent nephewes: his tyrannical usurpation: with the whole course of his detested life, and most deserved death."

Shakespeare has no more dramatic opening than the entry, in a London street, of "Richard Duke of Gloucester, *solus*". Today an optimistic society exists to clear his name, to explain that historians (especially Sir Thomas More in a section of Halle's chronicle) vilified him in the Tudor cause. Still, little can soften the impact of Shakespeare's blazing melodrama – which in effect it is – and that first scene when Richard limps downstage to reveal himself in a soliloquy that begins, "Now is the winter of our discontent/Made glorious summer by this sun of York", and goes on to an unflinching resolve, "I am determined to prove a villain/And hate the idle pleasures of these days." Richard has to dispose of six people who stand between him and the throne when his dying brother, Edward IV, has gone. When he takes the crown, he has removed only one of them: the others he will deal with later.

First, the dissimulation with his elder brother, the Duke of Clarence. By playing on Edward's fears he has Clarence sent to the Tower. Having seen this done and affected great concern ("I will deliver you"), he meets the bearers of the coffin of Henry VI (the King he murdered), followed by Henry's daughter-in-law, Lady Anne, whose husband he and his brothers had killed at Tewkesbury. Out of mischief or masochism, or both, he woos her over the coffin and she yields (I.2). Richard gloats:

> Was ever woman in this humour woo'd?
> Was ever woman in this humour won?
> I'll have her; but I will not keep her long.

Next, he stirs trouble at court while the former Queen Margaret – who, unhistorically, still prowls about – releases some of her fiercest invective: "Thou elvish-mark'd, abortive, rooting hog", "That bottled spider", "This poisonous hunchback'd toad." Clarence, by Richard's order (and despite a royal pardon), is murdered in the Tower and his corpse pushed into a butt of malmsey (sweet wine).

Overwhelmed by Clarence's death, King Edward dies (Act II); the young Prince of Wales is to be brought from Ludlow. By then Richard and his associates, notably Buckingham, have begun to direct affairs as they wish. When the Prince arrives (Act III) he and his younger brother, the Duke of York, are "lodged" in the Tower, presumably until the coronation. Various men of the Queen's party, dangerous to Richard, are executed, among them at a few minutes' notice the rash Lord Hastings. Buckingham, primed, gets the Lord Mayor and citizens of London to urge an apparently unwilling Richard to accept the throne. Once crowned (Act IV), Richard does all he can to safeguard himself, such as inciting Tyrrel to procure the death of the Princes in the Tower; forsaking his wife whose end is merely suggested ("Anne, my wife, hath bid this world good night"); and proposing, though this does not take place, to wed his niece, Edward IV's daughter Elizabeth. Buckingham revolts against him, raising an army; Henry, Earl of Richmond, lands from France. Richard, environed by enemies, must fight to keep the throne.

He goes to battle (Act V) when he meets the invader at Bosworth Field near Leicester. Buckingham has been captured and executed; but Richmond is the first danger. After a night during which Richmond has fair dreams and Richard is harassed by the ghosts of his victims – conscience is a dominant theme in the play – he fights desperately ("A horse! A horse! My kingdom for a horse!") only to be defeated and killed. All ends with Richmond's decision to marry Elizabeth: "We will unite the white rose and the red,/Smile heaven upon this fair conjunction."

In performance

Where *Henry VI* has too little stage history, *Richard III*, completing the tetralogy, and a tremendous advance on its forerunners, has almost too much. Since Burbage created Richard in Shakespeare's lifetime, hundreds of actors have been in thrall to one of the most theatrical parts ever written. True, too often these men would offer the mask without the mind, a grotesque strutting Crookback snatched from a child's history book. Shakespeare's *Richard III* may move to melodrama incarnadined; but its blood is the blood royal. The Red King is not simply an animated oleograph.

Curiously, for over a century and a half from 1700 the approved acting version was not Shakespeare's but a mosaic devised by the actor-dramatist Colley Cibber for production at Drury Lane. He was not much good himself; indeed, his performance was remembered, critically, as "the distorted Heavings of an unjointed Caterpillar". His text lived on; even in our period, a few traces of Cibber survive, e.g. in the Olivier film (1955). He wrote himself into the records with his notorious accretions – such a "claptrap" as "Off with his head! – so much for Buckingham!" An astute, coarse melodramatist, his composite version, with scraps from other histories and a great many additions of his own, could hold a theatre, though a few purists regretted the loss of (for example) Margaret and the wailing women, Clarence and his dream, and Stanley.

Among English Richards, David Garrick (from 1741, date of his anonymous London début at Goodman's Fields) was always a Cibber man: something to be remembered when we see the Hogarth picture of Richard waking after the phantoms ("Despair and die!") have encircled him on the night before Bosworth. Garrick was splendidly relaxed, sardonic and menacing: "He dwindles neither into the buffoon nor the brute", wrote a contemporary. The powerful George Frederick Cooke (Covent Garden, 1800) displeased Charles Lamb, who spoke of him in a letter: "The lofty imagery and high sentiments and high passions of *Poetry* come black and prose-smoked from his prose Lips."

John Philip Kemble's main performances (1783, 1811) had a far more refined villainy, and that "little, keenly-visaged man", Edmund Kean (Drury Lane, 1814) a *diablerie* that terrified. Hazlitt, to whom we owe so much of what we know of Kean as an artist – it has been said, cynically perhaps, that the critic invented the actor – reported the final combat in which Kean "fought like one drunk with wounds". William Charles Macready, who played the Cibber version at Covent Garden (1819) with a sharp theatrical intelligence and unexpected lightness, came nearer to Shakespeare in 1821 with a text that contained not more than two hundred Cibber lines; the production failed. Though he often acted Richard later, Macready was unhappy about it. (A frequently unnoticed line in his journal, December 23, 1838, when managing Covent Garden, reads: "Looked through the unused plays of Shakespeare for *cementing* lines for Richard III.") Samuel Phelps, restoring the original text at Sadler's Wells (1845) – he would later go back to Cibber – was "careful and judicious". Charles Kean, equally careful, and anxiously spectacular, had no luck with Cibber (Princess's, 1854), though he called the text more "striking and spirit-stirring" than Shakespeare's. At the Lyceum (1877) Henry Irving reverted to Shakespeare, very badly cut; in his short-lived revival, 1896, he played (said Henry James) "on the chord dominant of the sinister-sardonic, flowered over ... be with the elegant-grotesque".

Among many twentieth-century English actors (John Martin Harvey, for one) three would dominate, though Robert Atkins, during various Vic seasons (first in 1915; others in 1921 and 1923 when he was directing), had what James Agate called a "quiet ferocity": he diminished the man by acting him as an upstart instead of a princely usurper. A finer portrait was Baliol Holloway's pictorial, grimly royal devil (Old Vic, 1925; New, 1930). Donald Wolfit (Strand, 1941) offered a study in scarlet, never entirely melodrama, though he could verge on it.

The unexampled performance was Laurence Olivier's for the Old Vic company at the New Theatre (September, 1944), one of the major classical occasions of the century. Outwardly a limping panther, there was no lameness in his mind. Pale, lankly black-haired, evilly debonair, he preserved Richard's pride; he had a glittering irony, a frightening rage. History records the sharp-thrust, outflung gesture at "Set the murderous Machiavel to school", one of the lines (*Henry VI, Part 3*, III.2) inserted in the first soliloquy of the Old Vic text, the imperatively regal gesture to Buckingham in the very birth of majesty, the malice of the "giving vein", the swoop back to the throne at "Is the chair empty?", the strangled sobbing at "There is no creature loves me" and the doom in the distorted face on the lost field at Bosworth. Shaw had said (1896), when criticizing Irving: "The attempt to make a stage combat look as imposing as Hazlitt's description of the death of Edmund Kean reads, is hopeless. If Kean were to return to life and do the combat for us, we should very likely find it as absurd as his habit of lying down on a sofa when too tired or too drunk to keep his feet during the final scenes." But when he wrote this Shaw was nearly half a century too soon for Olivier's combat at the New in 1944.

Some other English actors: Emlyn Williams (Old Vic, 1937); Marius Goring (Stratford, 1953); Robert Helpmann (Old Vic, 1957); Paul Daneman (Old Vic, 1962); Ian Holm (*The Wars of the Roses*, Stratford/Aldwych, 1963–4), a not particularly demonic Richard playing the "power game"; Alan Badel (St George's, Islington, 1976); John Wood (National, 1979).

America, too, where Cibber was long popular, has had several eminent Richards. Edwin Booth, son of the English-born Junius Brutus Booth (whose Richard in London and New York had been roughly vigorous), made his name with a subtly potent performance (1852); acted in London (1861); developed his Richard more broadly over the years; and restored Shakespeare's text to New York (1876). As late as 1889 (in London; later in the United States) the American tragedian, Richard Mansfield, was remembering Cibber, beginning in *Henry VI, Part 3* and omitting Margaret: the portrait had a closely graduated malignancy shadowed by rising fear.

Robert Mantell (1904) kept to Cibber; John Barrymore (1920), using the Mansfield text, was a man spiritually warped, but of searching intellect; Walter Hampden (1934) retained "Off with his head! – So much for Buckingham!" and Hume Cronyn (Minneapolis, 1965) gave an almost "black-comedy" treatment for Tyrone Guthrie. Twelve years earlier, also for Guthrie, Alec Guinness – at the opening festival in Stratford, Ontario – was a dagger in the heart from his first appearance.

In other terms

Laurence Olivier's film performance (1955), dominating though it was in a production with a steady insistence on betrayal, could not match his Richard in the theatre. Margaret had been cut, but a silent personage, not in Shakespeare's cast list, was Jane Shore, Edward IV's mistress, whom the extrovert Hastings annexes. John Burrell had her on stage – "decorative but dumb" said *Punch* – in his production for Olivier (1944), and Pamela Brown played her in the film. Jane Shore has arrived on other occasions, notably Stratford (1970).

Chief characters

Richard, Duke of Gloucester (King Richard III). Misshapen in body as in mind, but facially handsome and sinister. After Hamlet, the longest part in Shakespeare (1,164 lines). Played by Garrick*** and Edmund Kean*** and – definitively in our period – by Laurence Olivier*** (1944). Also memorable: Baliol Holloway*** (1925, 1930).

Duke of Buckingham "The deep-revolving, witty Buckingham" (IV.2) who helps Richard to the throne, who is warned by the malice of the "giving vein" speech, and who is captured and executed just too early for his revenge. The second-longest part: 361 lines.

George, Duke of Clarence Cut from the Cibber text. Valued for his narrative of the dream in the Tower when the dead Prince of Wales – this is a haunted play – cries to him: "Clarence is come – false, fleeting, perjur'd Clarence,/That stabb'd me in the field by Tewkesbury." John Gielgud spoke this grandly in the Olivier film**. Others: Alec Clunes* when a young man at the Old Vic (1936), and Robert Eddison** (Old Vic, 1962).

William, Lord Hastings Incautious extrovert Lord Chamberlain, whose support of Edward's "heirs in true descent" leads to his sudden death.

Sir James Tyrrel The "discontented gentleman" who obtains the murder of the Princes. He speaks the soliloquy (IV.3), quoting one of the murderers who described the children as they lay in each other's arms: "Their lips were four red roses on a stalk,/Which in their summer beauty kiss'd each other." In Richard Mansfield's revival there was a suggestion that after reporting to Richard, Tyrrel had been murdered: a commotion (off) and a horrified, smothered cry.

Henry, Earl of Richmond (afterwards King Henry VII). Richmond fulfills Henry's prophecy in *Henry VI, Part 3*, IV.6; he is the Tudor equivalent of St George destroying the dragon. In the Old Vic/New Theatre programme for the Olivier first night, a collector's piece now, Richmond was described, remarkably, as "later King Edward VII". A Young Vic theatre-in-the-round production (1978), unable to face the fighting at Bosworth, ended with Richmond cutting implausibly into a boar's head.

Queen Margaret "Foul, wrinkled witch" (Richard, I.3); "Remember, Margaret was a prophetess" (Buckingham, V.1). Still at court, she acts as a dark chorus, especially in I.3 and IV.4 ("Here in these confines slily have I lurk'd/To watch the waning of mine enemies"). Cut from the Cibber version. Acted by Genevieve Ward in many productions, by Sybil Thorndike (e.g. at the New, 1944), Edith Evans (e.g. Stratford, 1961), and, above all, Peggy Ashcroft*** (Stratford/Aldwych, 1963–4).

Lady Anne Daughter-in-law of Henry VI; married to Richard after the wooing over the coffin (I.2). She vanishes from the play after she has been crowned Queen, though her end is mentioned meaningly and there is a salient passage (IV.2) when Richard says to Catesby: "Give out/That Anne, my Queen, is sick and like to die." In one postwar production by the Oxford University Dramatic Society Richard said this in Anne's hearing. Sarah

Siddons played Anne (1776) during her luckless first season in London, Garrick's farewell to Drury Lane. "As to most of the other characters," commented the *London Magazine*, "particularly the female ones, they were wretchedly played . . . Mrs Siddons a lamentable Lady Anne."

Ghosts In his tortured dream on the night before Bosworth they urge Richard to "despair and die" and Richmond, in his quiet sleep, to "live and flourish".

TITUS ANDRONICUS

1593–4

Saturninus, son to the late Emperor of Rome, afterwards Emperor	kinsmen to Titus
	Æmilius, a noble Roman
	Alarbus, Demetrius, Chiron, sons to Tamora
Bassianus, his brother	
Titus Andronicus, a noble Roman	*Aaron*, a Moor beloved of Tamora
Lucius, Quintus, Martius and *Mutius*, sons to Titus	*Tamora*, Queen of the Goths
	Lavinia, daughter to Titus Andronicus
Marcus Andronicus, Tribune of the people and brother to Titus	A Nurse, a Black Child, a Captain, a Messenger, a Clown (simple peasant), Romans, Goths, Senators, Tribunes, Officers, Soldiers, Attendants
Young Lucius, a boy, son to Lucius	
Publius, son to Marcus Andronicus	
Sempronius, Caius, Valentine,	

Scene: Rome and the neighbourhood

Synopsis

Two sons of the late Roman Emperor, Saturninus (the elder) and Bassianus, strive to succeed him, but Titus Andronicus, veteran general triumphant against the Goths, is chosen. He has just returned with his prisoners: Tamora, Queen of the Goths, her sons, and Aaron, her Moorish paramour. Heedless of entreaty, Titus orders her eldest son, Alarbus, to be sacrificed to appease the spirits of his own dead sons. He refuses the crown, urging the choice of Saturninus, to whom he gives his daughter Lavinia and yields his Gothic prisoners. Bassianus, secretly pledged to Lavinia, runs off with her; Saturninus, to curb the influence of Titus, announces that he will marry Tamora, who tells him to remain silent while she plans revenge upon the Andronici.

In a rush of events (Act II), Tamora's sons, Demetrius and Chiron, kill Bassianus during a hunt in the forest. They rape Lavinia, cut off her hands and cut out her tongue. Meanwhile, Aaron manages to implicate the sons of Titus in the murder of Bassianus. They are sentenced to death (Act III), and another son, Lucius, is banished. Titus, already overcome by the plight of Lavinia, is tricked into losing his hand as fruitless ransom for his sons.

While Lucius is raising a revenging army among the Goths, the mutilated Lavinia (Act IV), by the manipulation of a staff in the sand, accuses Chiron and Demetrius. Titus behaves like a madman ("Is not this a heavy case?" asks Marcus), despatching messages to the gods to redress his wrongs.

Tamora has had a black child by Aaron, who removes it for safety; captured by the Gothic army on its way, under Lucius, to attack Rome, he tells the whole story (Act V). Tamora, seeking to persuade Titus – whom she regards merely as crazed – to recall Lucius, has come to him dressed as Revenge, with her two sons as Murder and Rape. Having promised to invite "the Empress and her sons" and Saturninus, with Lucius, to a feast, Titus – who has seen through the charade – later kills Chiron and Demetrius and at the banquet serves their flesh baked in a pie. The end is a frenzy in which Lavinia, Tamora, Titus and Saturninus all die. Lucius becomes Emperor and after sentencing Aaron to be buried breast-deep and starved to death, resolves – not too soon – "to order well the state."

In performance

When, after an interval of at least two centuries, London's Royal Court Theatre (1979) revived a Restoration farce by Edward Ravenscroft, *The London Cuckolds*, no one remarked on another part of Ravenscroft's record. A barrister-dramatist, competent in the cuckoldry-based jests of the period's uninhibited theatre, he succumbed to the prevailing vice of adapting Shakespeare. The play he chose (acted in 1678) was one of the least-regarded, the tragedy of *Titus Andronicus*, which he claimed to have constructed from "rather a heap of Rubbish than a Structure".

We shall get back to him. Shakespeare's melodrama was much admired in its day, though in 1614 Ben Jonson, who could not endure potboilers, observed that anyone who swore *Jeronimo* (*The Spanish Tragedy*) or *Andronicus* were the best plays yet, must be a man "whose judgement has stood still these five and twenty, or thirty, years". *Titus Andronicus* may have been suggested by the Roman Seneca's *Thyestes* and *Troades*, Ovid's *Metamorphoses*, and a chapbook (discovered in 1936) of which only an eighteenth-century version exists. For a long time scholars, who have disagreed about dates and details, refused to think that Shakespeare could have written so horrific a play, an exercise in the sensational (more than a dozen violent deaths) that resembled the Senecan "tragedies of blood". Today there is little reason to believe that the drama is not Shakespeare's own – though George Peele, especially for Act I, has his supporters.

The play is to be acted rather than read. Even so, various secondary productions have failed to burnish a text that at Stratford (1955) needed the combined gifts of Peter Brook (director) and Laurence Oliver. A great actor is an alchemist; few – Betterton during the Restoration could have been one – have yet attempted Titus. Ravenscroft's version, which until its last frightful scene did not deviate as much from Shakespeare as the adaptor promised, was done now and then during the first quarter of the eighteenth century (James Quin often an applauded Aaron). Afterwards, silence until a Negro actor, Ira Aldridge, "the African Roscius", appeared in 1852 and 1857 at the Britannia Theatre, Hoxton, a flaring old melodrama house in East London. In what was mainly Aldridge's own highly emasculated text, Aaron – reasonably in the circumstances – became "a noble and lofty character." Certainly Aldridge did not use Ravenscroft's ferocious climax where the Moor is racked; the heads and hands of Tamora's sons hang on the wall and their bodies are "in chairs in bloody linen"; Tamora stabs her black child ("Give me the child, I'll eat it," cries Aaron); Saturninus, not unexpectedly, expires in horror; and Aaron is put to death onstage by racking and burning.

Shakespeare's text, directed by Robert Atkins, returned in 1923 (Old Vic; tercentenary of the First Folio) with such expert players as Wilfrid Walter, George Hayes, Ion Swinley and Florence Saunders: a gallant experiment remembered for Hayes as Aaron, his diabolism and the sudden moment of tenderness for his infant son. He and Walter had the same parts on BBC radio (1953), a period when – though there had been earlier stirrings – everything for *Titus Andronicus* began to happen at once. That year there was a Marlowe Society revival at Cambridge, one that tried to show how humanity and retribution balanced sadism and terror; and in the summer of 1955, on the Stratford stage at last, the play grandly re-entered the professional repertory. Peter Brook had organized the text, and its final succession of murders (V.3), so that his company could let drive without being deflected by derisive laughter. The grimness remained: at the same time Brook imposed a formalized dignity on these strong, uncomplicated emotions. With Olivier we found ourselves in the upper air of heroic acting; just as Lear was identified with the storm in his mind, Titus was identified with the sea, his constant image: "I *am* the sea; look, how her sighs do flow." The actor reached a meridian none could have divined from the printed word. Brook's *musique concrète* intensified the atmosphere in this "wilderness of tigers". His production, which toured Europe during 1957 – *"un spectacle stupéfiant"* they called it in Paris – was revived that year in the vast cavern of the now vanished Stoll Theatre, London.

No further attempt approached this, though we recognized the power of Barbara Jefford's Tamora (Old Vic, 1957); Derek Jacobi was a consistent Aaron (Birmingham Repertory, 1963); and John Wood's vicious Saturninus fortified a Stratford/Aldwych revival, 1972/3. A misguided effort to perform the tragedy on a staircase-set (Round House, London, 1971) had an inadequate cast.

Titus Andronicus is in peril of being as over-praised as it was once scorned. It was never much more than a roughly effective neo-Senecan melodrama; but after great acting and direction had transformed it, we had the customary follow-my-leader reaction.

In the United States a version by N.H. Bannister (1839), "altered into a beautiful play" said a local critic, ran four nights in Philadelphia. Joseph Papp presented *Titus Andronicus* for the New York Shakespeare Festival (1967).

In other terms

The only picture we have of an Elizabethan play in its own setting is in a manuscript at Longleat, Wiltshire, home of the Marquess of Bath. It is a pen-and-ink drawing of Tamora apparently pleading before Titus; the chief characters are in Roman dress, the minor ones in contemporary Elizabethan costume.

Chief characters

Titus Andronicus Laurence Olivier*** (Stratford, 1955; Stoll Theatre, London, 1957) turned the "sea" speech (III.1) into a great moment of the modern repertory. Elsewhere there are fine phrases among the fustian: "What fool hath added water to the sea,/Or brought a faggot to bright-burning Troy?" (III.1), and "The angry northern wind/Will blow these sands like Sibyl's leaves abroad" (IV.1). The longest part: 715 lines.

Saturninus An almost Neronic voluptuary. John Wood** (Stratford/Aldwych, 1972–3).

Marcus Andronicus The play is full of classical allusion. No doubt the Elizabethans, who did not think it odd to watch bear-baiting on the South Bank while lute music drifted over the Thames, would have seen nothing strange when Lavinia's uncle addressed the lopped and ravished girl in a stream of classical conceits instead of hurrying a surgeon to her. His long speech (II.4) includes the sometimes omitted lines:

> O, had the monster seen those lily hands
> Tremble like aspen leaves upon a lute
> And make the silken strings delight to kiss them,
> He would not then have touch'd them for his life.

Tamora The evil queen and empress, whom Aaron calls "this goddess, this Semiramis, this nymph", has one unexpectedly evocative speech in the forest, "The birds chant melody on every bush" (II.3). She is an involuntary cannibal in the final Thyestean feast. (*Thyestes* is a tragedy by Seneca where a father is deceived into eating his own sons.)

Aaron Tamora's Moorish lover ("your swarth Cimmerian") is a full-scale villain, with a passage of true affection for his black child. He puts the play in a few lines (V.1):

> For I must talk of murders, rapes, and massacres,
> Acts of black night, abominable deeds,
> Complots of mischief, treason, villainies,
> Ruthful to hear, yet piteously performed.

He could be a forerunner of Iago: "If one good deed in all my life I did, /I do repent it from my very soul" (V.3). George Hayes*** (Old Vic, 1923); Anthony Quayle*** (Stratford, 1955).

Lavinia Brook merely hinted at her mutilation. Thus she appeared (II.4) holding up her arms from which long ribbons of brilliant red velvet fell and wavered. Earlier (II.3) she speaks an exquisite detached line when pleading with Tamora: "Poor I was slain when Bassianus died." Vivien Leigh* (Stratford, 1955).

THE COMEDY OF ERRORS

Before 1594

Solinus, Duke of Ephesus	*Second Merchant*, to whom Angelo is a debtor
Aegeon, a merchant of Syracuse	
Antipholus of Ephesus, *Antipholus of Syracuse*, twin brothers, sons of Aegeon and Aemilia	*Pinch*, a schoolmaster
	Aemilia, wife to Aegeon, and Abbess at Ephesus
Dromio of Ephesus, *Dromio of Syracuse*, twin brothers and attendants on the Antipholus twins	*Adriana*, wife to Antipholus of Ephesus
	Luciana, her sister
	Luce, kitchenmaid to Adriana (also called Nell)
Balthazar, a merchant	*A Courtesan*
Angelo, a goldsmith	Gaoler, Officers, Headsman, Attendants
First Merchant, friend to Antipholus of Syracuse	

Scene: Ephesus

Synopsis

Aegeon, a veteran merchant of Syracuse, is in distress in Ephesus, his town's implacable enemy. Any Syracusian seen in Ephesus will be executed unless he can pay a ransom of a thousand marks. Aegeon's goods, at the highest rate, cannot reach a hundred marks. Then why has he risked the penalty? He explains to the Duke (sympathetic, but unable to break the law), that long before, at Epidamnum, where he had gone on business, his wife had borne him "two goodly sons,/And, which was strange, the one so like the other/As could not be distinguished but by names." Strangely, at that same hour and in the same inn, a peasant woman had given birth to indistinguishable twins whom Aegeon had bought so that they could attend as slaves upon his sons. But on the way home their vessel was shipwrecked; he was separated from his wife, one of his twins and one of the peasant boys, and heard no more of them. When the other twins were eighteen they asked to go in search of their lost brothers. They did not return, and Aegeon, alone, had spent five years looking for them, coming at last to Ephesus and his apparent fate unless, at the day's end, he could make up the ransom.

The second scene introduces the wanderers who happen to have arrived, unknown to him, at the same time as Aegeon. Very soon, Antipholus and Dromio of Syracuse are involved in a furious sequence of misunderstandings and false identifications with Antipholus and Dromio of Ephesus. (Oddly, four people but only two names.) Throughout the piece – which observes the unities of action, time and place – A is always being mistaken for B and C for D. Shakespeare keeps it up with fantastic ingenuity until (in Act V.1) when the plot seems impossible to disentangle, an abbess emerges from the priory in mid-Ephesus and observes:

> Speak, old Aegeon, if thou be'st the man
> That hadst a wife once called Aemilia,
> That bore thee at a burden two fair sons.
> O, if thou be'st the same Aegeon, speak,
> And speak unto the same Aemilia.

Within a short scene everything is more or less explained; and the Abbess invites the Duke, who has become progressively baffled, "To go with us into the abbey here,/And hear at large discoursed all our fortunes."

In performance

This, like "the flashing across and to-and-fro of dragonflies", is both the shortest of the plays (1,777 lines) and the most crowded. "In literature, as in life," the scholar Arthur Quiller-Couch said once, "he makes himself felt who not only calls a spade a spade, but has the pluck to double spades and re-double." Shakespeare, a daring technician already, had pluck enough when, earlier than 1594, though we cannot be exact, he wrote *The Comedy of Errors*, taking much of his plot from the *Menæchmi* by the Roman dramatist Plautus and a little from the *Amphitruo*. To complicate things he doubled slaves as well as masters. The play is necessarily farcical in plot, but it should not be underrated in the scamped and scurrying treatment it has often had. Few audiences will be patient enough to look beneath the surface; in performance, alas, *The Comedy of Errors* is always likely to be a director's punch-ball.

The earliest recorded production is one during a Christmas revel, a night of chaos at Gray's Inn on December 28, 1594; still, the play could have been written long before. It is set in Ephesus because the city was deemed to be the home of sorcerers and cheaters ("This town is full of cozenage", I.2); because it was the centre of the cult of Diana, goddess of childbirth; and because

27

(some propose, though this is arguable) it is relevant to remember Paul in the *Epistle to the Ephesians*: "Wives, submit yourselves unto your own husbands, as to the Lord." (Shakespeare would later have something to add to this in *The Taming of the Shrew*.)

Though there are certain lyrical passages (e.g. III.2), the play in the theatre has to exist first on its tangled skein, its cross-questions and crooked answers, which few directors have bothered to explore seriously. Indeed, not many have made even such a unity of the piece as Komisarjevsky did during an otherwise poor season at Stratford in 1938. His method was broad enough, operatic and balletic, the men in plumed pink bowler hats, the women in farthingales and carrying modern handbags. But with a large clock, its hands racing, always prominently in sight, Komisarjevsky did insist upon the passage of time that is here so important.

There were eighteenth-century adaptations. Later, the incorrigible Frederick Reynolds (1819) treated it as an operatic exercise; Samuel Phelps (Sadler's Wells, 1855) brought back Shakespeare; the Irish brothers, Charles and Henry Webb, were peas-in-the-pod Dromios (Princess's, 1864, and tercentenary revival at Stratford); and at Gray's Inn (1895) William Poel put it on, barebones fashion, with his amateurs of the Elizabethan Stage Society ("Huge and quite unnecessary cuts in the last act," said the critic, William Archer).

Not much has emerged from a cluster of twentieth-century revivals: played straight, as at the Old Vic (1914); heavily cut, as a curtain-raiser to *The Bells*, in Henry Baynton's provincial productions (and Savoy, 1924), with the Dromios in black-face; scampered through (Open Air, 1949) in a double bill with *The Two Gentlemen of Verona*; in Edwardian dress (Court, 1952); shortened to an hour and put on before *Titus Andronicus* (Old Vic, 1957). The most applauded versions were by Clifford Williams, with its mock-gravity (Stratford/Aldwych, 1962–3, and later), and by Trevor Nunn (Stratford/Aldwych, 1976–7), remorselessly semi-operatic and set in a modern Greek port.

The United States had popular nineteenth-century Dromios in the brothers Henry and Thomas Placide and (from 1878) William Henry Crane and Stuart Robson. The New York Shakespeare Festival staged the play in 1967.

In other terms

A bouncing musical, *The Boys from Syracuse*, by Rodgers, Hart and Abbott, ran in New York (1938–9, 1963–4), but failed in London at Drury Lane, 1963.

Chief characters

Brothers Antipholus The twin from Syracuse ties for the longest part with his brother's wife, Adriana (each has 264 lines). A fussily bland young man, he finds himself, as he thinks, in an extraordinary world of illusion. Alec McCowen** (Stratford, 1962), after listening gravely to the mistaken Adriana's thirty-seven lines of passionate blank verse, said, mildly puzzled: "Plead you to *me*, fair dame?" Antipholus of Ephesus is, reasonably, the more progressively worried of the brothers, with his home life in confusion.

Brothers Dromio These quibbling slaves, like their masters, have – remarkably – the same names. Dromio of Syracuse (263 lines) has been the more popular figure, probably because of his close geographical description of Nell, the kitchenmaid (III.2):

"She is spherical, like a globe; I could find out countries in her."

Aegeon His first-act exposition can be affecting if it is left alone, but any long speech of this kind, especially in a reputed farce, is a temptation to directors. Performances of Aegeon can be desperate, and he is not always helped by the Duke's interruptions ("Say, in brief, the cause/Why thou departed'st from thy native home", "Do not break off so", "Do me the favour to dilate at full").

Solinus He can be acted (old style) as a kind of stern Theseus, or more usually today, with a baffled gravity: "Why, what an intricate impeach is this?" (V.1).

Adriana The jealous Ephesian wife, about whom the Abbess (V.1) says everything. Sybil Thorndike's first part at the Old Vic (1914).

Luciana Her gentler sister.

Aemilia The redoubtable Abbess who has lines that can be difficult before a modern audience: "Whoever bound him, I will loose his bonds,/And gain a husband by his liberty" (V.1). The story of Aegeon and Aemilia, "nautically considered", is improbable, said John Masefield, poet and critic, who had been a sailor.

A courtesan Only thirty-two lines (IV.3), but rewarding to Peggy Livesey*, impudently drawling in Komisarjevsky's production (Stratford, 1938), and Elizabeth Spriggs (Stratford, 1965), like a romping bird of paradise.

Luce (also called **Nell**). Adriana's kitchenmaid. "Spherical, like a globe" (III.2).

Pinch The "conjuring" schoolmaster, "a needy, hollow-eyed, sharp-looking wretch,/A living dead man" (V.1). A part that has invited disastrous overplaying.

THE TAMING
OF THE SHREW
1593–4

INDUCTION	Gremio, *Hortensio*, gentlemen of
A Lord	Padua, suitors to Bianca
Christopher Sly, a drunken tinker	Tranio, Biondello, servants to
Hostess, Page, Huntsmen,	Lucentio
Players, Servants	Grumio, *Curtis*, servants to
THE PLAY	Petruchio
Baptista Minola, a wealthy citizen	*A Pedant*
of Pisa	Katharina (Kate), the Shrew;
Vincentio, a merchant of Pisa	daughter to Baptista
Lucentio, son to Vincentio, in love	Bianca, her sister
with Bianca	*A widow*; wife to Hortensio
Petruchio, a gentleman of Verona,	Tailor, Haberdasher, Servants
a suitor to Katharina	

Scene: Padua and Petruchio's country house

Synopsis

This is a play within another play that peters out after the Induction. There a nobleman and his hunting party discover a drunken tinker, Christopher Sly, establish him in transient luxury, tell him that he is a lord who has been dreaming for fifteen years, and bring in a group of strolling players – "pomping folk", as they used to be known in one part of England – to entertain him. The comedy they present might take as its epigraph a line spoken to Sly by the young page disguised as his wife: " I am your wife in all obedience."

The scene here could be Warwickshire, but the play proper has an Italian setting. It is about the marriage and consequent taming of the shrewish Katharina, elder daughter of a wealthy Paduan, Baptista. No one wants her, but everyone wants her sister Bianca, who cannot be given in marriage until Kate is off her father's hands. Hence the excitement when a swaggering adventurer, Petruchio, appears, seeking a rich wife.

The contest for Bianca involves a battery of impersonations; the Petruchio/Kate story goes straight on, beginning (Act II) with a first meeting, angry on Kate's side, determined on her suitor's, and reaching a wedding day (Act III) when Petruchio, dressed with deliberate absurdity, carries off an unwilling bride to his country house near Verona. Here (Act IV) Petruchio contrives to keep Kate hungry, sleepless and frustrated until she agrees to anything he says – and all "done in reverend care of her". Though Kate's agreement is severely tested on the homeward journey to Padua, the plot is resolved (Act V) when at a wedding feast for Bianca and her Lucentio – who have been married secretly – Kate lectures Bianca and another new bride on the whole duty of a wife.

In performance

Another play, *The Taming of a Shrew* (published 1594), may be either the source of Shakespeare's broad comedy or – and this is more probable – a corrupt, pirated edition of the original text. In any event, modern directors, except those who do not use the Induction (and this can still happen), usually tag on to the recognized play the last scene of *A Shrew* in which Sly, himself again, wakes outside the tavern and plans an experiment on his own wife: "I know now how to tame a shrew . . . I'll to my wife presently, and tame her, too, an if she anger me." The piece, which takes some hints (the Bianca plot) from the translation of an Italian comedy, has prospered down the years, though for a long time only in adaptations. One (1667) by a low comedian, John Lacy, vulgarized and called *Sauny the Scot*, had Grumio (Sauny) as the principal character. Samuel Pepys wrote of it in his diary (9 April 1667): "To the King's house, and there saw 'The Tameing of a Shrew', which hath some very good pieces in it, but generally is but a mean play." (Pepys could not follow Lacy's dialect.) David Garrick's three-act abbreviation, *Catherine and Petruchio* (1754), which managed without the Induction and Bianca's wooing, had a much longer life.

In fact, possibly the first return to Shakespeare's text was in 1844, when Benjamin Webster and J.R. Planché did the play at the Haymarket in neo-Elizabethan fashion, at that period astonishing. More than forty years later (1888), the American Ada Rehan, who was the Kate of all time and who had previously played the part in New York, came to London's Gaiety Theatre in Augustin Daly's production (in 1893 this also opened the new Daly's Theatre). Ada Rehan's portrait, by Eliot Gregory, now hangs in the Royal Shakespeare Picture Gallery at Stratford-upon-Avon; the Shrew, wearing a rose-coloured gown, stands with upflung head and folded arms, her eyes sparkling defiance. It was said of her after a Stratford appearance (1888); "Here is a girl with a fiery and unbridled temper . . . wrought to this pitch by uncongenial surroundings. She is a woman well worth taming."

Thenceforward the comedy was acted again and again in London and (with Frank Benson and his wife, who was an indifferent actress) at Stratford. Oscar Asche, a massive Old Bensonian, doubled Petruchio with Sly (Benson himself had a trick of lopping the Induction) at the Adelphi (1904). Martin Harvey (Prince of Wales's, 1913), in a production that had been influenced by the German director, Max Reinhardt, established Sly permanently in the conductor's place – though here it was a carved stone seat – above the orchestra well, with his back to the audience. Edith Evans (Old Vic, 1925) was a tornado, far better than she would be in a West End revival (New, 1937) when the part was dissipated in mannerism. Inevitably, the play reached modern dress. During Barry Jackson's Court season (1928), Frank Pettingell played Sly as a vagabond who watched all night from a stage-box, with Laurence Oliver as the Lord in attendance; Petruchio (Ralph Richardson) addressed "Come on, in God's name!" to the starting-handle of a battered Ford. Maurice Evans (his last London year) and Cathleen Nesbitt were at the Old Vic (1935). At Stratford (1939), in his last production there and by no means his best, Komisarjevsky relied on polychromatic artificiality. The stage was all carnation and blue and citron and apple-green, the costumes were *commedia dell'arte*-cum-Restoration, and Komisarjevsky provided a patchwork-quilt text with interpolated nonsense-songs.

The story continues. We cannot name everything, but history records a rough-house, Crazy-Gang treatment at Stratford (1948); Peggy Ashcroft and Peter O'Toole (Stratford, 1960) in a production (John Barton's) that according to Robert Speaight traced its pedigree right down from Chaucer and Langland; Vanessa Redgrave – in a surf of tangerine – and Derek Godfrey (Stratford, 1962); and Jonathan Miller's muted Chichester revival (1972), which appeared to study the power-structure in family life. The Stratford/Aldwych production (1978–9) was an oddly dispiriting modern-dress affair: Sly, emerging from the audience, knocked the set to pieces before the play began: the same actor, Jonathan Pryce, was later and confusingly Petruchio.

In North America, for more than a century from 1766 (Philadelphia), the play was *Catherine and Petruchio*. Daly's Shakespearian text, with the Induction and Ada Rehan, had 137 performances (New York, 1887); in her time Ada Rehan acted her unmatched Kate with many Petruchios, among them John Drew and George Clarke. Later revivals included E.H. Sothern and Julia Marlowe's (1907, no Induction, Kate "a lovely fish-wife"); and the century's richest (Guild, New York, 1935 and 1940), which had Alfred Lunt and Lynn Fontanne in relishing swirl, with Harry Wagstaff Gribble to direct. Stratford, Ontario, has staged the play (e.g. 1973) with vigorous enjoyment.

The Taming of the Shrew can be glumly over-analysed ("It manipulates the theme of misplaced identity in a way that can hardly be ignored," and so on). But, after all, it is being performed to divert a dazed tinker.

In other terms

Kiss Me, Kate, score and lyrics by Cole Porter, was a musical (New York, 1948; London, 1951) with Shakespearian echoes. There have been at least three films of *The Taming of the Shrew*: one by D.W. Griffith as early as 1908; one, resolutely extravagant, "written by William Shakespeare, with additional dialogue by Sam Taylor" (silent and in sound, 1929), and Mary Pickford and Douglas Fairbanks whirling about as tamed and tamer; and a third (1966), done by Zeffirelli as a free-for-all, with Elizabeth Taylor, Richard Burton, and a lopped text.

Chief characters

Petruchio The flamboyant young man from Verona announces himself in the Paduan marriage market (I.2): "Wealth is burden of my wooing dance." He tells Baptista that he "woos not like a babe", and throughout he is the ruler. His bullying and whip-cracking have lessened in recent years. Much the longest part (585 lines). Alfred Lunt*** (New York, 1935).

Katharina "The curst", the shrew, who very soon (in the modern theatre) is in love with her tempestuous tamer, though she has to endure a good deal before the last speech (V.2), "Fie, fie, unknit that threatening, unkind brow", which today is often gently tongue-in-cheek. Ada Rehan*** (New York, 1887; Stratford, 1888); Lynn Fontanne*** (New York, 1935). Laurence Olivier as a fourteen-year-old choirboy from All Saints, Margaret Street, swooped through Kate (1922; with a special matinée at Stratford), and Ellen Terry said in her diary that she had never seen the part done better by anyone except Ada Rehan.

Christopher Sly The drunken tinker of the Induction, "old Sly's son" from Barton-on-the-Heath ("Burton-heath" in the text), out to the south of Stratford, where Shakespeare had an uncle and aunt. Directors, often unsure what to do with Sly, sometimes cut the Induction altogether. In the text the man vanishes after I.1: "A good matter, surely; comes there any more of it?" – "My lord, 'tis but begun." – "'Tis a very excellent piece of work ... Would 'twere done." Stage direction: "They sit and mark." In today's theatre Sly often gets involved somewhere in the action; at the New (1937) Arthur Sinclair doubled him with the Pedant. Occasionally (e.g. Oscar Asche, 1904; Jonathan Pryce, Stratford/Aldwych, 1978–9) he has been doubled with Petruchio.

Biondello Lucentio's second servant – the first is Tranio – has one show-piece, the headlong description (III.2) of Petruchio's arrival for the mad wedding, something spoken in as few breaths as possible.

Gremio Bianca's veteran suitor, a pantaloon-figure who is out of luck, has two good acting scenes – the bidding for Bianca with the disguised Tranio (II.1) and the description of the wedding ceremony (III.2).

Tranio The servant disguised as his master Lucentio, he produces a fine flourish in the contest with Gremio for Bianca (II.1). "What," says Gremio, "have I chok'd you with an argosy?" Whereupon Tranio replies:

> Gremio, 'tis known my father has no less
> Than three great argosies, besides two galliasses,
> And twelve tight galleys. These I will assure her,
> And twice as much whate'er thou off'rest next.

Grumio Petruchio's man, the usual comic servitor.

Bianca Kate's apparently insipid younger sister who may be a shrew in embryo.

A lord He has, in the Induction, some of the most pictorial verse in the play, but he needs a sympathetic director to allow him to speak it. Ian Richardson** (Stratford, 1960).

For the rest, we can get some idea of the confusion from a stage direction (II.1) in a modern text: "Enter Gremio, with Lucentio, disguised as Cambio, in the habit of a mean man; Petruchio, with Hortensio disguised as Licio; and Tranio, disguised as Lucentio, with his boy Biondello bearing a lute and books."

THE TWO GENTLEMEN
OF VERONA

1594

Duke of Milan, father to Silvia
Valentine and *Proteus*, the two
    Gentlemen of Verona
Antonio, father to Proteus
Thurio, a foolish rival to Valentine
Sir Eglamour, agent for Silvia in
    her escape
Speed, a clownish servant to
    Valentine

Launce, a clownish servant to
    Proteus
Panthino, servant to Antonio
Host of Julia in Milan
Julia, a lady of Verona loved by
    Proteus
Silvia, the Duke's daughter, loved
    by Valentine
Lucetta, Julia's waiting-woman
Outlaws, Servants, Musicians

Scene: Verona, Milan, a forest between Milan and Mantua

Synopsis

Valentine, seeking to be "tutor'd in the world", goes with his servant Speed from Verona to Milan, saying goodbye to his friend Proteus ("Cease to persuade, my loving Proteus;/Home-keeping youth have ever homely wits"). Presently, Proteus, enamoured of Julia (as she is of him), is also ordered by his father to leave for Milan. There (Act II) Valentine falls in love with the Duke's daughter, Silvia; when Proteus arrives they tell him that because the Duke prefers a wealthier suitor, Thurio, they propose to elope.

Proteus, himself infatuated with Silvia, informs the Duke, who (Act III) finds a rope ladder under Valentine's cloak and banishes him. He becomes (Act IV) leader of a highly selective band of outlaws. Julia, who has followed Proteus disguised as a boy, hears Thurio's musicians serenading Silvia with "Who is Silvia? What is she,/That all our swains commend her?" Proteus is listening and after Thurio has gone, he proclaims his love, which Silvia scorns, asking Sir Eglamour to conduct her to Valentine. Proteus, taking the disguised Julia ("Sebastian") as his page, sends a message to Silvia who again rejects him.

The Duke (Act V) pursues his escaping daughter and is captured by outlaws while she is rescued by Proteus. The watching Valentine attacks his treachery, then for a moment becomes all too magnanimous by giving up Silvia to him. Julia/Sebastian, swooning, reveals herself, the outlaws bring in the Duke who pardons them, and there is a correct pairing-off. Last line: "One feast, one house, one mutual happiness."

In performance

If we need worry about sources, *The Two Gentlemen of Verona* is based, maybe indirectly, on *Diana*, a chivalrous and pastoral romance written in Spanish by a Portuguese (Jorge de Montemayor); this was the theme of a lost Elizabethan play. It is enough that the comedy of friendship and treachery, as we have it, is a Shakespearian notebook foreshadowing much to come. Herbert Farjeon, the critic, said rightly (1925) that we find in it hints for half a dozen later plays and the substance of some of the

33

Sonnets. Apprentice-work, careless in its facts but undervalued, it can have a lyrical gaiety.

Apart from an "improvement" (Drury Lane, 1762), the first recorded revival was in 1784 at Covent Garden. The notorious Frederick Reynolds as usual puffed it out operatically (1821) William Charles Macready played Valentine without marked enthusiasm – "imperfectly", he said – when he managed Drury Lane (1841). Through the century little enough happened. Ada Rehan "moved and spoke with imposing rhythmic grace" (Shaw) in a poor production by Augustin Daly (Daly's Theatre, 1895). Next, in April 1904, the young Granville Barker (not hyphenated then) directed the comedy at the Royal Court and even appeared as Speed, an arrangement made for the sake of what might, and did, follow – his famous sequence (1904–07) of mainly new plays by Shaw and others. Broadmindedly, the florid Beerbohm Tree invited William Poel, austere neo-Elizabethan zealot, to direct a few performances at His Majesty's in 1910; they came off well, for all Poel's oddities. Since then it has seldom been staged – except for Denis Carey's shining revival (Old Vic, 1952) of what he called a "wilful comedy", with John Neville as Valentine. Michael Langham tried a Regency setting (Old Vic, 1957), with Keith Michell as a Byronic Proteus. Eric Porter's gusty idea of the Duke is now the most potent memory of a revival (1960) at Stratford where ten years later Robin Phillips established the play in modern dress by a campus swimming-pool, a conception he repeated at Stratford, Ontario (1975).

In other terms

A musical based on *The Two Gentlemen of Verona* and borrowing its name ran in New York in various versions (1971 – at first there was a character called Sir Brilliantine – and 1973); also Phoenix, London (1973), for a moderate run.

Chief characters

Valentine The more magnanimous of the two gentlemen, who in a sudden access of generosity yields Silvia to his rival, though not for long: "And that my love may appear plain and free, / All that was mine in Silvia I give thee" (V.4). Macready (Drury Lane, 1841) decided that such an unimportant personage could scarcely injure his reputation.

Proteus Certainly a better theatrical chance than Valentine, besides being the longest part (448 lines) in the play. His name is symbolic, yet (II.4) Valentine believes in him resolutely: "His years but young, but his experience old; / His head unmellowed, but his judgement ripe.' Proteus has the famous lines (III.2);

> For Orpheus' lute was strung with poets' sinews,
> Whose golden touch could soften steel and stones,
> Make tigers tame, and huge leviathans
> Forsake unsounded deeps to dance on sands.

Launce Servant to Proteus, is usually the night's favourite person because of his low-comedy monologues with his dog Crab. Though these can be an acquired taste, Crab, among dog-stars of the drama, has become an unrivalled Sirius. In the theatre he is usually the mildest of wagging spaniels, but Launce speaks of him as "the sourest-natured dog that lives; my mother weeping, my father wailing, my sister crying, our maid howling, our cat wringing her hands, and all our house in a great perplexity; yet did not this cruel-hearted cur shed one tear" (II.3).

Speed Valentine's servant. A part bristling with tedious word-play. Acted, for business reasons, by the young Granville Barker (Court, 1904; see "In performance").

Thurio Like Cloten in *Cymbeline* fifteen or so years later, a foolish suitor who orders a song for his lady. Cloten's is an aubade, Thurio's a serenade, "Who is Silvia?" (IV.3), a lyric he would never have had the wit to write.

Julia The first Shakespearian heroine to be disguised as a page (Sebastian) – no trouble in an Elizabethan company. In her first scene, as herself and with her confidante Lucetta, she might be an early draft for Portia discussing the suitors with Nerissa. In II.7 she has the lovely lyric passage, "The current that with gentle murmur glides".

Silvia "What light is light, if Silvia be not seen?/What joy is joy, if Silvia be not by?" (Valentine, III.1).

Sir Eglamour "Valiant, wise, remorseful, well accomplish'd" (IV.3). The knight, who helps Silvia to escape, is generally caricatured in the modern theatre because of one unhappy line (V.3), the Second Outlaw's observation, "Being nimble-footed, he hath outrun us." In an RSC production (Stratford, 1970) he was a scoutmaster.

Outlaws The outlaws in the forest scenes – "the frontiers of Mantua" – are sheer comic-opera ("By the bare scalp of Robin Hood's fat friar,/This fellow were a king for our wild faction", IV.1). When in the final scene Valentine says to the Duke, "They are reformèd, civil, full of good,/And fit for great employment, worthy lord", one is reminded irresistibly of the end of *The Pirates of Penzance:* "They are no members of the common throng;/They are all noblemen who have gone wrong." At Covent Garden (1808) John Philip Kemble could not resist adding a special scene for the outlaws, whom he christened Ubaldo, Luigi, Carlos, Stephano, Giacomo, Rodolfo and Valerio.

LOVE'S LABOUR'S LOST

1594–5

Ferdinand, King of Navarre	*Dull*, a constable
Berowne, Longaville, Dumain, Lords attending on the King	*Costard*, a clown (peasant)
	Moth, Armado's page
Boyet, Marcade, Lords attending on the Princess of France	*The Princess of France*
	Rosaline, Maria, Katharine, Ladies attending on the Princess
Don Adriano de Armado, a fantastical Spaniard	*Jaquenetta*, a country wench
Sir Nathaniel, a curate	A Forester, Lords, Attendants
Holofernes, a schoolmaster	

Scene: Navarre

Synopsis

Ferdinand, King of Navarre, and three of his lords, Dumain, Longaville and Berowne, who have sworn to study for three years during which no woman shall come within a mile of them, are swayed almost at once by the arrival (Act II) of the Princess of France, with three of her ladies, to discuss her father's debts to the King.

The country youth, Costard, told (Act III) to deliver two letters, muddles them so that (Act IV) a letter from Armado, a "fantastical Spaniard" at court, to the village wench, Jaquenetta, is read to the Princess and her ladies, and a love sonnet from Berowne to Rosaline is read (for Jaquenetta) by Sir Nathaniel, the curate. Holofernes, the schoolmaster, tells the girl to show it to Ferdinand. She does so just when, in succession, the young men have caught each other reciting love-rhymes. Berowne, in an irresistible lyrical speech, claims that love belongs to study, and that women's eyes are "the books, the arts, the academes,/That show, contain, and nourish all the world."

Presently (Act V) they meet the ladies – who have taken pains to trick them – in an unsuccessful mock-Russian entertainment. At length they are all settled, watching the masque of the Nine Worthies, arranged by Armado and Holofernes, when Marcade brings news to the Princess that her father has died. She and her ladies prepare to leave, having put their lovers on probation, with tasks for a year and a day before they can come together. But before departing they listen in the twilight to the villagers' songs of spring ("When daisies pied and violets blue") and winter ("When icicles hang by the wall") – the cuckoo and the owl.

In performance

Love's Labour's Lost (the plot is Shakespeare's own, probably based on a report of a French diplomatic mission to Aquitaine) comes to us now as a young and zestful lyric comedy that in our century has been reborn. It might be described in two lines from Berowne's famous outburst: "Subtle as Sphinx; as sweet and musical/As bright Apollo's lute, strung with his hair." Its narrative is negligible. We know that the four young men who have sworn to flout love will be immediately forsworn; besides the flashing raillery of the lovers we have the "singular and choice epitaphs" of the pedants and the fantastic Armado. A German writer called the play "exessively jocular"; it has never suited the Holofernes type of critic, who is content to search for lost topicalities. Again, in a snatch from the play, we can think of it as, in the language of Armado: "Some delightful ostentation, or show, or pageant, or antic, or firework" (V.1).

Written probably about 1594 and altered in 1597 (to be acted before the Queen at Christmas), there were apparently no revivals until the nineteenth century. Then (1839) Madame Vestris, who also played Rosaline, did an elaborate production at Covent Garden. Little else counted except a Sadler's Wells revival (1857) with Samuel Phelps as Armado, until Ion Swinley and George Hayes acted Berowne and Armado at the Old Vic in 1923; the critic James Agate called the comedy "a Watteau ... of that significance in ordered beauty which unity alone can give".

From 1920 onwards, *Love's Labour's Lost*, "so picked, so spruce, so peregrinate" (as Holofernes more or less describes Armado, V.1), suddenly found its directors and its audiences. W. Bridges-Adams, a sustained admirer, did it in 1925 at Stratford, where there had been only two previous productions, and again (1934), now at the new Memorial Theatre before an immense oak tree, a permanent set for the park of Navarre. Tyrone Guthrie had put it on decoratively, in mood and scene, at the Westminster (1932); and in another of his revivals (1936) Ernest Milton was a marvellous peacock of an Armado. Open Air Theatre audiences appreciated it under Robert Atkins; but it was not until 1946 that the comedy, destined for a happy efflorescence on any stage, had one of its three major revivals of the century.

This was at Stratford-upon-Avon, where no one argued about a production by Peter Brook, then twenty years old. That spring in Paris he had seen the first French *Love's Labour's Lost* for thirty years, a translation that seemed to anticipate much of Molière, Marivaux and Musset, with certain scenes changed and rewritten. By this time Brook had fixed on his own treatment. Like Agate (whom he had not read) he thought of Watteau: his production, pictorial, witty and rhythmical, never cast out the verse, and though some harlequinade-comedy was unexpected, the revival as a whole came as a valuable gift to the Shakespearian theatre. Particularly fine was its Armado (Paul Scofield), meditatively detached, with generations of grandees speaking in his resolute, fragile tones. Brook had a long and daring pause at the last when, conceits and silken terms at an end, the messenger in Act V brought with his tidings of death the realities of life.

It seemed that it might be impossible to match this revival but Hugh Hunt (for the Old Vic at the New, 1949) achieved it in a production of great visual beauty, with a lakeside setting and costume designs (Berkeley Sutcliffe) that were inspired by the miniatures of Nicholas Hilliard and Isaac Oliver. Michael Redgrave's Berowne was in full flood, and Miles Malleson (Nathaniel) and Mark Dignam (Holofernes) were the most beguiling of their period, straight – one would have said – from Stratford-atte-Navarre. A third memorable production, John Barton's (Stratford/Aldwych, 1978–9) had the benefit of an exquisite screen of autumnal trees by Ralph Koltai.

Stratford, Ontario, presented the comedy in 1961 and 1974.

Chief characters

Ferdinand The graceful, mildly academic King of Navarre, who has a totally unworkable idea. "Necessity," says Berowne, "will make us all forsworn."

Berowne Most eloquent of the lords: the longest part (597 lines). He blazes into the glorious sophistry (IV.3) of "Have at you then, affection's men-at-arms." Rosaline's description of him (II.1) might be Shakespeare's self-portrait: "A merrier man,/Within the limit of becoming mirth,/I never spent an hour's talk withal." Michael Redgrave*** (New, 1949); Ian Richardson*** (Stratford, 1973).

Longaville In love with Maria. His name and those of Berowne and Dumain are from commanders in the French civil war, 1589–93. The Ducs de Longueville and de Biron supported Henry of Navarre; the Duc de Mayenne opposed him.

Dumain In love with Katharine.

Don Adriano de Armado A "fantastical Spaniard" at court. His name echoes the Armada, still fresh in English minds. A difficult part, especially in the opening scene with Moth, the page, but overcome triumphantly by such actors as Ernest Milton*** (Old Vic, 1936), Paul Scofield*** (Stratford, 1946), and the Quixote-type of Tony Church** (Aldwych, 1979). Hunters have suggested many Elizabethan originals for the part but these identifications are needless. Armado's language, his "mint of phrases", is in key with the affected "Euphuism" made fashionable by the dramatist, John Lyly (c.1554–1606).

Boyet Middle-aged and "honey-tongued" diplomatist.

Sir Nathaniel Unforgettably acted by Miles Malleson*** (New, 1949), whose curate, a milky mouse with only a score of speeches, was one of the richest Shakespeare-comedy creations of the period.

Holofernes The bristling village schoolmaster, all pedant, a man who cannot talk without unpeeling a Latin tag or pulling some curious word from the basket. Mark Dignam*** (New, 1949; Stratford, 1956).

Costard Mildest of country youths. Pompey the Great in the masque. "If your ladyship would say, 'Thanks, Pompey,' I had done."

Marcade The usually black-clad figure who brings the news of the King's death to the Princess of France. Three lines only, but a profoundly impressive entrance, often heightened – and especially in Brook's 1946 production – by a long pause before he speaks.

Dull The village constable who will expand one day into Dogberry of *Much Ado About Nothing*. "Thou hast spoken no word all this while," says Holofernes to him (V.1), and Dull replies: "Nor understood none neither, sir."

The Princess of France Witty and responsible, she will be a distinguished Queen. Brook (1946) gave to her the final speech, "The words of Mercury are harsh after the songs of Apollo. You that way – we this way." In the text it is attributed to Armado, who generally delivers it, though it has also been given to Boyet.

Rosaline The "whitely wanton with a velvet brow" (III.1), possibly another projection of the Dark Lady of the Sonnets.

Maria The youngest of the Princess's ladies.

Katharine Has a passing moment of sadness (V.2).

Jaquenetta The village hoyden. Ruby Wax* (Stratford/Aldwych, 1978–9).

KING JOHN

1594–6

King John, of England	*King Philip*, of France
Prince Henry, his son; afterwards King Henry III	*Lewis*, the Dauphin
	Lymoges, Archduke of Austria
Arthur, Duke of Bretagne, son of Geoffrey, late Duke of Bretagne, elder brother of King John	*Cardinal Pandulph*, the Pope's legate
	Melun, a French lord
Earl of Pembroke	*Chatillon*, Ambassador from France to King John
Earl of Essex	*Queen Elinor*, widow of King Henry II of England and mother of King John
Earl of Salisbury	
Lord Bigot	
Hubert de Burgh	*Constance*, mother of Arthur
Robert Faulconbridge, son of Sir Robert Faulconbridge	*Blanch of Spain*, daughter of the King of Castile and niece of King John
Philip the Bastard, his half-brother, illegitimate son of King Richard Coeur-de-Lion (Richard I of England)	*Lady Faulconbridge*, Sir Robert Faulconbridge's widow
	Lords, Citizens of Angiers,
James Gurney, servant to Lady Faulconbridge	Sheriff, Heralds, Officers, Soldiers, Executioners,
Peter of Pomfret, a prophet	Messengers, Attendants

Scene: England and France at the beginning of the thirteenth century
(John reigned from 1199 to 1216)

Synopsis

Chatillon, an ambassador from King Philip of France, demands King John's crown for Arthur, young son of John's dead elder brother, Geoffrey. Whereupon John declares war. He is followed to France by Philip the Bastard, who has been created Sir Richard Plantagenet on the revelation that he is the illegitimate son of King Richard I.

Before Angiers (200 miles south-west of Paris) the English and French armies meet (Act II). When the citizens declare that they will recognize only the rightful King of England ("he that proves the King,/To him will we prove loyal"), the two armies temporarily unite to assault the town. Peace of a sort is made after the citizens have suggested that Lewis, Dauphin of France, should marry John's niece, Blanch of Spain; Arthur is to become Duke of Bretagne (Brittany).

Constance, the boy's mother, assails King Philip and his ally, the Duke of Austria (Act III) for his treacherous bargain. The new-patched peace is brief; Cardinal Pandulph, the Papal legate, arrives to excommunicate John for disobedience to the Pope; and because King Philip is also to be excommunicated unless he breaks his pact with John, the battle begins afresh. The Bastard kills the Duke of Austria; Arthur is taken prisoner and sent to England, Constance mourning for him; and John secretly orders Hubert de Burgh to dispose of the boy.

Hubert (Act IV), receiving a royal command to blind Arthur, resolves instead to hide the boy and to announce his death, false news that takes from John the support of Lords Salisbury and Pembroke. All troubles press on him at once; the Dauphin is ready to invade England; John learns that his mother, Elinor, has died – so, too, has Constance – and now the barons fall away from him. Though he learns from Hubert that Arthur is alive, the boy has actually been killed in an attempt to escape from Northampton Castle.

John yields to the Pope (Act V), but the Dauphin refuses to obey Pandulph's order to return to France, and supported by the English barons, fights with John's army. Retiring to Swinstead Abbey in Lincolnshire, the King is joined again by Salisbury and Pembroke who have heard that the Dauphin intended to kill them. At Swinstead, John – poisoned, it is believed, by a monk – dies in the orchard; Lewis by then has withdrawn his army, leaving Pandulph to arrange terms for peace; and the Bastard, acknowledging the young Prince Henry as Henry III, ends with the speech:

> This England never did, nor never shall
> Lie at the proud foot of a conqueror,
> But when it first did help to wound itself.
> Now these her princes are come home again,
> Come the three corners of the world in arms,
> And we shall shock them. Nought shall make us rue,
> If England to itself do rest but true.

In performance

The Life and Death of King John was probably based upon an anonymous play in two parts, *The Troublesome Raigne of King John*. Shakespeare's chronicle is sometimes dismissed as a Little Arthur's History, simply because of the brief but affecting scene (IV.1) between the young Prince Arthur, in prison, and Hubert de Burgh whom he persuades not to blind him. The play is far from being a reliable historical document; it does not even mention the principal domestic event in John's reign, the signing at Runnymede in 1215 of Magna Carta, the charter of rights which the barons forced the King to accept. In his London production (1899) Herbert Beerbohm Tree, introduced this, typically, as a tableau which permitted John, according to legend, to gnaw the rushes in his rage. A dominant figure in *King John* is the no-nonsense Bastard, illegitimate son of Richard I (Coeur-de-Lion), who has the final patriotic outburst.

The play, better in performance than in the text, had the usual troubles in the theatre. After nearly a century and a half it was revived at Covent Garden (1737), and in 1745 there were two productions: Garrick's at Drury Lane (he played John) was the Shakespearian one, and the other was Colley Cibber's version called *Papal Tyranny in the Reign of King John*, which speaks for itself.

Sarah Siddons, who came to Constance at Drury Lane in 1783 (her brother John Philip Kemble was the King), was to give the definitive emotional performance. Another Kemble, Charles (as the Bastard), produced the play at Covent Garden (1823), everyone appearing "in the precise Habit of the Period, the whole of the Dresses and Decorations being executed from indisputable Authorities such as Monumental Effigies, Seals, Illuminated MSS, etc." J.R. Planché, the antiquarian (and dramatist), who looked after the staging, wrote years later: "Never shall I forget the dismay of some of the performers when they looked upon the flat-topped *chapeaux de fer* ... which they irreverently called *stewpans*. Nothing but the fact that the classical features of a Kemble were to be surmounted by a precisely similar abomination could, I think, have induced one of the rebellious Barons to have appeared in it." Still, the public approved. Macready revived the chronicle with magnificence at Drury Lane (1842), playing John himself.

So to the archaeological Charles Kean (Princess's, 1852); Tree's revival, with tableau (Her Majesty's, 1899); a number of Old Vic and Stratford productions; and the Old Vic company at the New (1941), with the best cast of our day (Ernest Milton, Sybil Thorndike, Lewis Casson as Pandulph). At the Birmingham Repertory (1945) the young Paul Scofield, already with extraordinary personal magnetism, acted the Bastard in Peter Brook's first Shakespearian production. Beginning with a bacchanal instead of the usual court tableau, Brook never let the play drift into a monotony of booming barons. In the Bastard's "commodity" speech (II.1) he inserted an early defining phrase ("That smooth-fac'd gentleman, *expediency, or, as they say,* tickling commodity, /Commodity, the bias of the world ..."), and no scholar grumbled.

There have been various more-or-less routine productions (George Devine's at the Old Vic, 1953, with Richard Burton competent as the Bastard); but the only one that caused any real alarm was John Barton's (Stratford, 1974). There he provided what was, in effect, a new and superfluous play based on *The Troublesome Raigne*, the earlier interlude of *Kynge John* by a Protestant apologist, John Bale, and *King John* itself. It had, at least, Richard Pasco as the Bastard.

The New York Shakespeare Festival presented *King John* in 1967. It was staged at Stratford, Ontario in 1961, and again in 1974, then with Edward Atienza as John.

Chief characters

King John A foxy monarch, one of the butts of English history, though at some time, as Holinshed says, he might have had "a princelie heart in him". Splendidly acted by William Charles Macready*** (Drury Lane, 1842) and by Ernest Milton*** (New, 1941), a fine intellect poisoned.

Philip the Bastard (becomes Sir Richard Plantagenet). The longest part (511 lines). An honest, impatient, realistic soldier, Coeur-de-Lion's illegitimate son by Lady Faulconbridge, he goes undeviatingly to the point at all times and has the last patriotic brag. Paul Scofield** (Birmingham Repertory, 1945); Richard Pasco*** (Stratford, 1974).

Arthur The scene with Hubert (IV.1), not just a popular show-piece, an Arthurian legend, can move all but the determinedly cynical. Arthur needs a good boy actor, though there is an actress-tradition, and Ann Casson was affecting at the New (1941).

Hubert de Burgh Arthur's warden; some editors believe that he was also the First Citizen of Angiers (II.1).

Archduke of Austria The pompous braggart whom the Bastard kills at Angiers. Direction in III.2: "Enter the Bastard with Austria's head." Usually it is enough to come on with the lion-skin. One theatrical variation has been "Austria's *hide*, lie there."

Lord Salisbury In Act IV.2, after John's second coronation, he has one of the most frequently misquoted phrases in English literature, "To gild refinèd gold, to paint the lily."

King Philip of France Among the more vacillating monarchs ("I am perplex'd and know not what to say"). He says too much in one of the less fortunate speeches (III.4) when observing that a tear has fallen on the distraught Constance's unbound hair: "Even to that drop ten thousand wiry friends/Do glue themselves in sociable grief."

Prince Henry The youth, who will be Henry III, speaks the lines that too often are either ignored or ill-delivered (V.7, before John's death in the Swinstead orchard):

> 'Tis strange that death should sing.
> I am the cygnet to this pale faint swan
> Who chants a doleful hymn to his own death,
> And from the organ-pipe of frailty sings
> His soul and body to their lasting rest.

Cardinal Pandulph "I, Pandulph, of fair Milan cardinal." Casuistical legate of the Pope, whose shadow, that of the Church Militant, falls across the play like the shadow of the great cross that in some productions is borne before him. He has been played as a massively arrogant prelate or as frail and silver-haired.

Lewis the Dauphin Heir to the French throne. His sudden willingness to love Blanch for politic reasons, but expressed hyperbolically (II.3), rouses the Bastard's sardonic contempt. Historically, the marriage is said to have been idyllic.

Constance Arthur's betrayed mother whom the stage knew as "crying Constance". Her part is a mixture of overburdened lines and such famous speeches as "I will instruct my sorrows to be proud" (III.1). Sarah Siddons*** (1783 and on); Sybil Thorndike*** (New, 1941).

Blanch of Spain "Whoever wins, on that side shall I lose:/Assurèd loss before the match be play'd" (III.1). A small part but haunting. Doreen Aris** (Stratford, 1947).

Queen Elinor John's mother; with little to say, she is far more than a cipher. Her son's evil inspiration, for ever at his ear: "An Até stirring him to blood and strife."

RICHARD II

1595

Historically, King Richard II, who was the grandson of King Edward III and the son of Edward the Black Prince, reigned from 1377 to 1399. Born at Bordeaux in 1367 – he was the same age as his cousin, Henry Bolingbroke, later Henry IV – he succeeded his grandfather as King in 1377 when only a child. Henry Bolingbroke deposed him in 1399 and he died early in 1400 while imprisoned at Pontefract (Pomfret) Castle.

King Richard the Second	*Lord Ross*
John of Gaunt, Duke of Lancaster,	*Lord Willoughby*
the King's uncle, and brother of	*Lord Berkeley*
the Duke of York and the late	*Earl of Salisbury*
Thomas of Woodstock, Duke	*Bishop of Carlisle*
of Gloucester	*Sir Stephen Scroop*
Henry Bolingbroke, Duke of	*Lord Fitzwater*
Hereford, son of John of Gaunt	*Duke of Surrey*
and afterwards King Henry IV	*Abbot of Westminster*
Thomas Mowbray, Duke of	*Sir Pierce of Exton*
Norfolk	*Lord Marshal*
Edmund of Langley, Duke of York;	*A Welsh captain*
uncle of the King	*Two gardeners*
Duke of Aumerle, son of the Duke	*A groom of the stable* to King
of York	Richard
Henry Percy, Earl of	*Keeper of the prison* at Pomfret
Northumberland	*Isabel*, King Richard's Queen
Harry Percy, surnamed Hotspur,	*The Duchess of York*
son of the Earl of	*The Duchess of Gloucester*, Thomas
Northumberland	of Woodstock's widow
Sir Henry Green	A Lord, Heralds, Ladies
Sir John Bushy	Attendant upon Queen Isabel,
Sir John Bagot	Guards, Soldiers, Servants

Scene: England and Wales

Synopsis

The play opens with Henry Bolingbroke, the King's cousin, accusing Thomas Mowbray, Duke of Norfolk, of the murder of the King's uncle, Thomas of Woodstock, Duke of Gloucester (a crime actually committed at the King's command). Richard orders Bolingbroke and Mowbray to a trial by combat at Coventry; there, as the fight is about to begin, he forbids it, sentencing Mowbray to exile for life and Bolingbroke for ten years, presently reduced to six.

Soon (Act II) Bolingbroke's father, John of Gaunt, Duke of Lancaster, dies after a noble panegyric on England ("This royal throne of kings"). At once, Richard, against the protests of his uncle York and the powerful nobleman Northumberland, seizes Gaunt's estates to pay for his coming Irish campaign. While he is in Ireland, Bolingbroke lands at Ravenspurgh in Yorkshire and joined by Northumberland, marches through England to Berkeley Castle, where the vacillating York, as regent, is obliged to receive them. Bolingbroke (Act III) executes two of Richard's favourites, "the caterpillars of the commonwealth", Bushy and Green. The country rises in his favour. When Richard lands in Wales he hears only a tale of woe; Bolingbroke takes him prisoner at Flint Castle where he has gone with York's son, Aumerle.

In London, at Westminster Hall (Act IV), Richard yields the crown to Bolingbroke (who becomes King Henry IV), and is sent to Pomfret Castle and his Queen to France. Aumerle and the Bishop of Carlisle join in a plot against the King, but Aumerle's part is discovered by his father (Act V). His mother pleads for his pardon, which Henry grants. Richard is murdered by Sir Pierce of Exton at Pomfret, a crime at once mourned by the King who had prompted it. "From your own mouth, my lord, did I this deed," says Exton; and Henry answers, "They love not poison that do poison need."

In performance

Richard II, with Holinshed's *Chronicles* as a main source, has become conspicuous in the theatre because so many expert speakers have responded to Richard's lyrical verse in a play predominantly lyrical and frequently rhymed. There are two methods of presenting Richard – as a man, luxuriating in his imagination, who is entranced by word and image and makes shivering music of his grief, or as a man who suffers profoundly with each new fall. In the theatre it can be often difficult to separate the two conceptions, but the play must always be a rare experience, given the right kind of unfussed production – one by Bridges-Adams at Stratford in the 1920s was sovereign – and a sensitive speaker who can present the King, moving from haughty insolence to contemplative artist, without blurring the arias. The night falters – and this happens seldom – only when a Richard, cannot find the harmonics.

Opposed to him is the strong man, the usurping and verbally unimaginative Henry Bolingbroke, "silent king" of the Westminster Hall scenes. Richard aside, the noblest passage (II.1) and possibly the most familiar, is John of Gaunt's inspired apostrophe to England, "This royal throne of kings" (II.1). Theatrically, the trickiest scene is the "Aumerle conspiracy" (V.2 and 3) which is worked uneasily into the pattern and used regularly to be cut: a pity because we must always miss the Duke of York's memory of Richard's entrance into London behind the conquering Bolingbroke. (Various directors, e.g. Charles Kean and Beerbohm Tree, tried superfluously to illustrate this.)

We know that Queen Elizabeth – who had her influential favourites as Richard had – was angry when she was compared with him. Presumably for political reasons (though Shakespeare had had no ulterior design) the abdication scene was omitted from printed editions during the Queen's reign, but restored after her death. One of her favourites, the foolhardy Earl of Essex, rose against her in 1601, the day after supporters of Essex paid the sum of forty shillings for a special performance of *Richard II* at the Globe, complete with deposition. The revolt was suppressed and Essex was executed. The next recorded performance of the chronicle was, remarkably, in the East India Company's ship, *Dragon* (commanded by John Keeling) off the coast of Sierra Leone in the autumn of 1607. The *Dragon* was in company with the *Hector*, under Captain William Hawkins, and Keeling's log has the note: "Sept. 30. Captain Hawkins dined with me, where my companions acted King Richard the Second." (The same versatile ship's company, it seems, would also play *Hamlet*.)

After the Restoration, Nahum Tate tried a short-lived adaptation (The Sicilian Usurper, 1680). Lewis Theobald put together a rather luckier one (1719); and Shakespeare's own text ran at Covent Garden in 1738. Among nineteenth-century Richards were Edmund Kean, who used an adapted text; Macready; and Charles Kean, whose much-cut version surrounded by all imaginable pomp, had eighty-five performances (Princess's, 1857).

The nineteenth century's only other important Richard was Frank Benson (Stratford, 1896), who at once took imaginative control of a man bred to autocracy, lord by divine right and prisoner by the right of Bolingbroke. It was a performance, inescapably poignant, of a haunted artist and lost, spoilt child, surrendering his life with his crown. Benson, who could be a far better actor than the too easily accepted legends suggest (legends die hard in the theatre) played Richard in Manchester (1899); he received from Charles Edward Montague of the *Manchester Guardian* one of the most famous theatre essays in the language, describing how Benson expressed "that half of the character which criticism seems always to have taken pains to hide – the capable and faithful artist in the same skin as the incapable and faithless king." Benson acted Richard in London (Lyceum, 1900) and frequently thereafter at Stratford.

Except for Tree's mannered and touching portrait (His Majesty's, 1903) in a much-decorated revival (real horses), there was no major Richard until that of George Hayes at the Old Vic (1925), which he repeated at Stratford (1929), the year when John Gielgud at the Old Vic first proved his mastery of a part he would make his own. Hayes created much excitement in Boston late in 1929 on the Stratford company's tour. The chronicle was then barely known in the American theatre (though Edwin Booth had done it in the 1870s), but it startled New York (St James's, 1937) when the English actor, Maurice Evans – who had been in an Old Vic revival of 1934 – appeared under Margaret Webster's direction. The play was unfamiliar and the Evans–Webster première is still remembered. "At the end of the 'death of kings' speech," the director said, "an outburst of applause stopped the action for almost a minute. I had never heard such a thing in the theatre before."

There were various other Richards in years ahead: Alec Guinness (Old Vic at the New, 1946), a proud weakling using irony as his defence; Michael Redgrave (Stratford, 1951); Paul Scofield (Lyric, Hammersmith, 1953; directed by Gielgud); John Neville (Old Vic, 1954–6); Jack May (Birmingham Repertory, 1955); Ronald Pickup (National company at Old Vic, 1972); and Ian Richardson and Richard Pasco, who alternated the King and Bolingbroke (Stratford, 1973). The record becomes a catalogue; but all of these players added something to the mosaic and all could sustain the great speeches, "Of comfort no man speak" (III.2), "We are amazed" (III.3), and the metaphysical "I have been studying" at Pomfret (V.5); Bernard Hepton (St George's, Islington, 1979) analysed the man with affecting clarity.

Zoë Caldwell directed the play at Stratford, Ontario (1979), using three Richards during the run.

In other terms

Derek Jacobi, sympathetic and intelligent, appeared on BBC television (1978), a production otherwise routine except for the John of Gaunt by John Gielgud, whose name is inseparable from the play.

Chief characters

Richard II Standing to the last for the divine right of kingship. So many actors have played – and, most important, spoken – Richard memorably that we have to be unusually selective. Frank Benson*** (Stratford, from 1896); George Hayes*** (Old Vic, 1925; Stratford, 1929 and 1933), in Westminster Hall a missal-figure in black velvet; John Gielgud*** (Old Vic, 1929; Queen's, 1937); Maurice Evans*** (Old Vic, 1934; St James's, New York, 1937); Ian Richardson*** alternating with Richard Pasco*** (Stratford, 1973). Gielgud insisted that "the actor's vocal effects must be contrived within the framework of the verse.... Too many pauses and striking variations of tempo will tend to hold up the action disastrously" and so ruin the text's symmetry and pattern.

Henry Bolingbroke John of Gaunt's son, who takes the throne as Henry IV. A long part (411 lines against Richard's 756), yet its strength can be in its silences. Pronounced "Bullingbrook"; the title "Hereford" is "Herford".

John of Gaunt "Old John of Gaunt, time-honoured Lancaster", though when the play opens (1398) he is only fifty-eight. The name is from his birthplace, Ghent in Flanders. One of the great Shakespearian elders, he has the salute to England, "This royal throne of kings" (II.1).

Thomas Mowbray, Duke of Norfolk Vanishes from the play after his exile (I.3). In the theatre often doubled with the Bishop of Carlisle who (IV.1) reports Mowbray's death in Venice. Eric Maxon* (Stratford, 1929).

Edmund, Duke of York The King's uncle, and regent during Richard's absence in Ireland, Vacillating, bemused and kindly. Should not be played for laughter at some difficult lines.

Duchess of York Historically, Aumerle was only her stepson.

Duke of Aumerle York's son, involved in the disastrous conspiracy (Act V), scenes that were probably added in Queen Elizabeth's time to atone for the loss of the deposition scene. In Westminster Hall (IV.1) he is at the centre of the quarrel in which so many gages are thrown down – an impossible passage in the theatre, unless it is judiciously cut.

Earl of Northumberland Richard's implacable enemy.

Henry (Harry) Percy Northumberland's son: the Hotspur of *Henry I, Part I* though one might never guess this from *Richard II*. Actually he was two years older than Bolingbroke himself.

Earl of Salisbury He has the famous line (III.2), "O, call back yesterday, bid time return", which has been varied so often in other plays down the years.

Captain of a band of Welshmen Briefly met (II.4), this superstitious Welshman can be reasonably identified with Owen Glendower, though some critics – Dr Stanley Wells for one – consider that he is a purely choric figure.

Groom He comes to the prisoner at Pomfret (V.5), telling him how Bolingbroke had ridden on Richard's favourite horse, roan Barbary. The part, at Stratford (1973–4), was represented capriciously as the disguised Bolingbroke.

Queen to King Richard Historically she was Isabella of Valois, daughter of Charles VI of France. In the Duke of York's garden at Langley (III.4) she overhears the symbolic talk of the two Gardeners (who must never be teased into comedy): "He that hath suffered this disordered spring/Hath now himself met with the fall of leaf."

Duchess of Gloucester Her scene with Gaunt (I.2) is not easy to understand without knowledge of her husband's murder.

45

ROMEO AND JULIET

1595–6

Chorus	*Balthasar*, Romeo's servant
Escalus, Prince of Verona	*Sampson*, *Gregory*, Capulet's
Paris, a young nobleman, the	servants
Prince's kinsman	*Peter*, servant to Juliet's Nurse
Montague and *Capulet*, heads of	*Abraham*, Montague's servant
two rival houses	*Lady Montague*, wife to Montague
An old man, of the Capulet family	*Lady Capulet*, wife to Capulet
Romeo, Montague's son	*Juliet*, Capulet's daughter
Mercutio, the Prince's kinsman and	*Nurse* to Juliet
Romeo's friend	An Apothecary, Three Musicians,
Benvolio, Montague's nephew and	Page to Paris, another Page, an
Romeo's friend	Officer, Citizens of Verona,
Tybalt, Lady Capulet's nephew	Kinsfolk of both Houses,
Friar Lawrence, a Franciscan	Masquers, Guards, Watchmen,
Friar John, of the same Order	and Attendants

Scene: Verona, Mantua

Synopsis

After a brawl between the rival Veronese families of Montague and Capulet ("Two households both alike in dignity"), the Prince threatens with death anyone who "disturbs our streets again". Romeo, Montague's heir, masked at a Capulet dance, becomes infatuated with Capulet's daughter, Juliet. From the garden (Act II) he overhears her avowal ("Take all myself") as she stands on her balcony: and their love scene follows (II.2). Next afternoon Friar Lawrence marries them in secret.

When (Act III) Romeo refuses to fight with Tybalt, a passionate Capulet (who is now his cousin by marriage), the gallant Mercutio takes the challenge himself. He is killed by mischance; and Romeo, enraged, kills Tybalt. In his absence the Prince banishes him; the Friar tells him to stay the night with Juliet and then wait in Mantua until recall is possible (III.3). When Juliet's father insists that she shall marry a young nobleman, Paris, and she gets no aid from either her mother or her nurse, the Friar (Act IV) gives her an opiate (to take on the following night) that will put her in a death-like trance for "two-and-forty hours". She will be laid in the Capulet vault; when she wakes, Romeo will be there.

Juliet is duly placed in the vault as dead, but the Friar's messenger to Mantua miscarries; hearing only of Juliet's "death" ("Then I defy you, stars!", Act V), Romeo hastens to the tomb at night and is surprised by Paris whom he kills; in the vault he drinks poison he has bought from a Mantuan apothecary, and dies by Juliet's side. She wakes as the desperate Friar enters, and on seeing Romeo dead, stabs herself. The Prince and the heads of the families are roused; over the bodies of their children Capulet and Montague are reconciled; and the Prince closes the play: "For never was a story of more woe/Than this of Juliet and her Romeo."

In performance

"A tragedy of youth as youth sees it," wrote Harley Granville Barker. Set in a Veronese high summer, it is both the tale of "star-crossed lovers" and the healing of their parents' feud: Shakespeare's principal source was a poem by Arthur Brooke (1562), a version of a story long popular. The play is what Bernard Shaw, unassailable for once, called "an irresistibly impetuous march of music", though the "two hours' traffic of our stage" (a phrase from the Prologue) cannot be taken literally.

Few plays have been acted so often; but it had much ado to find itself. Thomas Otway (1679) provided a travesty, *The History and Fall of Caius Marius*; Theophilus Cibber's version (1744), less distorted, also supplied what was (for the taste of the period) an obligatory farewell dialogue in the tomb; David Garrick (1748), in a text enormously successful, was also far too self-indulgent. "Bless me," said the waking Juliet. "How cold it is! Who's there?" Whereupon Romeo replied: "Thy husband. 'Tis thy Romeo, raised from despair to joy unutterable." Joy was brief; the apothecary's poison worked: "My powers are blasted. 'Twixt death and life I am torn, I am distracted." Listeners were not; indeed, the alterations were in use as late as 1845. Through many mid-eighteenth-century seasons London's two principal theatres competed with each other in performances of the tragedy; Garrick himself played Romeo for eleven years from 1750.

A long sequence of revivals continued. Charles Kemble (Romeo first in 1803) became Mercutio in 1829. Eliza O'Neill (1814), nineteen-year-old Fanny Kemble (1829) and Helen Faucit (1836) were historic Juliets. The American Charlotte Cushman, as Romeo to her sister Susan (Haymarket, 1845), omitted the interpolated dialogue in death; Adelaide Neilson was Juliet for fifteen years (in England and the United States) from 1865; and the realistic Lyceum décor (1882) meant more than the playing of Henry Irving and Ellen Terry. In spite of a procession of distinguished names (e.g. Forbes-Robertson and Mrs Patrick Campbell, Lyceum, 1895) there would be no memorable excitement until the veteran Ellen Terry (as the Nurse) had her last triumph (Lyric 1919). Eric Portman and Jean Forbes-Robertson (Old Vic, 1928) caused the author and artist, Graham Robertson, to say: "The two very young lovers made the whole thing so poignant and real that you longed to wait for them at the stage door with a double perambulator to wheel them home to bed."

Seven years later, the century's most exciting revival brought the John Gielgud-Laurence Olivier alternation of Romeo and Mercutio (New, 1935), with Peggy Ashcroft's Juliet magically right, and Edith Evans as the Nurse described definitively by W.A. Darlington: "Earthy as a potato, slow as a cart-horse, cunning as a badger." In spite of not wholly justified criticism of his verse-speaking, Olivier's impetuous adolescent moved straight from Renaissance Italy; Gielgud found more in the Queen Mab flourish than Mercutio himself might have guessed; and when they changed parts each actor still had passionate adherents.

Nothing since has shadowed that revival; but Peter Brook's Stratford production (1947, on the note of "The mad blood stirring") is recalled for Paul Scofield's Mercutio. There were Old Vic performances by Alan Badel and Claire Bloom (1952); and John Stride and the impulsively young Judi Dench (1960). Franco Zeffirelli, who directed, chopped the Mab speech into untidy little cubes and opened the Mantuan scene at "Then I defy you, stars!" Best Stratford Juliet: Dorothy Tutin (1958 and 1961).

There is a record of American productions since the mid-eighteenth-century. In the nineteenth century Charlotte Cushman's Romeo and the Juliets of Adelaide Neilson and Mary Anderson (New York, 1885, with Forbes-Robertson as Romeo) were all applauded. Julia Marlowe (1904), was ardent and heroic. Rollo Peters and Jane Cowl had more than 150 performances at the Henry Miller Theatre (1928); and of other players – e.g. Eva Le Gallienne and Donald Cameron (1930) and Olivia de Havilland and Douglas Watson (1951) – probably the most satisfying was Katharine Cornell (1934, Basil Rathbone as Romeo, Edith Evans as the Nurse; 1935, Maurice Evans as Romeo).

In other terms

None of the Romeo and Juliet films has been of much lasting value: Hollywood's (1936), with Norma Shearer (on a "wedding-cake balcony") and Leslie Howard, was ardent and heroic; a British-Italian production (1954) by Renato Castellani; and a second (1968) by Franco Zeffirelli, with two very young lovers, Leonard Whiting (aged sixteen) and Olivia Hussey (aged fifteen).

Vincenzo Bellini composed the opera of I Capoletti ed i Montecchi (1830) and Charles Gounod (1867; revised, 1881), Roméo et Juliette. Hector Berlioz wrote an extended Roméo and Juliet symphony, with soloists and chorus (1839). We have also Tchaikovsky's Romeo and Juliet fantasy (1880) and Delius's A Village Romeo and Juliet (1907). The play has also been the subject of elaborate ballets, such as Serge Prokofiev's (1934), and an American gang-war musical, West Side Story (1957). It was acted, on BBC television (1978) with an inexperienced pair of lovers.

Chief characters

Romeo Juliet's passionate lover has always a premonition of disaster. Before he has ever seen her, on the night of the Capulet ball, he says:

> My mind misgives
> Some consequence, yet hanging in the stars,
> Shall bitterly begin his fearful date
> With this night's revels. [I.4].

Hearing of Juliet's supposed death (V.1), he cries: "Then I defy you, stars!"; and in the tomb he prepares to "shake the yoke of inauspicious stars/From this world-wearied flesh" (V.3). It is no part for a timid actor: Romeo is a youth who, in grief, must not fear to "fall upon the ground as I do now,/Taking the measure of an unmade grave" (III.3). Strangely few Romeos are remembered. Those from history, apart from the eighteenth-century Garrick and Spranger Barry, are Charles Kemble*** (1803 onwards), Laurence Olivier*** and John Gielgud*** (New, 1935).

Juliet "O, she doth teach the torches to burn bright." She is thirteen; she would have been fourteen on Lammas Eve, soon after her death. In performance she must come from the right latitude – no hint of northern skies – and she needs far more than a child's experience: experiments with very young actresses have usually failed. Four Juliets safe in record are Eliza O'Neill*** (1814), Fanny Kemble 1829), Peggy Ashcroft*** (New, 1935) and Judi Dench*** (Old Vic, 1960). Few Victorian players spoke the lines beginning "Gallop apace" (III.2) because they were deemed immodest ("Lovers can see to do their amorous rites/By their own beauties").

Mercutio Romeo's friend, a kinsman of the Prince. Mercurial (hence his name), gallant (he jests to the end), imaginative (the Queen Mab speech), and doomed: Tybalt strikes him under Romeo's arm. John Gielgud*** and Laurence Olivier*** (New, 1935), Paul Scofield*** (Stratford, 1947): Ian Richardson*** (Old Vic, 1979).

Tybalt "Talk of peace! I hate the word/As I hate hell, all Montagues, and thee" (I.1). He goes on from there.

Benvolio Romeo and Mercutio's friend, vanishes from the play after his description of the duel (III.1).

Paris Kinsman of both the Prince and Mercutio. An amiable young man and desperately unlucky.

Escalus, Prince of Verona. Three times the voice of much-troubled authority (I.1, III.1, V.3).

Capulet Juliet's father; much older than his wife. Proud, hospitable, unimaginative and at the end honest in his grief.

Friar Lawrence "Ghostly confessor" (II.6). Happier as a botanist than a conspirator; full of helpful maxims.

Lady Capulet Juliet's mother, and a thankless part. She is, we gather, not yet thirty but speaks of "my old age" (V.3).

Nurse There is no need for the Nurse, garrulous, bawdy and fickle, to be an ancient. She could be fifty though we are used to the type of bulky, voluble peasant played by Edith Evans*** (New, 1935). Elizabeth Spriggs*** (Stratford, 1966) was a younger version. So was Brenda Bruce*** (Stratford, 1980).

Apothecary Romeo describes him in detail. "Meagre were his looks./Sharp misery had worn him to the bones" (V.1). It is a dangerous invitation to a young actor; but Alec Guinness* (New, 1935) was perfectly credible and did not carry about the dram of poison as if he were expecting a customer.

Rosaline Does not appear (though much talked about, and some directors have brought her to Capulet's ball); Romeo's first love and Juliet's cousin. Mercutio calls her a "pale, hard-hearted wench" (II.4).

A MIDSUMMER NIGHT'S DREAM

1595–6

Theseus, Duke of Athens	*Hermia*, daughter of Egeus, in
Egeus, father of Hermia	love with Lysander
Lysander and *Demetrius*, each in	*Helena*, in love with Demetrius
love with Hermia	*Oberon*, King of the Fairies
Philostrate, master of the revels to	*Titania*, Queen of the Fairies
Theseus	*Puck*, or Robin Goodfellow
Quince, a carpenter	*A Fairy*
Snug, a joiner	*Peaseblossom, Cobweb, Moth,*
Bottom, a weaver	*Mustardseed*, fairy attendants on
Flute, a bellows-mender	Titania
Snout, a tinker	Attendants on Theseus and
Starveling, a tailor	Hippolyta; other fairies attending
Hippolyta, Queen of the	the King and Queen
Amazons, betrothed to Theseus	

Scene: Athens, and a wood near it

Synopsis

While Theseus, Duke of Athens, and the Amazon Queen Hippolyta, whom he has defeated in battle, are contemplating their marriage, Theseus has to judge a matrimonial dispute. Egeus wishes his daughter Hermia to wed Demetrius when her heart is set upon Lysander. Though warned of the consequences if she disobeys, Hermia resolves to elope and on the next night to meet Lysander in a wood close to Athens. They tell Helena who is herself in love with Demetrius and who promptly reveals the plan to him.

In the wood (Act II) the goblin Puck and one of the Fairy Queen's train talk of the quarrel between Oberon and Titania over the changeling boy she has adopted and he desires for a henchman. She refuses to yield, whereupon Oberon orders Puck to fetch a flower whose juice, squeezed on Titania's sleeping eyelids, will cause her on awakening to love the first live creature that she sees. Helena has followed Demetrius to the wood; Oberon, invisible and sympathetic, orders Puck to squeeze the flower on the lids of the "Athenian youth", while he himself anoints Titania. But Puck, mistaking, chooses Lysander, who when he wakes immediately pursues Helena.

Puck (Act III) mischievously gives an ass's head to Nick Bottom, the weaver, one of a group of "mechanicals" rehearsing a play for the wedding of Theseus. Titania, waking, falls in love with Bottom. Presently confusion is worse than ever because Demetrius (who has now been anointed) and Lysander fight over Helena, to Hermia's distress. The only thing to do is to get the lovers to sleep and to restore Lysander's sight before he wakes.

Oberon (Act IV) releases Titania; Puck removes the ass's head, and one quarrel is settled as Fairy King and Queen leave before the dawn. Theseus and Hippolyta, hunting early, rouse the lovers who, back as they were, are assured by Theseus that they shall be wedded that day. Bottom, baffled by his apparent dream, goes off to find his fellows.

In Act V they perform, in all sincerity, their interlude of Pyramus and Thisby before the amused court audience. Midnight sounds. When all have retired the fairies return to give their blessing to house and lovers, and Puck says the final word.

In performance

It has been suggested, without proof, that the magical play of *A Midsummer Night's Dream*, with some of Shakespeare's loveliest lyric verse, was written for a wedding. Its tripartite narrative of Romantics, Immortals and Mechanicals is an enchanted fantasy possessed by moonlight, though one or two modern critics perversely reduce it to an erotic nightmare. So much has happened to it through the centuries that we are often surprised now to find a straight performance. It has been the basis of masque, opera (someone described it as a libretto for Mendelssohn), ballet and film; it has been smothered in scenery or used for experiment. There have been live rabbits in one wood and gilded fairies in another. Oberon has often been a woman, with songs; the 'interlude' has been raw material for self-indulgent clowning; the richest twentieth-century revival was influenced by circus legerdemain.

Samuel Pepys (1662) called it "the most insipid, ridiculous play that I ever saw in my life." It was the core of a Restoration operatic version, *The Fairy Queen*, with Purcell's music and a last act choked by a near-demented efflorescence of spectacle, a dance of six monkeys, and a chorus of "Chineses" in a Chinese garden. A Midsummer Night's Dream did not return to the stage, almost as itself – after various song-crowded versions in the eighteenth century – until Madame Vestris and her husband, Charles Mathews, put it on at Covent Garden (1840). Samuel Phelps (who was Bottom) did it beautifully at Sadler's Wells in 1853, a production more Shakespearian than Charles Kean's desperately archaeological effort at the Princess's (1856); there a nine-year-old child, Ellen Terry, was Puck, belted and garlanded with flowers. For a long time any revival involved a proliferation of needless accessories (e.g. Tree's rabbits and bluebell thickets at Her Majesty's, 1900). Nothing much counted until Harley Granville Barker (Savoy, 1914) rejected Mendelssohn and muslin ballet skirts, peopling the wood with gold-and-bronze Cambodian-idol fairies. The Mechanicals were charmingly earnest, working against fate without any sequence of venerable gags.

Later, there were dozens of revivals: at the Old Vic; in central London (Basil Dean's Drury Lane production, 1924, was one of the last predominantly spectacular); at the Open Air Theatre in Regent's Park; and in Stratford. The most evocative performances in those years were the Jacobean-masque treatment (Old Vic, 1929), with the young Gielgud as Oberon and Leslie French as Puck ("I go, I go; *look* how I go"); and the patrician courtliness, under Bridges-Adams, at Stratford's new theatre (1932). There a critic described the Norman Wilkinson sets as "a nocturne in blue and silver, Elizabethan figures in alabaster stepping through some fold of time."

At Christmas 1937 Tyrone Guthrie delighted most people with his Old Vic album of Victoriana, flying fairies and tarlatan skirts, and Vivien Leigh's Titania like an engraving of the ballerina Taglioni. Gielgud and Peggy Ashcroft were Oberon and Titania at the Haymarket (1945). Peter Hall tried various Stratford/Aldwych versions, the last in 1963; and at length in 1970 Peter Brook's Stratford production invited us to consider the play as though it were entirely new. The setting, a white cube, became a wood when coils and tendrils of helical steel wire were released; Oberon and Puck were on trapezes; Titania and Oberon doubled with Hippolyta and Theseus, their other selves released in dream and night; the interlude was not a repository for the myriad accretions of the years; and in general the company spoke the verse better than one had ever known it.

The United States had its first performance in New York (1826); Charlotte Cushman at twenty-five played Oberon (Park Theatre, 1841), and Laure Keene, Puck (at her own theatre, 1859, a production scenically adventurous). Later, Augustin Daly took charge with three revivals between 1873 and 1890; he brought the last to Daly's, London (1895), with Ada Rehan's Helena: an occasion when Bernard Shaw wrote rudely that the panoramic illusion of Theseus' barge on its way to Athens seemed "more absurd than anything that occurs in the tragedy of Pyramus and Thisby." Granville Barker's Savoy production, as contentious as in London, reached Broadway at Wallack's in 1915.

Numerous later revivals included Max Reinhardt's spectacle (Century, 1927), acted in German, with Alexander Moissi's Oberon; and Joseph Papp's for the New York Shakespeare Festival, 1961. Douglas Campbell directed the comedy at Stratford, Ontario (1961), and Maggie Smith doubled Titania and Hippolyta for Robin Phillips (1977).

In other terms

A Midsummer Night's Dream has been filmed twice: in Hollywood (1935) in Reinhardt's much-cut grandiose romantic version; and in Britain (1969) by Peter Hall with his Royal Shakespeare Company, using the house, park and lakes of Compton Verney, near Stratford. Ian Richardson and Judi Dench were Oberon and Titania; Paul Rogers, Bottom. Hall said of the play: "It is about an English summer in which the seasons have gone wrong.... The King and Queen of the Fairies, embodying animal nature, are quarrelling, and their quarrels have upset the balance of nature."

Mendelssohn's music (1826–43) was used for many years. In 1826 Weber based his opera *Oberon* on the play. Benjamin Britten's opera, *A Midsummer Night's Dream*, came in 1960.

Chief characters

Theseus Legendary Duke of Athens. He will reappear in *The Two Noble Kinsmen* (see p. 126). Unexpectedly the second longest part.

Egeus Hermia's heavy father. Brook (1970) doubled the part with Quince; each is an example of paternalism.

Lysander He and Demetrius are practically interchangeable; Lysander has a "widow aunt, a dowager of great revenue" (I.1).

Demetrius Lysander calls him rudely a "spotted and inconstant man". Today the lovers' scenes are always played for comedy; until the mid-1920s they were usually straight.

Quince Peter Quince, the carpenter (the name is from "quines", or blocks of wood) is the Mechanicals' producer. Usually a benevolent martinet, thoroughly nervous when he speaks the prologue to "Pyramus and Thisby" instead of playing Thisby's mother. Much of the casting planned in I.2 is ignored, not that anyone notices it. Miles Malleson*** (Haymarket, 1945) was miraculously apt as a kind of parish council chairman.

Snug The joiner (hence his name, "close-fitting"). Frequently plays "the lion's part" with a mild purr.

Bottom Nick Bottom, the weaver, whose name is from the "bottom" or core of the skein upon which the weaver's yarn was wound. He has the longest part which is only right. Ralph Richardson*** (Old Vic/Sadler's Wells, 1931) was a moony triumph; Charles Laughton (Stratford, 1959) disappointing.

Flute Francis Flute, the bellows-mender. Cast as Thisby, with an intermittent tendency to become gruff and masculine.

Snout Tom Snout, the tinker. Originally the father of Pyramus. Ends as a rather sulky Wall.

Starveling Robin Starveling, the tailor, was possibly created by John Sincklo, who in Shakespeare's company was noted for parts requiring a thin man (e.g. Apothecary in *Romeo and Juliet*). Cast as Thisby's mother; finally a deaf, garrulous Moonshine with lantern, dog and bush of thorns.

Hippolyta, Queen of the Amazons, conquered by Theseus before the play opens and later wedded to him. Surprisingly, at the Old Vic (1960) appeared at curtain-rise in manacles.

Hermia Smallest of the lovers; probably acted by the boy who would play Maria in *Twelfth Night*. "You bead, you acorn", says the bemused Lysander (III.2).

Helena Taller of the two girls. In these days a comedienne's joy, she was acted seriously little more than half a century ago. Edith Evans, playing for comedy, failed at Drury Lane (1924). Coral Browne* (Old Vic, 1957) would have worried Granville Barker, who said in 1914 that Shakespeare meant the passage beginning "We, Hermia, like two artificial gods" (III.2) to be spoken "with a meticulous regard to its every beauty."

Oberon, King of the Fairies, with much of the finest verse ("Well, go thy way" and "I know a bank where the wild thyme blows" – both II.1 – and "We are spirits of another sort", III.2). There have been various Oberon fashions; at one period he was an actress who would sing "I know a bank"; today he can have sinister overtones, but he is a figure of great dignity and power. Ian Richardson*** (Stratford, 1962); Alan Howard*** (Stratford, 1970).

Titania, Queen of the Fairies, who has the key speech, though it can be unwisely clipped, "These are the forgeries of jealousy" (II.1). Peggy Ashcroft*** (Haymarket, 1945), a "spirit of no common rate", with an exquisite play of her hands. Shakespeare omitted a last-act song for the visiting fairies ("...will we sing and bless this place", V.1), so we often get "Roses, their sharp spines being gone" from *The Two Noble Kinsmen*.

Puck or Robin Goodfellow, Oberon's attendant and messenger. Unless discreetly acted, he can be trying; probably the best this century was Leslie French*** (Old Vic, 1929; and Open Air).

THE MERCHANT
OF VENICE

1596–7

Duke of Venice	servant, later servant to
Princes of Morocco and *Arragon*,	Bassanio
suitors to Portia	*Old Gobbo*, his father
Antonio, a merchant of Venice	*Leonardo*, servant to Bassanio
Bassanio, his friend, suitor to	*Balthasar*, *Stephano*, servants to
Portia	Portia
Solanio, *Salerio*, *Gratiano*, friends	*Portia*, a rich heiress of Belmont
to Antonio and Bassanio	*Nerissa*, her gentlewoman
Lorenzo, in love with Jessica	*Jessica*, daughter to Shylock
Shylock, a rich Jew	*Magnificoes of Venice, Officers of*
Tubal, a Jew, his friend	the Court of Justice, Gaolers,
Launcelot Gobbo, Shylock's	Servants, Other Attendants

Scene: Venice, and Portia's house near Belmont

Synopsis

Bassanio, needing money to woo Portia, heiress of Belmont, asks his friend Antonio, a Venetian merchant, for three thousand ducats. Having no money by him, and with all his ships at sea, Antonio goes to a Jewish moneylender, Shylock, who hates him for his loathing of usury. Shylock proposes what he calls a "merry bond" by which, if the money is not repaid within three months, he may take a pound of Antonio's flesh; and foolishly Antonio agrees.

Portia at Belmont (Act II) receives the Prince of Morocco, come to make his choice under the will of Portia's father. All suitors must choose from three caskets (gold, silver and lead) the one that contains her portrait; those who fail can never contemplate marriage again. Morocco fails with the golden casket, and the Prince of Arragon with the silver. Meanwhile, Bassanio and his friend Gratiano are on their way to Belmont; and Jessica, Shylock's daughter, in the disguise of a boy, has eloped with Lorenzo, taking rings and ducats with her.

Shylock (Act III) is furious about his losses. But Bassanio, choosing the correct (leaden) casket, prepares to wed Portia (and her gentlewoman Nerissa and Gratiano also plan to marry). Then Salerio, Lorenzo and Jessica bring news that Shylock is demanding his due and that Antonio's ships have "all miscarried". There must be a trial; Portia arranges to be present at the court as a young lawyer (Balthasar), Nerissa as "his" clerk. There (Act IV.1), admitting that the bond is flawless, she begs mercy from Shylock, who refuses and rejects all offers of money. He is about to take his pound of flesh when Portia turns on him: "Tarry a little; there is something else." She warns him that according to the bond, he is not entitled to "one jot of blood". Baffled, he will take his three thousand ducats – only to be told that as an alien who has conspired against a Venetian's life, his own life is forfeit. However, he is pardoned and allowed half his fortune on the pledge that he will become a Christian and bequeath the money to Lorenzo and Jessica at his death.

When he has left the court the play is practically over except (Act V) for the tranquil coda (it used often to be cut) in the moonlight at Belmont, some comedy with rings, and tidings that Antonio's "argosies" (ships) are safely come to port.

In performance

Once more the full title of a Quarto text, that of 1600, gives a useful simplified summary: "The most excellent Historie of the Merchant of Venice. With the extreame crueltie of Shylocke the Jewe towards the sayd Merchant, in cutting a just pound of his flesh; and the obtayning of Portia by the choyse of three chests." Shakespeare – as so often – took suggestions from various sources, Italian and English, for the pound-of-flesh and casket stories which he amalgamated and transmuted. Marlowe's *The Jew of Malta* might have given some hints; the Royal Shakespeare Company valuably staged this at Stratford (1965) in the same season as a revival of *The Merchant of Venice*, Eric Porter playing both Shylock and the monstrous Barabas. Gratiano's trial scene outburst (IV.1), "Thy currish spirit/Govern'd a wolf ... hang'd for human slaughter", could be a reference to Roderigo Lopez, a Jewish-Portuguese physician to the Queen, who in 1594 was hanged for conspiring against her.

The play has long been a show-piece: Portia's "quality of mercy" speech (IV.1) is as worn as anything in Shakespeare, though in *Measure for Measure* (II.2) Isabella is even more eloquent on the same subject. However often it is heard, Portia's "Tarry a little; there is something else" at the climax of the trial can remain startlingly dramatic. Shylock, of the alien minority in Venice, is the governing figure: in spite of the title of the play, Antonio is secondary to both his enemy and his saviour. The text bristles with "quotations' (as in much of the trial and, at V.1, Lorenzo's pæan to the power of music); but its main quality is dramatic, and Shylocks and Portias have multiplied.

Between 1605 and 1741 there was no recorded performance of Shakespeare's text. Instead, a silly version (1701) by George Granville, afterwards Lord Lansdowne, held the stage for some years; it began with Shakespeare and Dryden rising laurel-crowned. There was also a masque of Peleus and Thetis, besides a banquet with a comic Shylock drinking a toast to money. Charles Macklin (Drury Lane, 1741) brought back what was hailed as "the Jew that Shakespeare drew", a ferocious, revengeful, red-wigged figure that Macklin acted (as "the Nestor of the stage') until he was nearly ninety. Garrick (unimportant), John Henderson, John Philip Kemble (who for many years from 1786 at Drury Lane had Sarah Siddons as Portia) and George Frederick Cooke (like a depraved demon) were all Shylocks of variable quality.

The most astonishing was Edmund Kean (Drury Lane, 1814) who, in black beard and wig, changed Shylock from a malignant fiend to a man of racial pride, plausibly resentful ("Hath not a Jew eyes?", III.1), an avenger through force of circumstance. Macready (Covent Garden, 1823) added touches of nobility to his harshness. More than half a century later Henry Irving's Shylock (a long Lyceum run, 1879, with Ellen Terry's radiant Portia) was intensely proud, gently menacing, the type of a persecuted race.

The twentieth century brought many versions: hysterical, extravagantly theatrical (Tree, His Majesty's, 1908); repulsively realistic (Maurice Moscovitch, Royal Court, 1919, his first part in English); dignified and implacable in the Irving manner (Ernest Milton, St James's, 1932); and so on, through performances by such players as Gielgud (in the manner of Granville-Barker's "sordid little outsider, passionate, resentful"), Donald Wolfit, Paul Rogers, Michael Redgrave, to Laurence Olivier's prosperous private banker (for the National company, Cambridge Theatre, London, 1970). His dance of triumph on hearing of Antonio's ill-fortune lingers in memory, with the offstage cry of anguish after Shylock had left the court (Jonathan Miller directed). The Portia of her day has been Peggy Ashcroft (Old Vic, 1932; Queen's, 1938; particularly Stratford, 1953). The most capricious production, Terence Gray's at Cambridge aside (Gray was thoroughly bored with the play and showed it), was Komisarjevsky's (Stratford, 1932), a wild fantastication in which Randle Ayrton's unyielding Jew seemed out of key.

There have been productions in the United States since 1752. George Frederick Cooke came to New York from London in 1810, and Edmund Kean, Charles Kemble, Charles Kean and Henry Irving were other nineteenth-century English visitors. Prominent American players were Edwin Booth (1867, grim and self-centred); Richard Mansfield, at first (1893) highly sympathetic, but growing into extreme malevolence in later years; and John Drew (with Ada Rehan, 1898) in a revival of Augustin Daly opulence. After E.H. Sothern (melodramatic), Robert Mantell and David Warfield, the Shylock of his day was probably Walter Hampden (New York, 1925, with Ethel Barrymore as a lovely Portia), a lonely, dominating, totally vindictive man. Most succeeding actors, George Arliss (1928) among them, were fairly colourless until Boris Tumarin (Gate Theatre) and George C. Scott (New York Shakespeare Festival), both in 1962, re-animated Shylock, Scott especially in a sardonic and obsessive performance. The play has been done at Stratford, Ontario (e.g. Frederick Valk, 1955) and Stratford, Connecticut (1957; with Morris Carnovsky and Katharine Hepburn in the main parts.)

Reinhardt had an uncommonly spectacular production in the Campo San Trovaso, Venice (1934, with Memo Benassi and Marta Abba).

In other terms

Play: St John Ervine, the critic and dramatist, wrote a sequel to Shakespeare, *The Lady of Belmont* (1923), set ten years after the trial, with Shylock now a Venetian senator and the Doge's friend. Opera: *Merchant of Venice* (1922), written by Adrian Welles Beecham at the age of fifteen and directed by Sir Frank Benson at the Duke of York's. Music: "Tell me where is fancy bred" (1821), a setting for voices and guitar, by Weber; Serenade for Music (1938), Act V, by Ralph Vaughan Williams.

Chief characters

Shylock Second longest part (359 lines), probably created by Richard Burbage. Usurer – the name is a transliteration of the Hebrew word for "cormorant" – outraged father, avenging creditor: the precise emphases must vary with the actor, and also with the changing responses to Jewry across the centuries. Shylock is both villain and victim. Charles Macklin*** (1741 and for nearly fifty years), Edmund Kean*** (1814), Henry Irving*** (1879), Laurence Olivier*** (1970).

Antonio The unselfish, serious, patient merchant, who in the theatre must have personality enough not to be a cipher before the obliterating Shylock. He is not just a distillation of melancholy.

Bassanio "A Venetian, a scholar, and a soldier"; nobly spoken; deeply remorseful at the news of Antonio's misfortune. Though critics have abused him, he is more than a fortune-hunter.

Gratiano "Let me play the fool/With mirth and laughter let old wrinkles come" (I.1). Overplayed, he can be tedious, and he needs great tact in performance, especially in those trial scene interpolations.

Duke of Venice A purely functional character; but he should be imposing enough to distract us from the bizarre workings of the so-called "strict court".

Prince of Morocco The sonorously rhetorical suitor ("a tawny Moor all in white") who chooses the gold casket.

Prince of Arragon This affected Spanish suitor (man of the silver casket) used frequently to be cut, but his scene can take the theatre, if kept within bounds. Ian Richardson* (Stratford, 1960).

Lorenzo Jessica's lover lives almost entirely on his praise of music in the Belmont epilogue (V.1).

Solanio and **Salerio**. In theatre jargon these gentlemen of Venice are "the Sals" or "the Salads". Once they were Salanio and Salarino; but they have not changed with any adjustment of their names. Their phrasing is magnificent; its effect too often dissipated by minor actors.

Launcelot Gobbo One of Shakespeare's dreariest clowns, especially in the scene (II.2) with his father, Old Gobbo. Still, Jessica calls him a "merry devil".

Balthasar Portia's servant – whose name is shared, carelessly, with the young "lawyer". He depends in the theatre on one line, "Madam, I go with all convenient speed" (III.4), which means a snail's pace.

Portia The great lady of Belmont, patrician, witty, adventurous, is at the heart of the fantasy: first the casket-story, then her trial masquerade (we never know about the conference with Bellario, learned doctor of Padua); finally, after the ring-time comedy, her splendidly unexplained bonus to Antonio (V.1):

Unseal this letter soon;
There you shall find three of your argosies

> Are richly come to harbour suddenly.
> You shall not know by what strange accident
> I chancèd on this letter.

Portia needs no explanation; she moves in her own golden world. Ellen Terry*** (1879 and later); Peggy Ashcroft*** (particularly Stratford, 1953).

Nerissa Portia's gentlewoman (a first draft was Lucetta in *The Two Gentlemen of Verona*). She is "echoing merriment; not much more", said Granville Barker. We can agree; but she has to be a capable lawyer's clerk.

Jessica The eloping daughter exists less when she is on the stage than in Shylock's passion when she is absent. A small part, usually made smaller by the cutting of III.5.

HENRY IV
PART 1

1596–7

Historically, the period of the action is the summer of 1402 to the summer of 1403. When the play opens, Henry IV, who reigned from 1399 to 1413, has been on the throne for three years. Hotspur was twenty-three years older than Prince Hal; but Shakespeare, for his own purposes, treats them as contemporaries.

King Henry the Fourth	*Owen Glendower*
Henry, Prince of Wales and *Prince*	*Sir Richard Vernon*
John of Lancaster, (his sons)	*Sir John Falstaff, Poins, Bardolph,*
Earl of Westmoreland and *Sir Walter*	*Peto, Gadshill*, irregular
Blunt, friends of the King	humorists
Thomas Percy, Earl of Worcester	*Francis*, a drawer (potboy)
Henry Percy, Earl of	*Lady Percy*, wife of Hotspur and
Northumberland	sister of Mortimer
Henry Percy, surnamed *Hotspur*,	*Lady Mortimer*, Mortimer's wife
his son	and daughter of Glendower
Edmund Mortimer, Earl of March	*Hostess Quickly*, of the Boar's
Archibald, Earl of Douglas	Head, Eastcheap
Scroop, Archbishop of York	Lords, Officers, Attendants,
Sir Michael, friend of the	Sheriff, Vintner, Chamberlain,
Archbishop	Drawers, Carriers, Travellers

Scene: England

Synopsis

King Henry IV ("So shaken as we are, so wan with care") is deeply troubled by affairs national and domestic. Nationally, he has to meet a rebellion raised by the Welshman, Glendower, who is joined by the fiery Harry Percy (Hotspur), and Hotspur's uncle (Worcester) and father (Northumberland). Domestically, the King mourns the behaviour of his son, the Prince of Wales (Prince Hal), who is always in the most dubious company, the fat knight Sir John Falstaff and his associates. Hal, in a soliloquy at the end of Act I, promises to redeem himself when the need comes

> Like bright metal on a sullen ground,
> My reformation, glitt'ring o'er my fault,
> Shall show more goodly and attract more eyes
> Than that which hath no foil to set it off.

The companions (Act II) join in a robbery, after which Hal and Poins, disguised, scare away Falstaff and Bardolph, though Falstaff at the Boar's Head boasts of his enterprise before Hal exposes him. During a long tavern charade Falstaff and Hal in turn impersonate the King, and Hal speaks with uncomfortable candour. In Wales (Act III) the rebels are assembled: Glendower, his former prisoner Mortimer, Hotspur's brother-in-law (now married to Glendower's daughter), Hotspur himself, and Worcester. Between them they plan how to divide the kingdom when victory is won. Meanwhile in London the King admonishes his son, comparing his behaviour with the splendour of Hotspur ("Mars in swathling clothes"). Hal promises him that there will be a change, and before leaving with his father to fight the rebels, offers to Falstaff a command of foot soldiers.

The rebels find that their forces are depleted (Act IV), but Hotspur urges battle. Though (Act V) the King offers pardon if the rebels disband, Worcester distrustfully keeps the news from Hotspur. In the battle of Shrewsbury Hal kills Hotspur in single fight (Falstaff, who earlier in V.1 has had his famous cynical soliloquy on honour, claims that he is responsible). After the royal army has won and two of the rebels have been sent for execution, Hal and his brother Prince John set off on various punitive expeditions.

In performance

Henry IV is Falstaff's play, the record of the fat knight who was not only witty in himself, but the cause of wit in other men: "the voice of spontaneous anarchy," said Robert Speaight, "opposed to calculating order". He and his irregular humorists supply only a secondary plot in the great twin brethren of the chronicle plays; but Falstaff stands – not by sheer bulk alone – at stage centre, something that in Part 1 can be a little unfair to the captains and the kings, the Prince of Wales and Hotspur, both grand theatrical parts. The fusion of high dramatic verse and robust comedy is almost unmatched in the Shakespeare Folio.

Part 1 has always been first in two senses. It has had more productions than its even finer sequel; and only in recent years have we found them played together in consecutive performances. (This, even so, is not invariable). The sources here are Holinshed and a play which was the first half of the surviving and anonymous *Famous Victories of Henry V* (1598). Clearly there must have been a great many early performances. We cannot say for certain who were the first Prince and Falstaff (in 1596 or 1597) – Burbage, perhaps, and Kemp, but this is speculation. In 1682 Betterton was Hotspur and in 1700 Falstaff, "hitting the humour better than any that have aimed at it before", said a playgoer. James Quin (first half of the eighteenth century) was praised as a Falstaff of intellect and breeding; John Henderson, always laughing, was the best of a later plethora.

Stephen Kemble, John Philip's brother, arrived early in the nineteenth century with an apparently unimaginative portrait much liked – as other Falstaffs had been – because he could play without padding. Macready, Hotspur at first, became a majestic King in Part 2. Phelps, as Falstaff, put on Part 1 often at Sadler's Wells. Tree ("he will never be even moderately good," said Shaw) was Falstaff at the Haymarket (1896). Matheson Lang,

Hotspur for Tree at His Majesty's (1914), probably began the tradition of stammering. The only warrant for this is Lady Percy's line (Part 2, II.3), "Speaking thick/Which nature made his blemish", something that means merely "thick and fast", pelting speech. Tree/Lang's notion remained fashionable for some decades.

Stratford audiences loved Roy Byford's convulsively laughing Falstaff – like Stephen Kemble, free from padding – on several "festival" occasions for Bridges-Adams in the 1920s and 1930s. The two most acclaimed revivals were Robert Atkins's (His Majesty's, 1935), with the comedian George Robey in a sack-and-sugar performance inevitably overpraised at the time; and a marvellous 1945 production (Old Vic company at New Theatre, under John Burrell), with Ralph Richardson's Falstaff and Olivier's Hotspur. No one had driven more surely than Richardson into the knight's wise, agile mind or examined the richly textured prose with a livelier zest. Laurence Olivier, who played Hotspur with stabbing, darting fire, chose to stammer on the letter "w" so that he died with his last word struggling for utterance: "Thou art dust/And food for—" To which the Prince replies: "For worms, brave Percy. Fare thee well, great heart." Michael Redgrave, six years later at Stratford, ignored the stammer and chose a thick Northumbrian accent. Falstaffs have included such actors as Anthony Quayle (Stratford, 1951), Donald Wolfit (King's Hammersmith, 1953), Hugh Griffith (Stratford, 1964), Brewster Mason (Stratford/Aldwych, 1975–6).

Part 1 appeared at the Chapel Street Theatre, New York, in December 1761. William Warren and Thomas Abthorpe Cooper (Philadelphia, 1796) were a famous pair as Falstaff and Hotspur. But probably the most accomplished American Falstaff was James Henry Hackett, between 1828 and 1871. Not everyone liked him, for he held that the man had neither refinement, intellect nor breeding, but even mere length of service would have kept him in the records. Maurice Evans was Falstaff in Philadelphia (1937) and New York (1939). Part 1 was staged at Stratford, Ontario in 1958, 1965 and 1979.

Scenes most susceptible to cutting at various times, though not lately, have been the charade in II.4, the Glendower scene (III.1), and the brief passage for the Archbishop of York and a priest, Sir Michael (IV.4).

Chief characters

Henry IV Historically, he is thirty-seven years old, but in the play he seems nearly twice that age, though there is no reason to present him as a glum neurotic. He speaks nobly in the scene with the Prince (III.2), "I know not whether God will have it so/For some displeasing service I have done." Randle Ayrton** (especially Stratford, 1932); Nicholas Hannen*** (New, 1945).

Henry, Prince of Wales Determined, as it has been said, to be a be a prince for all seasons. Actors emphasize his "I do, I will" in reply to Falstaff's charade-speech (II.4).

Henry Percy (Hotspur) Not a mere romantic blazon, but a man hurtling and passionate. He has the great cry (I.3), "By heaven, methinks it were an easy leap/To pluck bright honour from the pale-fac'd moon." Laurence Olivier*** (New, 1945).

Sir John Falstaff In comedy, Shakespeare's fullest creation and a prodigious coiner of phrases. Roy Byford*** (Stratford, 1930, and other times); Ralph Richardson*** (New, 1945); Hugh Griffith** (Stratford, 1964).

Sir Richard Vernon Remembered for the speech (IV.1), de-

scribing the Prince, "I saw young Harry, with his beaver on."
Bardolph Falstaff's follower, whose red-purple face inspires his
master to a prose aria (III.3), "I never see thy face but I think upon
hell-fire."

Owen Glendower "That great magician, damn'd Glendower."
We must assume that someone in Shakespeare's company had a
gift for Welsh character.

Earl of Worcester Hotspur's uncle ("Your presence is too bold
and peremptory," says the King, I.3).

Earl of Northumberland Hotspur's father; he disappears after
the first act. Formerly the tyrant of *Richard II*, he speaks now (I.3)
of "the unhappy king."

Lady Percy Hotspur's wife, with two very brief but – especially
the first – rewarding scenes. Fabia Drake*** (Stratford, 1932).

Hostess Quickly Angry, infatuated, voluble. Elizabeth
Spriggs*** (Stratford, 1966)

Lady Mortimer Edmund Mortimer's Welsh-speaking wife,
Glendower's daughter. Her song (III.1), in a passage that was
formerly too often cut, is a wistful moment in a twilit scene
miraculously evoked by Bridges-Adams (Stratford, 1930, 1932).

HENRY IV
PART 2
1598

Historically, Henry IV (Henry Bolingbroke) died in 1413. Shakespeare
presents him (IV.5) as urging his son "to busy giddy minds/With
foreign quarrels, that action, hence borne out,/May waste the memory
of the former days."

King Henry the Fourth	*Harcourt*
Henry, Prince of Wales, afterwards	*The Lord Chief Justice*
King Henry V	*Sir John Falstaff, Edward Poins,*
Prince John of Lancaster, Prince	*Bardolph, Pistol, Peto, Falstaff's*
Humphrey of Gloucester and	*Page,* irregular humorists
Thomas, Duke of Clarence, his	*Robert Shallow, Silence,*
brothers	Gloucestershire country justices
OPPOSING THE KING	*Davy,* Shallow's servant
Earl of Northumberland	*Ralph Mouldy, Simon Shadow,*
Scroop, Archbishop of York	*Thomas Wart, Francis Feeble,*
Lord Mowbray	*Peter Bullcalf,* countrymen
Lord Hastings	*Fang* and *Snare,* Sheriff's officers
Lord Bardolph	*Francis,* a drawer (potboy)
Sir John Colville	*Lady Northumberland*
Travers and *Morton,*	*Lady Percy,* Hotspur's widow
Northumberland's retainers	*Hostess Quickly,* of the Boar's
FOR THE KING	Head, Eastcheap
Earl of Warwick	*Doll Tearsheet,* a whore
Earl of Westmoreland	*Rumour,* the Presenter
Earl of Surrey, Earl of Kent, Sir	Lords, Attendants, Porters,
John Blunt, do not speak	Drawers, Beadles, Grooms,
Gower	Servants

Scene: England

Synopsis

In his castle at Warkworth the Earl of Northumberland learns, after previous false tidings, that Hotspur has been killed and that royal troops, commanded by Prince John of Lancaster and the Earl of Westmoreland, are advancing towards him. In London the Lord Chief Justice warns Falstaff of his behaviour and reminds him that he is to join Prince John's forces. Falstaff (Act II) persuades Hostess Quickly of the Boar's Head Tavern to lend him still more money; the old man, at supper with Doll Tearsheet, speaks unguardedly of Prince Hal and Poins who, disguised as potmen, overhear it all.

The King (Act III) is told of Owen Glendower's death; and Falstaff, recruiting in the Cotswolds, meets an old friend, Justice Robert Shallow (and another country justice, Silence). The northern rebels, who are without Northumberland, are tricked (Act IV) into surrendering to Prince John's army. King Henry is ill at Westminster: Hal, finding him asleep and believing him to be dead, takes the crown from the pillow. Later, deeply moved, he is rebuked by the awakened King. They are reconciled (IV.5): "God put it in thy mind to take it hence, / That thou mightst win the more thy father's love."

Down in Gloucestershire (V.3), Falstaff (who has returned that way to visit Shallow) hears from Pistol that the King is dead and Hal has succeeded him. Certain of fortune, Falstaff sets out for London with his followers (and Shallow); but when he calls to the new King, Henry V, coming from the coronation, he is rejected and sent with his party to the Fleet prison until – "their conversations / Appear more wise and modest to the world."

In performance

The sixth longest of the plays, with nearly twice as many characters as Part 1, *Henry IV, Part 2*, relatively autumnal, has lagged behind its partner. Falstaff, if a little quieter, is no whit diminished (the Cotswold scenes are incomparable comedy); and Prince Hal's character grows with his accession as Henry V. There is, of course, no Hotspur; the northern rebellion is a sour interlude; and moralists, especially in the nineteenth century, were affronted by that "abandoned creature, Doll Tearsheet", with (said *The Athenaeum* in 1853) "certain freedoms not exactly in accordance with the prevailing taste in modern stage manners". Probably the play was not performed between the pre-Civil War period and early in the eighteenth century, when a distorted version reached Drury Lane. Later, Part 2, though never as popular as Part 1, had numerous productions (James Quin and John Henderson were sometimes its Falstaff); John Philip Kemble played the King at Covent Garden (1804); a revival there (1821) mocked George IV's coronation; Macready, a superb Hotspur in Part 1, often acted the King in Part 2 with his hypnotic grandeur; and Phelps, at Sadler's Wells, contrived to double the King and Hotspur on various occasions from 1853.

Frank Benson, who had special affection for Part 2, often staged it at Stratford with a comedian of gusto, George Weir, as Falstaff. Barry Jackson, in 1913, did what was then a rarity, a full text of Part 1 at the Birmingham Repertory; and on Shakespeare's birthday, nine years later, he put on both parts consecutively. So did Bridges-Adams in 1932, at the opening of the present theatre in Stratford-upon-Avon (Roy Byford as Falstaff, Randle Ayrton as the King beneath the throne's crimson canopy, and Gyles Isham as Hal). In later years, when possible, the two parts would be acted in conjunction at the Old Vic and Stratford. Nothing would excel the Vic company's performance at the New (1945; Ralph Richardson as Falstaff and Laurence Olivier as Shallow in Part 2); and at Stratford (1964), a production by Peter Hall, John Barton and Clifford Williams (Falstaff, Hugh Griffith).

Tony van Bridge played Falstaff at Stratford, Ontario, in 1965; and the chronicles were revived there in 1979.

In other terms

Orson Welles's *Chimes at Midnight* (1966: *Falstaff* in USA) was an inadequately telescoped version of the histories. Elgar's symphonic study, *Falstaff*, was composed in 1913.

Chief characters

Henry IV Macready*** used to glorify the part. With its apostrophe to Sleep (III.1) and its rebuke to Hal (IV.5) it can be darkly impressive; midway there is such a sudden leap in the mind as "O Westmoreland, thou art a summer bird,/Which ever in the haunch of winter sings/The lifting up of day" (IV.4). Nicholas Hannen*** (New, 1945).

Henry, Prince of Wales After one relapse into the old mood, he is a graver figure, finding maturity with the succession to the throne. In the circumstances, the rejection of Falstaff (V.5) is inevitable.

Prince John of Lancaster The unlikeable prince ("this same young sober-blooded boy") who quells the northern rebellion (Act IV).

Lord Chief Justice Early in the play he is coping with Falstaff; at the end he is the new King's adviser ("You shall be as a father to my youth").

Sir John Falstaff A trifle quieter than in Part 1, but still sovereign. "I am as poor as Job, my Lord, but not so patient" (I.2), "I can get no remedy against this consumption of the purse" (I.2), "We have heard the chimes at midnight" (III.2), the sherris-sack soliloquy (IV.3). We think of him when he suddenly turns aside at the Boar's Head with "Peace, good Doll! ... Do not bid me remember mine end" (II.4). Ralph Richardson*** (New, 1945), Hugh Griffith** (Stratford, 1964).

Bardolph Now with Falstaff in the wars and in Gloucestershire. Shakespeare is as careless as ever with names. The cast includes an inconsiderable Lord Bardolph, who comes from Shrewsbury to Warkworth.

Pistol A "swaggering rascal", whose Marlovian histrionics are in the *Tamburlaine* manner: "Packhorses/And hollow pamper'd jades of Asia,/Which cannot go but thirty miles a day" (II.4), "Under which King, Bezonian! speak, or die" (V.3).

Robert Shallow The husk of a man who remembers, in his Cotswold orchard, the mad days he knew when he and all the world were young and Jack Falstaff was "a crack not thus high" and page to Thomas Mowbray, Duke of Norfolk. Shallow lives for ever in our first sight of him ("And is old Double dead?" III.2), and in that warm silver night-piece with Silence jetting into song, and Falstaff sitting by, contemplative (V.3). Laurence Olivier*** (New, 1945); Alan Badel** (Stratford, 1951).

Silence The other Gloucestershire justice, "Cousin Silence", who is in more or less unquenchable song throughout the orchard scene. "Now comes in the sweet o'th'night" (V.3). Miles Malleson** (New, 1945).

Feeble The women's tailor, chosen as a recruit in the first

Cotswold scene (III.2): "I will do my good will, sir; you can have no more." His natural courage is opposed to the cowardice of the roaring "Peter Bullcalf o'th'green".

Lady Percy Her single scene (II.3) used regularly to be cut, a sad loss, for the widowed Kate uses the unforgettable phrase about dead Hotspur, "By his light/Did all the chivalry of England move"; she goes on to the line, "speaking thick which nature made his blemish", the misinterpreted suggestion that set a fashion for Hotspur's stammer. Fabia Drake*** (Stratford, 1932); Barbara Jefford* (Stratford, 1951).

Hostess Quickly Talkative to the bitter end, which has to be bitter indeed (V.4). Hers is the line, "He hath eaten me out of house and home" (II.1). Elizabeth Spriggs*** (Birmingham Repertory, 1960; Stratford, 1966).

Doll Tearsheet The boisterous Boar's Head whore endeared to us for her moments of affection for Falstaff (II.4). But we have to leave her (V.4) near the whipping-post.

Rumour, "painted full of tongues", is the Prologue, or Presenter. A surging pictorial speech, it has often been cut; once, too, split capriciously among a whole corps of players. Never done better than by Vivienne Bennett** (Old Vic, 1935).

THE MERRY WIVES
OF WINDSOR

1597–8

Sir John Falstaff	*Bardolph, Nym, Pistol*, Falstaff's
Fenton, a young gentleman	followers
Robert Shallow, a country justice	*Robin*, a page to Falstaff
Abraham Slender, Shallow's cousin	*Simple*, Slender's servant
Frank Ford and *George Page*,	*John Rugby*, servant to Dr Caius
citizens of Windsor	*Mistress Alice Ford*
William Page, a boy; Page's son	*Mistress Margaret Page*
Sir Hugh Evans, a Welsh parson	*Anne Page*, her daughter
Doctor Caius, a French physician	*Mistress Quickly*, servant to Caius
Host of the Garter Inn	Servants to Page, Ford etc.

Scene: Windsor and the neighbourhood

Synopsis

Sir John Falstaff, in Windsor and short of money, decides to woo both Mistress Ford and Mistress Page, prosperous citizens' wives, and sends identical letters to them. Two of Falstaff's discharged followers, Pistol and Nym, reveal this (Act II) to the husbands, though only the jealous Ford takes real notice. Going to the Garter Inn, disguised as a "Master Brook", he asks Falstaff to woo Mistress Ford on his behalf and learns that the knight already has an assignation. The wives prepare to trick Falstaff. At the same time other complex love-matters are in progress. The French physician, Caius, in love with Anne Page, has challenged Parson Hugh Evans to a duel, simply because Evans has asked the doctor's housekeeper, Quickly, to help the foolish Abraham Slender to Anne's hand. Actually, Anne – as we have seen in Act I

– is in love with Master Fenton who has already enlisted the versatile Quickly as an ally. Caius and Evans (Act III) are reconciled by the Host of the Garter who has neatly prevented the duel.

In III.3 Falstaff is carried from Ford's house (just as Ford arrives to search it) in a laundry-basket of dirty linen; later, as "Brook", Ford discovers what has happened and hears of a new assignation between Falstaff and Mistress Ford (III.5). This time (IV.2) Falstaff escapes in the clothes of a maid's aunt whom Ford, still unknowing, beats unmercifully as a witch. At length, the jest revealed to their husbands, the wives get Falstaff, disguised as the ghost of Herne the Hunter, to meet Mistress Ford in Windsor Forest at midnight. There (Act V) all is settled when Falstaff is assailed by a group of Windsor children, disguised as fairies and hobgoblins. Caius and Slender are each tricked into running off with boy "fairies", thinking them to be Anne. Fenton and Anne appear, just married; and the end will be a journey home "to laugh this sport o'er by a country fire."

In performance

Legend says that Queen Elizabeth wished to see Falstaff in love, and this predominantly prose comedy is the result, doubtless written in a hurry (tenuous legend, again, suggests a fortnight). One idea is that it was written early in 1597 and performed for a Garter celebration at Windsor. Never a favourite with academic critics, it usually goes well in the theatre, in its repetitive method, once we have realized that some of the characters (Falstaff himself, Shallow, Pistol, Bardolph, Quickly) have the names of great originals and little else. Falstaff, so mercilessly deceived by the merry wives, is an ample acting part, though the sharpest character is Ford, the Windsor citizen, who might be described as Leontes (*The Winter's Tale*) in the key of comedy, and who works himself into a glorious rage never better managed than by Ian Richardson at Stratford (1975).

The piece used to be acted in a summer setting; but many points ("sea-coal fire", "this raw rheumatic day", and so on) show that it is a winter piece influenced, no doubt, by the season when Shakespeare wrote it. The speech on the Order of the Garter (V.5), assigned to the "Fairy Queen" (often, and oddly, Mistress Quickly), is frequently cut; so, too, with more reason, though they did appear at e.g. the Mermaid (1975) and Stratford/Aldwych (1979–80), are the references (IV.3 and IV.5) to horse-stealing "Germans" which had a purely topical significance as dead now as so many topical jokes can be.

The comedy was approved in eighteenth-century London (James Quin a notable early Falstaff; John Henderson a later one), and through the nineteenth century as well. Charles Kean, who played Ford at the Princess's (1851) was better than usual. Tree was a rather juiceless Falstaff at the Haymarket (1889) and – here with Ellen Terry and Madge Kendal as the wives – at His Majesty's (1902). Oscar Asche was brave enough to do the piece in its proper winter setting (Garrick, 1911); Bridges-Adams directed it famously (Lyric, Hammersmith, 1923, with Edith Evans and Dorothy Green, as the wives, Roy Byford as Falstaff, Randle Ayrton as Ford); Theodore Komisarjevsky (Stratford, 1935) fantasticated it into something like a Viennese operetta, though remaining – he said cheerfully – "faithful in word and gesture to Shakespeare". The best of the Old Vic and Stratford performances were in 1951 (Old Vic, Roger Livesey as Falstaff, Peggy Ashcroft as Mistress Page), 1955 (Paul Rogers at the Old

Vic, Anthony Quayle at Stratford) and 1975 (Stratford, Brewster Mason as Falstaff, Ian Richardson as Ford).

The first American production was in Philadelphia, 1770; the first in New York, 1789. James Henry Hackett, for nearly forty years until 1871, was the definitive American Falstaff (described as "exorbitantly funny") in the comedy and in *Henry IV*. Ada Rehan was Mistress Ford for Daly (1885 and 1898; originally with Charles Fisher, later with George Clarke). Otis Skinner was Falstaff at the Knickerbocker (1928). Stratford, Ontario: Douglas Campbell, 1956; Tony van Bridge, 1967.

In other terms

Frederick Reynolds made a wild musical adaptation (Drury Lane, 1824). Otto Nicolai's opera, *The Merry Wives of Windsor*, was composed in 1849; Verdi's *Falstaff* in 1893; and Vaughan Williams's *Sir John in Love* in 1929.

Chief characters

Sir John Falstaff The knight of the Garter Inn at Windsor is, intellectually, only a wraith of the knight of the Boar's Head in Eastcheap. The Falstaff of *Henry IV* would never have submitted to these humiliations, but the part (496 lines) is theatrically useful at the centre of a farce; the old wit can flicker: "Think'st thou I'll endanger my soul gratis" (II.2), and "A man of continual dissolution and thaw" (III.5). Actors such as Baliol Holloway*** (many times in the 1920s and 1930s) and Paul Rogers*** (Old Vic, 1955) have played him for all he is worth.

Slender A minor Sir Andrew (*Twelfth Night*), invariably in peril of burlesque.

Shallow Only the name connects this thin sketch with Falstaff's Cotswold host in *Henry IV, Part 2*.

Ford The jealous husband who – as himself and as "Master Brook" – runs a high temperature throughout. Acted masterfully by Ian Richardson*** (Stratford, 1975) as if he were being bounced on a trampoline. Ben Kingsley** (Stratford/Aldwych, 1979–80).

Page A bluff, intelligent contrast with the hysterical Ford.

Parson Hugh Evans Another Welsh part for the actor in Shakespeare's company who, we must surmise, played Glendower in *Henry IV, Part 1* and Fluellen in *Henry V*.

Caius A parodied Frenchman represented by a series of fizzing verbal rockets.

Host of the Garter Heartily jovial, but too often boomed out of existence.

Fenton A personable blank, though Gyles Isham* (Stratford, 1931) found some character.

Simple Slender's man who at least can remind his master that Alice Shortcake borrowed his copy of the Book of Riddles "upon All-Hallowmass last, a fortnight afore Michaelmas" (I.1).

Bardolph Becomes a tapster at the Garter Inn.

Pistol Still speaking inflated blank verse, he fades away feebly in Act II, though he returns as a Hobgoblin at Herne's Oak. One familiar observation: "The world's mine oyster/Which I with sword will open" (II.2).

Nym Makes tedious play with the fashionable word "humours", and also disappears.

Mistress Alice Ford She is the wife who three times traps Falstaff. When he first enters her house she should be asleep. His greeting, "Have I caught thee, my heavenly jewel?" is the first line of a sonnet by Philip Sidney that the Elizabethan audience would know and which goes on: "Teaching sleep most fair to be?"

Mistress Page The other laughing conspirator, and the longer part.

Anne Page "Sweet Anne", much courted, would live if only for her protest on hearing her mother's support of Caius as a husband: "I had rather be set quick i'th'earth and bowl'd to death with turnips" (III.4). Kate Nicholls* (Stratford, 1979).

Mistress Quickly The third longest part, and no wonder, for she is a desperately loquacious "she-Mercury". Here she is house-keeper to Dr Caius, and the play's go-between. Nothing (except the name and the verbosity) to do with Hostess Quickly.

MUCH ADO ABOUT NOTHING

1598–9

Don Pedro, Prince of Arragon	*Dogberry*, a constable
Don John, his bastard brother	*Verges*, a headborough (parish
Claudio, a young lord of Florence	officer or petty constable)
Benedick, a young lord of Padua	*A Sexton*
Leonato, Governor of Messina	*A Boy*
Antonio, his brother	*Hero*, Leonato's daughter
Balthasar, attendant on Don Pedro	*Beatrice*, Leonato's niece
Borachio and *Conrade*, followers of	*Margaret*, *Ursula*, gentlewomen
Don John	attending on Hero
Friar Francis	Messengers, Watch, Attendants

Scene: Messina (Sicily)

Synopsis

Leonato, Governor of Messina, is host to Don Pedro, the Prince of Arragon, who has come from suppressing a rebellion by his bastard brother, Don John. With Pedro are John, now "reconciled" to him; Claudio, a young Florentine lord, of whom John is bitterly resentful; and a Paduan lord, Benedick, said to be a confirmed bachelor and engaged in a "merry war" with Leonato's niece, Beatrice, apparently a confirmed spinster. Claudio loves Leonato's daughter, Hero; Don John swears to thwart him. After a masked ball (Act II) the wedding of Claudio and Hero is planned. Borachio, Don John's follower, tells him that having seen that the Prince and Claudio are listening, he will exchange love vows by night with Hero's gentlewoman, dressed in her mistress's clothes, at Hero's bedroom window.

Pedro, Claudio and Leonato ensure that Benedick (hidden in a garden arbour) hears them discuss Beatrice's presumably passion-ate love for him. In Act III Hero and Ursula play a similar trick on the listening Beatrice (here the passion is Benedick's). On the night before the wedding Don John offers to give the Prince and Claudio proof of Hero's unfaithfulness. Later, Borachio, heard boasting about his successful deceit to a drunken comrade, is arrested by the Watch and taken to Dogberry, the constable. Before Leonato can know anything, the wedding ceremony (Act

IV) is due. In the church Claudio denounces Hero, who faints. Friar Francis, disbelieving the charge, proposes – when the Prince and Claudio have gone – that Hero should be reported dead and hidden until the truth is known. Beatrice, much grieved, urges Benedick to kill Claudio. At length (Act V) all is revealed, and the penitent Claudio promises to marry a niece of Leonato, said to be the image of "dead" Hero. She is, of course, Hero herself; Beatrice and Benedick, as expected, resolve their "merry war", and news comes that Don John has been taken prisoner.

In performance

Just as Falstaff steps out in front of the chronicle-figures in *Henry IV*, so Benedick and Beatrice, fighting their "merry war", rule the patrician comedy of *Much Ado About Nothing* (which is also a comedy of eavesdropping). Based on a traditional Italian tale, the play is a work of glittering artifice that needs in performance a style sometimes absent. Too many directors in the last thirty years have sought to vary it by changing the period: thus it has been put into British Regency fashions, Italy in the mid-nineteenth century (the Risorgimento), Sicily of eighty years ago, somewhere in Latin America, and – most daring and curiously effective of all – post-Mutiny India in some counterpart of Simla or Darjeeling, with Dogberry as a babu.

Nothing of this has much damaged what the critic, A.B. Walkley, writing in 1891, called a "composite picture of the multifarious, seething, fermenting life, the polychromatic phantasmagoria of the Renaissance", and what Bernard Shaw (1905) preferred to dismiss as "a hopeless story, pleasing only to lovers of the illustrated police papers." One passage has become a test of technique: the moment after the spurning of Hero when Benedick and Beatrice are left alone (IV.1). "Come," he urges, "bid me do anything for thee." She turns on him sharply with "Kill Claudio", and his spontaneous answer is "Ha! Not for the wide world." Mishandled, the exchange will bring jarring laughter – never better avoided than by John Gielgud and Diana Wynyard in the Phoenix production (Gielgud's own) of 1952. At Benedick's demand Beatrice paused in charged silence. Then "Kill Claudio" was almost forced from her, and Benedick's response, quick, low-toned, came as the near-incredulous exclamation of a man who had not realized how friendship must struggle with love and honour.

The other play-stealers are Dogberry, the portentous bullfrog constable; his timid lieutenant, Verges; and members of their Watch (who are straight from Warwickshire). Dogberry is a master of what, two centuries on, grew into a "malapropism" (because of Sheridan's Mrs Malaprop in *The Rivals*). The misapplication of words – e.g. "For the watch to babble and to talk is most tolerable and not to be endured" (III.3) – has long been a stage cliché, but Dogberry's exercises, when spoken unselfconsciously, remain comic ("Comparisons are odorous", III.5).

Much Ado About Nothing was among the plays acted at Court during the festivities for the betrothal and marriage of Princess Elizabeth and the Elector Palatine (May 1613), and in early years it was exceedingly popular. For all that, it vanished until 1721, and it did not really regain itself until Garrick, who had rehearsed himself for two months, played Benedick to Mrs Pritchard's Beatrice at Drury Lane (1748) and continued, off and on, until retirement in 1766. Various eminent Beatrices (among them Frances Abington and Mrs Jordan) appeared during the last two decades of the century; the major Benedick was John Philip Kemble (Drury Lane, 1788–1802), his brother Charles taking over in 1803. There was little else of note until Irving's shining Lyceum revival (1882); Ellen Terry, more than any Beatrice before her, seemed to have been born under a dancing star. In the 1903 revival (Imperial) her designer son, Gordon Craig, indicated the church simply by the widening light that illuminated the many colours of a huge cross.

Other West End names were George Alexander and Julia Neilson (1898), Tree and Winifred Emery (1905), Henry Ainley and Madge Titheradge (1926), Robert Donat and Renée Asherson (1956). Except for intermittent Old Vic revivals, the piece belonged, in effect, to Stratford-upon-Avon. There, in 1879, Barry Sullivan, with Helen Faucit (who left retirement for this performance), acted at the opening of the Memorial Theatre. Benson often did the comedy during his long management of the festivals; it was the jubilee choice of 1929; and afterwards the most complete production in a long sequence was Gielgud's (1949, Anthony Quayle, Diana Wynyard). Next year Gielgud himself and Peggy Ashcroft took over; and in 1952 Gielgud with Diana Wynyard (and Paul Scofield's Pedro) were in a London run at the Phoenix. There was a New York season (1959, Lunt-Fontanne Theatre, with Gielgud and Margaret Leighton). Michael Redgrave and Googie Withers (Stratford, 1958, set in mid-nineteenth-century Italy) and Donald Sinden and Judi Dench (Stratford/Aldwych, 1976–7, "Anglo-Indian") were all engagingly right. Zeffirelli's exhaustingly exuberant turn-of-the-century Sicilian romp (National company, Old Vic, 1965), with needless textual revision by Robert Graves, had Robert Stephens and Maggie Smith in the "merry war". The comedy has come to Stratford, Ontario, e.g. in 1971 and (Alan Scarfe, Martha Henry) in 1977.

In other terms

Opera (1862): *Béatrice et Bénédict* by Hector Berlioz. It cut out Don John altogether and brought in a comic musician, Somorone, instead of Dogberry and Verges.

Chief characters

Don Pedro, Prince of Arragon. A Renaissance nobleman, who believes too easily what he is told. Bridges-Adams, the Stratford director (1919–34), one of whose favourite plays this was, insisted that we should always be mindful in Shakespeare of what the dramatist called "degree": thus, "no one should touch Pedro on the arm, or sit in his presence without his gesture of assent."

Don John The bastard malcontent whose almost motiveless malice springs the main plot; his excuse is envy of Claudio, but he has a restless desire for mischief.

Benedick With the longest part (471 lines), he might be called a mature Berowne (*Love's Labour's Lost*). A figure of high comedy acted by so many famous players that it is enough to name John Gielgud*** (Stratford, 1950; Phoenix, London, 1952; New York, 1959).

Claudio Difficult to make sympathetic; but we can feel for him in the brief elegiac scene (V.3: "Done to death by slanderous tongues/Was the Hero that here lies").

Leonato He has a sometimes too lightly regarded speech in the Church scene (IV.1): "Why, doth not every earthly thing/Cry shame upon her?"

Dogberry The massively complacent constable created in Shakespeare's company by Will Kempe. John Aubrey said in *Brief Lives* – though he got the play wrong – that Shakespeare took Dogberry's humours from a man at Grendon in Buckinghamshire "which is the road from London to Stratford".

Verges Dogberry's lieutenant. A wisp of a man.

Borachio A functional minor villain.

Hero A wronged innocent.

Beatrice "Dear Lady Disdain", wittiest of Shakespeare's women; born under a dancing star (II.1). Professor Dover Wilson described Beatrice as "the first women in our literature ... who has not only a brain but delights in its constant employment." Ellen Terry*** (Lyceum, 1882), Diana Wynyard*** (especially Phoenix, 1952), Peggy Ashcroft*** (especially Stratford, 1950), Judi Dench*** (Stratford/Aldwych, 1976–7).

AS YOU LIKE IT

1599

Duke, living in exile	jester
Frederick, his brother, usurper of his dominions	Sir Oliver Martext, a vicar
	Corin, Silvius, shepherds
Amiens, Jaques, lords attending on the banished Duke	William, a country fellow, in love with Audrey
Le Beau, a courtier attending upon Frederick	A person representing Hymen
	Rosalind, the banished Duke's daughter
Charles, wrestler to Frederick	
Oliver, son to Sir Rowland de Boys	Celia, Frederick's daughter
	Phebe, a shepherdess
Jaques, his younger brother	Audrey, a country wench
Orlando, the youngest brother	Lords, Pages, Foresters, and Attendants
Adam, Dennis, Oliver's servants	
Touchstone, Frederick's court	

Scene: Oliver's house, Frederick's court, the Forest of Arden (which, though probably intended for the Ardennes, is more easily identifiable with Arden in Warwickshire – that is, if identification is needed)

Synopsis

The late Sir Rowland de Boys had three sons: Oliver, the eldest, hates the youngest, Orlando ("It is the stubbornest young fellow of France", I.1), whom he has steadily humiliated. Orlando is matched against the usurping Duke Frederick's deadly wrestler, Charles; the fight, which the youth wins, is watched by Rosalind, the banished Duke's daughter, and her cousin, Frederick's daughter Celia. Orlando and Rosalind fall immediately in love; Frederick, jealous of her popularity, banishes her; and in the disguise of a boy (Ganymede) she leaves with Celia (as Ganymede's sister) and the jester Touchstone, to find her father in the Forest of Arden. There he lives with a company ("my co-mates and brothers in exile") that includes the melancholy courtier, Jaques.

Orlando and his faithful old Adam have also gone to Arden. The travellers (Act II) arrive severally: Rosalind and Celia overhear the shepherd Silvius declaring his love for Phebe, a scornful shepherdess. Orlando becomes a member of the Duke's court, and (Act III) hangs on the trees his love poems to Rosalind. When he meets her, unknowing, as Ganymede, she promises to cure him of infatuation "if you would but call me Rosalind, and come every day to my cote to woo me".

Meanwhile Phebe falls in love with "Ganymede", and Touchstone condescends to the country wench, Audrey. Oliver (Act IV), whom Frederick has summarily banished to find Orlando, arrives in Arden; on hearing how Orlando has rescued his brother from a lioness – and seeing a bloodstained napkin – "Ganymede" faints. Oliver and Celia (Act V) are now in love. Presently all the couples in Arden are united: Rosalind reveals herself to Orlando; and Oliver and Celia, Touchstone and Audrey, and even Silvius and Phebe, are in harmony. Frederick has decided to retire from the world into contemplation; the banished Duke is restored; and Rosalind speaks an epilogue.

In performance

As You Like It, a glistening comedy of love (often at first sight), is derived principally from Thomas Lodge's novel, *Rosalynde* (1590), though Shakespeare invented such people as Jaques and Touchstone. A pastoral (and satirical) romance, it belongs first of all to its bewitching Rosalind, a deity on whom the forest airs attend and one of the great testing parts for an actress. Early in the eighteenth century (Drury Lane, 1723) a stupid adaptation, *Love in a Forest*, left out half a dozen characters – including Touchstone and Phebe – added a mosaic from other comedies, and brought Jaques in love with Celia.

From 1740, when the genuine text returned, until today, there has been a long splendour of Rosalinds: Hannah Pritchard, Peg Woffington, Dorothy Jordan, the American Ada Rehan (London, 1890), Athene Seyler (Stratford, 1919; Lyric, Hammersmith, 1920), Fabia Drake (Stratford, 1932; Phoenix, London, 1933), Edith Evans (particularly Old Vic and New, 1936–7), Margaret Leighton (Stratford, 1952), Peggy Ashcroft (Old Vic, 1932, when Walter Sickert sketched her, and Stratford, 1957), Vanessa Redgrave (Stratford/Aldwych, 1961–2), Dorothy Tutin (Stratford/Aldwych, 1967), Janet Suzman (Stratford, 1968), Kate Nelligan (in a superfluously semi-operatic production, Stratford, 1977), Sara Kestelman (National, 1979). All had their qualities: history may decide on Edith Evans in a forest that could have been designed and peopled by Watteau, with arching boughs, vague silvery distances and ornamental water. It was the Rosalind of an uncommonly sophisticated pastoral, but every word was caressed and no other players could have so danced up and down the scale on "Alas the day! What shall I do with my doublet and hose?" Forty years on, when Rosalinds multiplied (late 1970s, early 1980s), Susan Fleetwood (Stratford, 1980) was most genuinely and happily from Arden, with Sinead Cusack's Celia to partner her.

Of many New York Rosalinds since 1786, possibly the most memorable were Mary Anderson (1885–6); earlier, she had given a special Stratford performance), the near-classical achievement of Ada Rehan (1890, Augustin Daly's production), Katharine Hepburn (1950) – though John Mason Brown said she seemed "to have mistaken the Forest of Arden for the campus of Bryn Mawr" – and Nancy Wickwire (1958). At Stratford, Ontario: Irene Worth (1959), Carole Shelley (1972), Maggie Smith, in late eighteenth-century costume (1977).

Oscar Asche (His Majesty's, London, 1907) strewed the stage with a collection of moss-grown logs, two thousand pots of fern, large clumps of bamboo, and leaves by the cartload from the previous autumn. Jacques Copeau (1938) staged the play in the Boboli Gardens in Florence, on the site where Reinhardt had done *A Midsummer Night's Dream*. Michael Elliot's production (Stratford, 1961) was staged against a stylized tree on a green knoll. Ronald Pickup was, bravely, Rosalind for an uninspiring all-male *As You Like It* (National at Old Vic, 1967).

In other terms

Dr Paul Czinner directed a British-made film (1936), with Elisabeth Bergner as a coy Rosalind, Laurence Olivier as Orlando, and Henry Ainley as the banished Duke.

Chief characters

Banished Duke A man of patient nobility, apt at special pleading. "Happy is your Grace," says Amiens (II.1), "That can translate the stubborness of fortune/Into so quiet and so sweet a style."

Frederick The usurper who undergoes an unlikely but convenient spiritual conversion when meeting "an old religious man" (offstage) on the borders of the forest.

Jaques "The melancholy Jaques" is the banished Duke's sardonic and misanthropic courtier, who has a murky past, and whose future will be spent in philosophical argument with the reformed Frederick. A part often over-praised: it includes "All the world's a stage" (II.7). Richard Pasco*** (Stratford, 1973); Michael Bryant** (National, 1979); Derek Godfrey** (Stratford, 1980).

Le Beau Frederick's courtier who bids farewell to Orlando with "Hereafter, in a better world than this,/I shall desire more love and knowledge of you" (I.2). In the Stratford/Aldwych revival (1977–8) he defected to Arden.

Charles The "sinewy" wrestler who has the unexpected lines in which he tells Oliver that many young men flock daily to the banished Duke "and fleet the time carelessly, as they did in the golden world" (I.1).

Oliver The eldest de Boys brother, who passes during the night from villain to lover, and who meets in Arden a green and gilded snake and a hungry lioness.

Jaques de Boys Again Shakespeare does not bother about names. This Jaques is "the second son of old Sir Rowland"; here to settle everything with a last-act speech so awkward at that time of night that Frank Benson's company would give a shilling to every youth who spoke it without fault.

Orlando The youngest brother. An expert wrestler, a versifier and an agreeable young man who cannot recognize Rosalind when she is dressed as a boy (though one or two directors have tried to suggest that he does).

Adam Conscientious, teetotal veteran, who slips from the play once he has safely reached Arden with Orlando. Traditionally, Shakespeare might have acted him.

Touchstone Arguably the least amusing of Shakespeare's jesters, a pedantic professional whose marriage to Audrey may be one of his jokes. His speech on "the degrees of the lie" (V.4) was inserted presumably to give Rosalind time to change from her boy's disguise.

Silvius A shepherd obsessed by his love for Phebe.

Corin A veteran shepherd whose rural philosophy contrasts with the worldly-wise artifice of Touchstone (III.2).

Amiens The banished Duke's singing courtier.

Rosalind The longest woman's part in Shakespeare (736 lines), obviously created by a remarkable boy "actress". Wise, rapturously in love, a woman who "by heavenly synod was devised". Played by leading actresses through the centuries. Fabia Drake*** (Stratford, 1932), Edith Evans*** (Old Vic and New, 1936–7), Susan Fleetwood*** (Stratford, 1980).

Celia The "gentle Aliena", Frederick's daughter, who is Rosalind's foil and who will marry Oliver.

Phebe This disdainful shepherdess who scorns Silvius and loves Rosalind–Ganymede, speaks the tribute to Marlowe (III.5): "Dead shepherd, now I find thy saw of might:/'Who ever lov'd that lov'd not at first sight?'" (the quotation is from *Hero and Leander*). Her description – inky brows, black silk hair – may be yet another Dark Lady reference. Doreen Aris* (Stratford, 1957).

Audrey The country hoyden seized by Touchstone from her yokel William.

HENRY V

1599

Henry V, who succeeded his father in 1413, died in 1422. The English army won the battle of Agincourt, against the French, in 1415; Henry married Princess Katherine of France (historically, in 1420).

Chorus	*Boy*
King Henry the Fifth	*A Herald*
Dukes of Gloucester and *Bedford*,	*Charles the Sixth*, King of France
the King's brothers	*Lewis*, the Dauphin
Duke of Exeter, the King's uncle	*Duke of Burgundy*
Duke of York, the King's cousin	*Duke of Orleans*
Earl of Salisbury	*Duke of Berri*
Earl of Westmoreland	*Duke of Britaine*
Earl of Warwick	*Duke of Bourbon*
Archbishop of Canterbury	*The Constable of France*
Bishop of Ely	*Rambures*, *Grandpré*, French lords
Earl of Cambridge	*Governor of Harfleur*
Lord Scroop and *Sir Thomas Grey*,	*Montjoy*, a French herald
conspirators against the King	*French Ambassadors* to Henry V
Sir Thomas Erpingham	*Isabel*, Queen of France
Gower (English), *Fluellen* (Welsh),	*Princess Katherine*, her daughter
Macmorris (Irish), *Jamy*	*Alice*, Katherine's attendant lady
(Scottish), captains in the	*Hostess* of the Boar's Head,
King's army	Eastcheap, formerly Mistress
Bates, *Court*, *Williams*, *Nym*,	Nell Quickly, now Pistol's wife
Bardolph, *Pistol*, soldiers in the	Lords, Ladies, Officers, Soldiers,
King's army	Messengers, Attendants

Scene: England and France

Synopsis

Henry V hears the Archbishop of Canterbury's explanation of the "Salic Law", which justifies the royal claim to the French throne;

and he sends word to the Dauphin that he will fight in France. Before the army sails (Act II), Bardolph, Nym and Pistol learn of Falstaff's death from Nell Quickly, now Pistol's wife (II.3); and at Southampton the King sentences three traitors to death.

Henry (Act III) takes Harfleur; Princess Katherine of France has an early English lesson from her confidante, Alice; and Henry's outnumbered army prepares to fight at Agincourt. Walking among his troops, disguised, on the night before battle (Act IV) – "a little touch of Harry in the night" – the King debates with three soldiers, prays for success, and at sunrise delivers his rallying cry:

> Crispin Crispian shall ne'er go by,
> From this day to the ending of the world,
> But we in it shall be remembered;
> We few, we happy few, we band of brothers.

The battle is fought and won, with great losses to the French, and "of our English dead", fewer than thirty.

Fluellen, the Welsh captain (Act V) forces the braggart Pistol to eat a leek for mocking the Welsh. At a final meeting in the palace of the French King, peace is made; Henry, with attractive gaucherie, proposes to Princess Katherine and she accepts him. Chorus, who has set the scene on five occasions, now comes out to end the play: "Small time, but, in that small, most greatly lived/This star of England."

In performance

"O, for a Muse of fire!" cries Chorus in the most resounding opening to any chronicle. Chorus might well have been Shakespeare himself (at the end, V.2, there is a reference to "our bending author"): if so, he gave himself a sequence of grand set-pieces that, apologizing for failure to show the fury of the French wars "on this unworthy scaffold ... within this wooden 'O'" (the Globe Theatre, Southwark), can fire an audience's imagination at every phrase. Derived principally from Holinshed, the plan is a patriotic utterance throughout. Some modern criticism may undervalue it as an exercise in chauvinism; but as Dr Dover Wilson said, "Heroism is the theme, and Henry the hero." In the theatre, when he is speaking on the morning of Crispin's Day before Agincourt, the piece has unerring power. So, too, that moment of quieter emotion, the reading of the casualty lists after battle. If we do not search too deeply (the speech at III.3, describing the dire threat to captured Harfleur, is an example) Henry will come to us, unfashionable though it may be, as his old adversary, Hotspur, did – "the light by which the chivalry of England moved."

Records are not particularly helpful until 1735 (there had been a botched adaptation a dozen years earlier). Thenceforward the play was always familiar on the stage – for over a century at Covent Garden and Drury Lane. The principal Henry (from 1789 to 1811, in a bad text) was John Philip Kemble. Macready, between 1819 and 1839, acted with sustained spirit, and in the last year (Covent Garden) added spectacular effects that fortified the words of Chorus.

After Phelps (Sadler's Wells, 1852) and Charles Kean (Princess's, 1859), with his prolific pageantry, the major performances were Frank Benson's – from 1897 usually at Stratford but in some London seasons as well – and Lewis Waller's (Lyceum, 1900, and afterwards). Benson was, without complication, the "star of England" the Elizabethan theatre might have known; but he did not slide over the night-speeches that remind us the piece is more than battle music. (Strangely, he had a habit of omitting Chorus.) Lewis Waller, an eloquent paladin, would hurtle downstage for the Crispin crescendo. Between the wars Ralph Richardson (Old Vic, 1931) and Laurence Olivier (Old Vic, 1937, chiselling away at the dead wood of tradition), were most triumphant; Robert Atkins, valiant always, directed the play under hard white light during his experimental season (1936) at the Ring, Blackfriars; and unexpectedly (1938) Ivor Novello returned Shakespeare with sincerity to Drury Lane. After the war Alec Clunes (Old Vic, 1951, Glen Byam Shaw's production) never merely banged Henry over an assault course of rhetoric; and Alan Howard (Stratford/Aldwych, 1975–6) also thought his way into the part and regilded much that had been taken for granted.

Christopher Plummer played Henry at Stratford, Ontario (1956; Edinburgh Festival, 1957). French parts played by French Canadians.

In other terms

Films: *Henry V* (1944) was the first of Laurence Olivier's three Shakespeare films (score by William Walton). He produced and directed it, and acted Henry, with a comparably valuable cast (Chorus, Leslie Banks; George Robey was seen for a few moments as the dying Falstaff). Though it suited the temper of the time, it was a lesser experience than the more uncompromising stage version at the Vic in 1937.

Chorus, in the film, was a gallant Elizabethan. Among other things down the years he has been Clio, the Muse of History, an Elizabethan youth, an actor in a duffle coat, and the semblance of Shakespeare himself. He is no longer sonorous and so detached. Television: (BBC, 1979): David Gwillim as Henry.

Chief characters

Henry V Third longest part (1105 lines) in Shakespeare: "the warlike Henry", "the mirror of all Christian kings", "the star of England". A series of famous speeches: before Harfleur (III.1), the argument with the soldier Williams (IV.1), "Upon the King!" (IV.1), the Crispin's Day speech (IV.3), rarely treated now as an oration, the wooing (V.2). Frank Benson*** (many Stratford seasons from 1897); Alan Howard*** (Stratford/Aldwych, 1975–6).

Duke of Exeter The King's uncle, he brings English defiance to Charles VI (II.4).

Duke of York Two lines only: but the King's cousin, who falls when leading "the vaward", is the former Aumerle (*Richard II*). Exeter (IV.6) describes his death.

Archbishop of Canterbury His verbose and thankless genealogical versification (I.2) is frequently abridged, or the Archbishop is burlesqued to the detriment of such a line as "The singing masons building roofs of gold."

Bishop of Ely Often suffers as Canterbury does, which means the loss of the tribute to Henry "in the very May-morn of his youth" (I.2).

Gower The steady average Englishman: one of four captains (Fluellen for Wales, Jamy for Scotland, Macmorris for Ireland) who represent national characteristics.

Fluellen The Welsh captain, a fiery little dragon and the richest of Shakespeare's Welsh parts. Robert Speaight** (Old Vic, 1931).

Williams A blunt soldier who, at the camp-fire before Agincourt, argues with the disguised Henry about the King's responsibility.

Bardolph Lieutenant Bardolph, with his flame-coloured face, and Corporal Nym are hanged for looting (III.6, IV.4).

Pistol Last of Falstaff's "irregular humorists", the roaring coward is at length humiliated by Fluellen and proposes to return home as a bawd and cutpurse (V.1). Baliol Holloway** (Stratford, 1934).

Boy Killed by the French soldiers escaping from battle (IV.7).

Charles VI Formerly, and quite unnecessarily, played as something of a feeble wander-wit.

Lewis the Dauphin Sends Henry the insulting tennis balls (I.2).

Duke of Burgundy Makes a fervent appeal for peace in V.2.

Mountjoy Chivalrous and lonely French herald, often doubled with the French ambassador (I.2).

Katherine Bubbling French princess who in the English-lesson scene (III.4) appears already to be looking forward; and who (V.2) is clearly Henry's own: "Your Majestee ave *fausse* French enough to deceive de most *sage damoiselle* dat is *en France*.'

Alice Katherine's gentlewoman who has been in England.

Hostess Nell Quickly She is now Pistol's wife. In two brief scenes (II.1 and II.3), the first only a fragment, she describes Falstaff's death in an affecting passage ("'A went away an it had been any christom child") which contains the eighteenth-century reading of a debated text, "'a babbl'd of green fields". We hear from Pistol (V.1) that Nell herself has died.

Chorus He has half a dozen expository speeches, asking for his hearers' imagination to supply "the vasty fields of France", the English fleet as "a city on th'inconstant billows dancing", the armies waiting in the night before battle, the King's return in triumph to England and again to France. He ends – we like to think it is Shakespeare's voice – "Thus far, with rough and all-unable pen, / Our bending author has pursued the story." Michael Redgrave*** (Stratford, 1951).

JULIUS CAESAR

1599

Julius Caesar	*A Soothsayer*
Octavius Caesar, his great-nephew,	*Cinna*, a poet
Marcus Antonius and	*Another poet*
M. Aemilius Lepidus, triumvirs	*Lucilius, Titinius, Messala, Young*
after Julius Caesar's death	*Cato, Volumnius*, friends to
Cicero, Publius, Popilius Lena,	Brutus and Cassius
Senators	*Varro, Clitus, Claudius, Strato*,
Marcus Brutus and *Caius Cassius*,	*Lucius, Dardanius*, servants to
principal conspirators against	Brutus
Julius Caesar	*Pindarus*, servant to Cassius
Casca, Trebonius, Ligarius, Decius	*Calphurnia*, wife to Caesar
Brutus, Metellus Cimber,Cinna,	*Portia*, wife to Brutus
other conspirators	Senators, Citizens, Guards,
Flavius, Marullus, tribunes	Attendants, etc.
Artemidorus, a sophist, of Cnidos	

Scene: Rome, near Sardis, near Philippi

Synopsis

A powerful faction fears the growing strength of Julius Caesar in republican Rome. As he walks to the festival games, a soothsayer warns him of the Ides of March (March 15). On a night of storm, Cassius and Casca go to visit Marcus Brutus whom they must win to their party. He receives them and other conspirators (Act II) in his garden, and Caesar's murder is planned for the next morning. Portia, wife of Brutus, observes his unrest.

Caesar's wife, Calphurnia, seeks to prevent her husband from going to the Capitol, but he does so, and (Act III) upon the Ides of March is stabbed to death. Brutus, in the Forum, tells the mob his reasons; then Mark Antony, permitted to speak as Caesar's friend, rouses the people of Rome in a speech of searching and calculated irony and passion. Antony, Caesar's great-nephew Octavius and the feeble Lepidus form a triumvirate (Act IV) against the conspirators. Brutus and the firebrand Cassius quarrel in their camp at Sardis; the quarrel is resolved, and Cassius learns that Portia, wife of Brutus, has committed suicide in Rome. The meeting of the armies will be at Philippi; the ghost of Caesar appears to Brutus, saying that he also will be there.

Cassius (Act V), believing the final battle to be lost, orders his servants to stab him; Brutus falls on his own sword; and Antony speaks the epitaph over his foe:

> This was the noblest Roman of them all.
> All the conspirators, save only he
> Did that they did in envy of great Caesar.

In performance

In the fifth Chorus speech of *Henry V*, London pours out her citizens, "like to the senators of th'antique Rome,/With the plebeians swarming at their heels", to "fetch their conquering Caesar in." Already Shakespeare was contemplating his next play, based on Plutarch (Sir Thomas North's translation of a French version). It proved to be a tragedy of two men, the murdered Caesar who dominates after death, and one of his murderers, the liberal patrician, Marcus Brutus ("He only in a general honest thought/ And common good to all made one of them", V.5). The speaker is Mark Antony, no longer in the theatre a romantic orator but an astute and masterful tactician. This is the most direct of the tragedies, speaking (in a phrase from *Timon of Athens*) "bold, and forth on". Though Caesar dies midway, his ghost rises; modern directors keep him always in our minds, Glen Byam Shaw (Stratford, 1957) through the single star ("I am constant as the northern star") that shone at the last above Philippi. It is wrong to imagine that the play tails off after the Quarrel scene between Brutus and Cassius (IV.3).

We know that a Swiss traveller in England, Thomas Platter, a doctor of Basle, saw the tragedy at the Globe in September 1599; that the poet Leonard Digges (1640) was writing of Brutus and Cassius "at half-sword parley"; and that for more than a century from the Restoration, the play – spared by improvers – was in constant service. John Philip Kemble acted Brutus at Covent Garden between 1812 and 1817, and Charles Mayne Young, who was his Cassius, became an even finer Brutus. Macready, at various times, played Cassius and Brutus with acute understanding (his last Brutus, Haymarket, 1851); and a steady run of later performances included Tree's marmoreal spectacle in its Alma-Tadema sets (from 1898, Her Majesty's); Henry Ainley as Antony (St James's, 1920) in the downright rhetorical manner and a gleaming classical Rome; Gielgud as Antony, Donald Wolfit as Cassius (Old Vic, 1930); a modern-dress treatment (emphasis on Fascism), Embassy and His Majesty's 1939. Among many Stratford nights: Baliol Holloway as Cassius on various occasions between the wars, Gielgud as Cassius (1950), Alec Clunes as Brutus (1957), John Wood as Brutus (1972). At the Old Vic in 1962, when a Greek director, Minos Volanakis, and his designer saw Caesar's Rome as a world of rough and rusty scaffolding, with its citizens most shabbily arrayed, they did have one important figure, the Cassius of Robert Eddison, always a grand Shakespearian speaker. A National production (1977; Olivier Theatre) was distinguished by Gielgud's Caesar, lofty without being intolerable; and Bernard Hepton played Caesar splendidly at St George's, Islington (1979).

In America the tragedy first arrived (1774) at Charleston, South Carolina; there have been frequent New York revivals since 1817. Great performers were Edwin Booth as Brutus and Laurence Barrett as Cassius (together in 1871–2). Richard Mansfield, a surprisingly fanatical Brutus, staged the play (1902), moving through the part "not like a man who is painfully making up his mind, but as one fatally predestined to assassinate his friend" (Robert Speaight). A production of Orson Welles, before blood-red walls, in modern dress and "tinged with fascism", had 157 New York performances in 1937. Welles saw Brutus as "the bewildered liberal, the man of character and principle in a world threatened by fascist destruction." In a collectors' piece among American productions (1864), the brothers Edwin Booth, Junius Brutus Booth and John Wilkes Booth – later Lincoln's assassin – were, respectively, Brutus, Cassius and Antony.

In other terms

Films: *Julius Caesar* has been filmed several times (beginning in silent days). Most valuable: the American production of 1953 (Joseph L. Mankiewicz), remembered for Marlon Brando's Antony and John Gielgud's scorching Cassius; and a lesser English film (1969, directed by Stuart Burge), with Gielgud (Caesar), Charlton Heston (Antony), Jason Robards (Brutus). Television (BBC 1978): Richard Pasco's Brutus particularly good.

Chief characters

Julius Caesar Much must depend on the actor. The dictator's portrait is more reasonable in Shakespeare than in Plutarch; and given a John Gielgud*** (National, 1977), we are aware that Caesar is "mighty yet".

Octavius Caesar Julius Caesar's great-nephew and the coming strong man. "Within *my* tent tonight his bones shall lie" (V.5).

Marcus Antonius A highly theatrical part (the Forum speech: "Friends, Romans, countrymen"). But the eloquently improvising opportunist is often less exciting in today's theatre than Brutus and Cassius. Ion Swinley*** (Old Vic, 1935; Open Air, 1937).

Marcus Brutus The liberal idealist at war with himself. Charles Mayne Young *** (Covent Garden, 1819).

Caius Cassius "Such men are dangerous", said Caesar; and he was right. Passionate and jealous, Cassius – as many actors have found – can speak like the Tiber in flood. Laurence Barrett*** (New York, 1870s), John Gielgud*** (Stratford, 1950).

Lepidus One of the triumvirs after Caesar's death. "A slight unmeritable man," says Antony (IV.1), "meet to be sent on

77

errands." He reappears in *Antony and Cleopatra*.

Casca Disappears after the murder. His opening prose scene (I.2) is bluntly persuasive; afterwards it is left to the director to heighten him.

Cinna The poet; innocent victim of mob vengeance in a brief and agonizing scene (III.3). Once frequently cut, a casualty when so much time was spent in scene-changing.

Calphurnia Caesar's wife is a study in fear and anxiety.

Portia She is Cato's daughter, to Brutus a "true and honourable wife", proud, loving, brave. Joan Miller*** (Stratford, 1957).

TWELFTH NIGHT; OR, WHAT YOU WILL

1601–2

Orsino, Duke of Illyria	Olivia
Sebastian, brother to Viola	*Malvolio*, Olivia's steward
Antonio, a sea captain, friend to Sebastian	*Fabian*, in the service of Olivia
Sea Captain, friend to Viola	*Feste*, Olivia's Fool
Valentine, Curio, gentlemen attending on the Duke	*Olivia*, a rich countess
	Viola, sister to Sebastian
Sir Toby Belch, uncle to Olivia	*Maria*, Olivia's gentlewoman
Sir Andrew Aguecheek, suitor to	Lords, A Priest, Sailors, Officers, Musicians and Attendants

Scene: a city in Illyria and the seacoast near it

Synopsis

Viola, "of Messaline", wrecked on the Illyrian shore and believing wrongly that her twin brother Sebastian has been drowned, becomes (in the male disguise of Cesario) a page to Orsino, the Duke. She bears his reiterated and scorned love message to the young countess Olivia, who is mourning affectedly for a dead brother. Olivia falls in love with Viola/Cesario. Meanwhile (Act II) Olivia's parasitic uncle Sir Toby, her gullible suitor Sir Andrew, encouraged by Toby, her gentlewoman Maria, her "allowed fool" Feste, and Fabian, also in her service, join to trick Malvolio, her sombre, haughty and puritanical steward, an enemy of them all. "Dost thou think because thou art virtuous there shall be no more cakes and ale?" Toby asks him. Presently, told by a forged letter (ostensibly Olivia's, actually Maria's) that Olivia is infatuated with him, Malvolio takes to himself the phrase: "Some are born great, some achieve greatness, some have greatness thrust upon 'em."

Obeying the false command to appear before his mistress smiling and in absurdly cross-gartered yellow stockings ("a fashion she detests", "a colour she abhors"), Malvolio is carried off (Act III) to a dark cell as a presumed madman. Sebastian, whom we have realized by now was saved (he believes his sister lost), has reached the town with his rescuer Antonio, a piratical captain who had once fought against Orsino's ships. The plotters, "more matter for a May morning", have persuaded Andrew, jealous of Olivia's obvious love for Cesario, to challenge the page to a duel; while this is being scrambled through, Antonio arrives, mistakes Cesario for Sebastian, draws his sword to help, and is arrested by the Duke's officers.

Soon afterwards (Act IV), Toby, believing Sebastian to be Cesario, attacks him and is sternly rebuked by Olivia. Also mistaken, she begs the young man to go with her; he does so, pleasantly bewildered, and in a brief later scene she urges marriage ("Plight me the full assurance of your faith") and they follow a priest to the chantry. Finally (Act V), confusions are resolved: the twins recognize each other; Viola, herself again, will be Orsino's Duchess, his "fancy's queen"; Toby weds Maria; Malvolio, released, swears revenge on "the whole pack of you"; and the comedy fades in Feste's twilit song.

In performance

Twelfth Night, as topical references suggest, was probably written about 1601. Shakespeare invented the Malvolio sub-plot, but the fable of the twins and of Orsino and Olivia could have been derived from an old Italian comedy. Shakespeare's "Illyria" is simply a high-fantastical invention, a stage for the roaming of identical twins, the presentation of various shades of love, and the sub-plot's May-morning skirmish.

It has been proposed, not too plausibly, that the first performance was at Whitehall on Twelfth Night (January 6) 1601, in the presence of a visiting Italian nobleman, Don Valentino Orsino, Duke of Bracciano, in whose honour Shakespeare named the Illyrian duke. The comedy was certainly acted on Candlemas Day (February 2) 1602, in Middle Temple Hall, where "at our feast" a barrister named John Manningham saw and recorded it. Now one of the most loved and familiar romantic comedies, it had to struggle through several adaptations before being accepted for itself in the mid-eighteenth century. "But a silly play, and not related at all to the name of the day," Samuel Pepys had said (in 1662) to Sir William Davenant's version. He was wrong, for *Twelfth Night* in the words of Anne Barton, was "a period of holiday abandon ... in which serious issues and events mingled perplexingly with revelry and apparent madness."

Revivals of the Shakespearian text have flourished since Charles Macklin and Hannah Pritchard were Malvolio and Viola at Drury Lane in 1741. In the late nineteenth century – according to the production's Viola (Ellen Terry) – Henry Irving's Malvolio (Lyceum, 1884) was "fine and dignified, but not good for the play" in a production oddly dull. During the Edwardian period, Herbert Beerbohm Tree, firmly realistic, filled the stage of His Majesty's with Olivia's terraced garden; less realistically, he had four minor Malvolios to follow him wherever he went. Granville Barker broke with tradition in his famous Savoy Theatre revival (1912) in a black-and-silver setting, with Henry Ainley and Lillah McCarthy as Malvolio and Viola.

After the First World War most revivals were divided between Stratford (and from 1960 the Aldwych), the Old Vic and pastorals at the Open Air Theatre, Regent's Park. In these days directors have been only too ready to experiment with costume variations, assorted modern dress, even "hippy" fashions – and such caprices as turning Sir Andrew, on the strength of his name, to a Scot. Olivia has changed most radically; no longer a static great lady in early middle age, she is often a coquettish girl. Her gentlewoman, Maria, too frequently reduced in rank, should correspond to Nerissa in *The Merchant of Venice*.

In the United States *Twelfth Night* was staged first in Boston (1794). Among numerous New York productions were Augustin

Daly's (1894), with Ada Rehan, E.H. Sothern and Julia Marlowe's between 1905 and 1919, and one in 1940 with Maurice Evans and Helen Hayes. A Stratford, Connecticut, revival (1960), with Katharine Hepburn insecurely cast as Viola, was set in a nineteenth-century English seaside town. In Canada (1957) Tyrone Guthrie opened the permanent theatre at Stratford, Ontario, with an exhilarating treatment in Stuart costume.

In other terms

An operatic version at Covent Garden (1820) included "Songs, Glees, and Choruses, the poetry selected entirely from the Plays, Poems, and Sonnets of Shakespeare." There is an opera, *Viola* (1881) by Smetana. Brahms composed a setting for "Come away, death" and Schubert for "The wind and the rain". Songs and incidental music (1909) by Sibelius. A musical called *Your Own Thing*, at a long distance from *Twelfth Night*, ran briefly at the Comedy, London, in 1969. A celebrated French production by Jacques Copeau (Vieux-Colombier, Paris, 1914) had Suzanne Bing as Viola. Jakow Frid directed a Russian film (1955) with a distorted text and Viola and Sebastian doubled.

Chief characters

Orsino The high-romantic Duke of Illyria, who is in love with love, but his raptures should not be theatrically heightened.

Sebastian He should look enough like Viola not to make nonsense of Antonio's perilous comparison in Act V: "An apple cleft in two is not more twin/Than these two creatures."

Antonio Sea captain and pirate. Granville-Barker called him "an exact picture of an Elizabethan seaman-adventurer. ... I am always reminded of him by the story of Richard Grenville chewing a wine-glass in his rage."

Sir Toby Belch With the longest part in the play, he is a boisterous reprobate but a gentleman, Olivia's uncle ("Am I not of her blood?" he asks). Notable performances: Arthur Whitby** (Savoy, 1912), Cedric Hardwicke** (New, for Old Vic, 1948).

Sir Andrew Aguecheek Olivia's gullible wooer, "a very fool and a prodigal" whose hair "hangs like flax on a distaff". He has a wistful line – "I was ador'd once" – at the end of the drinking scene, and ought not to be unwisely burlesqued. Notable: James Dodd (eighteenth century), Michael Redgrave (Phoenix, 1938), Paul Scofield** (Stratford, 1947).

Malvolio Olivia's self-loving and pompous steward: "Contemplation makes a rare turkey-cock of him." His ultimate treatment, as even Toby realizes ("I would we were all rid of this knavery"), goes beyond a joke. Best postwar performance: Donald Sinden***, a towering major-domo, who could have had a military background (Stratford/Aldwych, 1969–70). Other players: Robert Bensley (1780s), Samuel Phelps (from 1848), Henry Irving (1884), Herbert Beerbohm Tree (especially from 1902, His Majesty's), Henry Ainley** (Savoy, 1912), Randle Ayrton and Baliol Holloway (between the wars, Ayrton at Stratford, Holloway in Stratford and London), Donald Wolfit (many times from 1937, with a last superfluous return to Olivia's favour), Laurence Olivier** (Stratford, 1955, sour and thin-lipped plebeian), Eric Porter*** (Stratford, 1960, St George's, Islington, 1976), Nicol Williamson (Stratford/Aldwych, 1974–5).

Feste Olivia's Fool, never a twirling, conventional clown, but a mature, privileged and bitter-sweet onlooker, guardian of the play's latent melancholy. He sings the famous songs, "O mistress

mine" (II.3), "Come away, death" (II.4), and the "When that I
was and a little tiny boy". Created by Robert Armin, the subtle
comedian who joined Shakespeare's company in 1599. Celebrated performances: George Hayes*** (Stratford, 1929) and pre-
eminently Robert Eddison*** (Old Vic, 1978).

Olivia This "virtuous maid", at first in love with grief, was once
acted as a stately contralto, but is now usually an affected girl.
Geraldine McEwan**, amusing at Stratford (1958), was a *poseuse*
who seemed to have escaped from a columbarium for slightly
cracked doves.

Viola Dressed as a male page like her brother, she must not be
simply a pert masquerader. Best postwar performance: Judi
Dench***, with an enchanged dream-like quality and an appealing break in her voice (Stratford, 1969, 1971; Aldwych, 1970).
Other players: Peg Woffington (1746), Dorothy Jordan (1780s),
Ellen Terry (1884), Ada Rehan (1894), Lillah McCarthy (Savoy,
1912), Jean Forbes-Robertson**, grave and rapt (New, 1932),
Edith Evans**, dazzling in the long vocal scherzo of II.2,
"Fortune forbid my outside have not charm'd her" (Vic/Wells,
1932), Peggy Ashcroft**, with the charged pause before she
answered Sebastian's questions in Act V, when Viola's name is
spoken for the first time (Phoenix, 1938, and especially Old Vic,
1950), Vivien Leigh (Stratford, 1955), Barbara Jefford (Old Vic,
1958), Dorothy Tutin (Stratford, 1958 and 1960), Diana Rigg
(Stratford, 1966), Vanessa Redgrave (Shaw, 1972), Eileen Atkins
(Old Vic, 1978), Cherie Lunghi (Stratford/Aldwych, 1978–80).

Maria A gentlewoman and not a kitchen soubrette. She says of
herself: "I can write very like my lady. . . . On a forgotten matter
we can hardly make distinction of our hands." Supposed to be
small, possibly a reference to the original boy player.

HAMLET,
PRINCE OF DENMARK

1601–2

Claudius, King of Denmark	*Players*
Hamlet, son to the former King and nephew to Claudius	*Two Clowns* (peasants), gravediggers
Polonius, Lord Chamberlain	*Fortinbras*, Prince of Norway
Horatio, Hamlet's friend	*A Norwegian Captain*
Laertes, son to Polonius	*English Ambassadors*
Voltemand, Cornelius, Rosencrantz, Guildenstern, Osric, Courtiers	*Ghost* of Hamlet's father
A Gentleman	*Gertrude*, Queen of Denmark, Hamlet's mother
A Priest	*Ophelia*, daughter to Polonius
Marcellus, Bernardo, Officers	Lords, Ladies, Officers, Soldiers,
Francisco, a soldier	Sailors, Messengers
Reynaldo, servant to Polonius	

Scene: Denmark

Synopsis

Hamlet, Prince of Denmark, has not succeeded his father as King.
On the throne is his uncle Claudius, who married Queen

Gertrude immediately upon the death of her husband, the first King Hamlet. At midnight the ghost of the dead King (whom Claudius had poisoned) appears to his son on the battlements of the castle and commands revenge. "If thou hast nature in thee, bear it not."

Hamlet, unsure at first, simulates madness (Act II) which overwhelms Ophelia (daughter of the Lord Chamberlain, Polonius) whom he loves. When a company of actors arrives, Hamlet asks for the performance of a play with a plot much like his father's murder, so that he can see how the King responds. Claudius, deeply alarmed, plans (Act III) to send Hamlet at once to England. Before this can be done, Hamlet, going to his mother's closet, fiercely reviles her for yielding to Claudius; then, hearing a noise, he stabs through the curtain, killing Polonius who had concealed himself there.

Two courtiers (Act IV) conduct Hamlet towards the voyage to England, bearing letters that order his death when he arrives. Meanwhile, Laertes, son of Polonius, enraged by news of his father's end finds that his sister Ophelia is helplessly mad, and swears to kill Hamlet (now coming home after a sea-fight in which he was saved by pirates).

Ophelia drowns herself; Hamlet is in time to see her burial (Act V). Later, at a fencing match where Laertes, after plotting with the King, seeks to stab Hamlet with a poisoned rapier, both men are wounded; Queen Gertrude drinks, in error, the poisoned wine Claudius had ready for Hamlet as a second device. Laertes and Gertrude die; Hamlet, after killing Claudius, collapses in the arms of his friend Horatio ("The rest is silence"). Here Fortinbras, Prince of Norway, whose army has invaded Denmark, enters to take the throne that Hamlet, with his "dying voice", has bequeathed. Fortinbras orders him to be borne up with military ceremonial: "For he was likely, had he been put on,/To have prov'd most royal."

In performance

"This is I, Hamlet the Dane." As we hear the actor's challenge (V.1), we must always ask if he is entitled to it. A Hamlet must be stricken to the heart; no superficial grief. Everything he speaks has been argued and tested in the mind. He is a young man in the darkest mental fight, balancing and indeterminate, swayed – as Matthew Arnold said long ago – by a thousand subtle influences, physiological and pathological. This study of the divided mind in a play of revenge deferred is probably the most famous part in the world's drama. Shakespeare, it is supposed, based his tragedy, among other sources, on a vanished play known as the *Ur-Hamlet*.

It is all marvellously theatrical; nothing has been so often acted or more stringently analysed. A standard dictionary of quotations contains 210 references to *Hamlet*, covering well over 800 lines. Full-scale productions in the theatre (this is the longest of all Shakespeare's plays) take about five hours. Though these are far more frequent than they used to be, as a rule we get a cut version of about three and a half to four hours. Cuts are fairly stereotyped, e.g. Polonius with Reynaldo (II.1), some of IV.7, the beginning (always a sad choice) of the Hamlet–Horatio colloquy (V.2). In recent years one of the least expected cuts was the opening on the guard-platform of Elsinore, the challenge and counter-challenge in the midnight cold, the hushed questioning, the sudden "Peace, break thee off; look where it comes again." – "In the same figure, like the king that's dead."

Hamlet moves forward in a sequence of astonishments, unfailing however familiar (and many Shakespearians have met them forty or fifty times). The great speeches flower in fire; the play endures, not simply for its wisdom or its acted excitements, but because (though he is by no means Everyman) there is at least a trace of Hamlet in us all.

Every actor sees the man differently. But none of them must forget – and there is a current trick of forgetting – that Hamlet should not differ in essence from the Prince Ophelia remembers (III.1): "Th'expectancy and rose of the fair state", "That unmatch'd form and feature of blown youth". He is sometimes over-subtilized; it is a pleasure now and then to find an actor who has the voice, the bearing and the intelligence, and who is not afraid to simplify.

Hamlets, in all their variations, defy pigeonholing. But any record of the seventeenth century must name Thomas Betterton, whose face, when he saw the Ghost, turned as white as his neckcloth; and, of the eighteenth century, David Garrick, with his rhetorical pauses and quick transitions, and John Philip Kemble (Drury Lane, 1783; black velvet court dress, powdered wig), a nobly introspective romantic. From the nineteenth century we may think of Edmund Kean (not at his meridian); Macready's intellect; Charles Fechter's naturalism; Henry Irving*** (Lyceum, 1874), princely, tender, hypnotic; Tree (Haymarket, 1892), dying to the sound of an angelic chorus; Johnston Forbes-Robertson (Lyceum, 1897), with "the courtier's, scholar's, soldier's, eye, tongue, sword."

Nearly every speech can be fitted into a mosaic of effects from the acting of the part. From myriad English Hamlets this century we can choose Ernest Milton*** (Old Vic, 1919 and later), "lonely, prehensile, mysterious"; Colin Keith-Johnston in modern dress (Kingsway, 1925), "the prose side of the medallion", said Ivor Brown; John Gielgud*** (Old Vic, 1930; New, 1934; Lyceum, 1939; Haymarket, 1944), lofty in spirit and mind, violin-music searchingly scored; Donald Wolfit* (Stratford, 1936; various stages), forcible without physical grace; Laurence Olivier** (Old Vic and Elsinore, 1937), desperately on the note, "I do not know/Why yet I live to say 'This thing's to do'"; and players of such contrasting methods as Paul Scofield*** (Stratford, 1948; Phoenix, 1955), with his doomed gentleness; Alec Guinness (Old Vic, 1938; New, 1951); Michael Redgrave*** (New, 1950; Stratford, 1958), who could have been a Double First and Double Blue of Wittenberg; John Neville*** (Old Vic, 1957), David Warner (Stratford/Aldwych, 1965–6), Peter O'Toole (National at Old Vic, 1963), Alan Howard (Stratford, 1970), Ian McKellen (Cambridge, 1971), Derek Jacobi (Old Vic, 1977), Albert Finney (National at Old Vic, 1975, and the National itself, 1976), and Jonathan Pryce (Royal Court, 1980).

The New York sequence is comparable. We can name here Edwin Booth*** (from 1857), patrician, gentle, melancholy, probably the nonpareil of American Hamlets); John Barrymore*** (1922; London, 1925), powerful and original; Walter Hampden (e.g. 1925, 1929); the English actor, Maurice Evans (New York, 1938), who had acted it at the Old Vic three years earlier; Donald Madden (1961); Richard Burton (modern dress, 1964). Christopher Plummer played Hamlet at Stratford, Ontario (1957); and Kenneth Welsh (1969).

Among European Hamlets have been Sarah Bernhardt, Jean-Louis Barrault (France), Alexander Moissi (Germany), Giorgio Albertazzi (Italy), and Miklós Gábor (Hungary, early 1960s), a great actor little known outside his country.

In other terms

Films: three Hamlet films have been particularly debated. Laurence Olivier's (1948), in black and white, was set elaborately in a combination of Doubting Castle and Castle Dangerous, with some odd textual shredding and patching. Innokenti Smoktunovsky was Hamlet in a Russian colour film directed by Grigori Kozintsev (1964) with music by Shostakovich, and Nicol Williamson in a British one (1969) directed by Tony Richardson. Opera: Scarlatti (1715); Ambroise Thomas (1868); Humphrey Searle (1968). Ballet: Robert Helpmann (1942). Music: Tchaikovsky (1891); symphonic poem, Franz Liszt (1861).

Chief characters

Hamlet "The time is out of joint. O cursed spite,/That ever I was born to set it right" (I.5). This (1,530 lines in the uncut text) is the longest part in Shakespeare. Soliloquies: "O, that this too too solid flesh would melt" (I.2); "O, what a rogue and peasant slave am I!" (II.2); "To be, or not to be" (III.1); "How all occasions do inform against me" (IV.4).

Claudius Murderer, seducer, drunkard, "bloat king"; yet on stage he can be a suave and regal diplomatist. Alec Clunes*** (Phoenix, 1955).

Polonius An elder statesman some critics say was based on Lord Burghley. Garrulous and shrewd, as in the precepts to Laertes (I.3). Miles Malleson*** (Haymarket, 1944).

Horatio Personification of loyalty, who need not be turned into a veteran tutor. He is a man of Hamlet's own age (about thirty). Leo Genn* (Old Vic, 1935).

Laertes The grieving son and brother is as impetuous as Hamlet is indecisive.

Rosencrantz and **Guildenstern** One of Shakespeare's "pairs", Hamlet's Wittenberg fellow-students; court spies for the King. Nothing to tell them apart, but they have had more luck in a modern play, *Rosencrantz and Guildenstern Are Dead*.

Osric The affected "water-fly", sometimes presented in these days as a mildly sinister man-about-court.

Bernardo (or Barnardo). Has arguably the most tingling lines in the world's drama, the two words "Who's there?", which begin the play in the Elsinore midnight.

Marcellus He has the "bird of dawning" speech (I.1).

First Player More than an opportunity for old-school declamation; Shakespeare delighting in a chance to talk shop (II.2).

Gravediggers Not an enthralling pair of clowns; but the First Gravedigger at least provides Hamlet with Yorick's skull (V.1).

Fortinbras The Norwegian prince who will reign in Denmark after Hamlet's death, and who makes a commanding entry in the last few minutes. Restored, after a long absence, in Forbes-Robertson's production (Lyceum, 1897).

Ghost Worrying in today's theatre (where there have been sundry experiments with echoes, offstage speaking and vast shadows). Still, an imaginative actor can hold us without seeming, in Shaw's words, to have anything else to "while away eternity".

Gertrude Hamlet's foolish, sensual mother is allowed one pictorial speech, the description of Ophelia's death, "There is a willow grows aslant the brook" (IV.7).

Ophelia The "rose of May". Best acted simply, with no superfluously embarrassing developments of her madness. Ellen Terry*** (1878).

TROILUS AND CRESSIDA

1601–2

Priam, King of Troy	*Diomedes* and *Patroclus*, Greek
Hector, Troilus, Paris, Deiphobus	commanders
and *Helenus*, his sons	*Thersites*, a deformed and
Margarelon, a bastard son of Priam	scurrilous Greek
Aeneas and *Antenor* Trojan	*Alexander*, Cressida's servant
commanders	*Helen*, wife to Menelaus
Calchas, Cressida's father, a	*Andromache*, Hector's wife
Trojan priest taking part with	*Cressida*, daughter of Calchas
the Greeks	*Cassandra*, Priam's daughter; a
Pandarus, Cressida's uncle	prophetess
Agamemnon, the Greek general	Trojan and Greek soldiers;
Menelaus, his brother	Attendants; Servants
Achilles, Ajax, Ulysses, Nestor,	

Scene: Troy and the Greek camp before it

Synopsis

Seven years after the army of the Greeks has landed to seek Helen, beautiful Spartan queen who was carried off by a Trojan prince, Troy is still beleaguered. Young Troilus loves Cressida, niece of Pandarus and daughter of a Trojan priest who has defected to the Greeks. Hector, Priam's son, sends to the Greeks a challenge of single combat; but because the great Achilles, "the sinew and the forehand of our host", is sulking in his tent, Ulysses suggests that if the chance is offered to the "blockish" Ajax, Achilles will return to reason. Once more the Greeks offer to abandon the siege if Helen is returned; but though Cassandra prophesies woe if the offer is refused, the Trojans (Act II) decide to continue the fight.

The Greeks consent (Act III) to exchange a Trojan prisoner for Cressida, and Diomedes is despatched to bring her from the city. Troilus and Cressida, who earlier have sworn everlasting faith, part sadly; but in the Greek camp (IV.5) Cressida responds to every salute, to the distaste of Ulysses who calls her a "daughter of the game". Achilles boasts that in the next day's fighting he will meet Hector "fell as death". Troilus learns during a brief truce that Diomedes has wooed Cressida. Conducted by Ulysses, and unobserved, he sees her give his love-token to the Greek (Act V). In the next day's battle Troilus fails in his vengeance on Diomedes; Achilles, treacherously, kills the unarmed Hector. Wearily, the Trojans retire.

In performance

This magnificent, long-ignored play – Chapman's translation of Homer's *Iliad* is among the sources – had to wait more than three centuries for its quality in the theatre, as in the text, to be rightly recognized. Though its classification – comedy, history or tragedy – has been in doubt, it is above all a satire. A First Quarto edition (1609) said that it had been acted at the Globe; a second edition, in the same year, said nothing about this and in a preface added that it was "a new play never staled with the stage". Probably – though we can only surmise – it had been performed at one of the Inns of Court before a sophisticated audience. After some perplexity, the First Folio editors (1623) inserted it between the histories and the tragedies.

Here, in effect, Shakespeare is a traitor inside the walls of Troy. The heroes of the *Iliad* are lost in harshest satire and the thorny mazes of debate; the great contention over Argive Helen turns to "cormorant war". And yet, among this, the play can move miraculously into the love scenes of Troilus and Cressida or shape the ice-flowers of Ulysses in those speeches on Degree (I.3) and Time (III.3). Its examination of values, its quick splendours, its dark mocking at love and strife, the ultimate confusion in the dying day – a director in the theatre has somehow to sort out this complexity. When he manages to do so the play (as in certain RSC productions) can be a stage marvel. Shakespeare had always been fascinated by the Troilus story: consider only a long section of *The Rape of Lucrece*, and a number of incidental references, e.g. Pistol calls Doll Tearsheet a "lazar kite of Cressid's kind" (*Henry V*, II.1).

Theatre history until the present century is brief. The play was performed, during the Restoration, at the Smock Alley Theatre in Dublin. Dryden cut and expanded the text to *Troilus and Cressida; or, Truth Found Too Late* (Dorset Gardens, 1679), acted on several occasions until 1734. A gap then until an insignificant production at the Great Queen Street Theatre, London (1907, Lewis Casson as Troilus), and William Poel's eccentrically cut version (King's Hall, Covent Garden, 1912) which at least brought to the stage the twenty-four-year-old amateur, Edith Evans, as Cressida with her pennon-fluttering voice and eloquent hands, the perfect "encounterer glib of tongue".

Afterwards (1922) the Marlowe Society of Cambridge – which this century has been a foster-parent of the play – staged it (also at the Everyman, London): one of several Marlowe revivals, later under George Rylands. Professional work was undistinguished, except for Ion Swinley's Troilus (Old Vic, 1923), and Pamela Brown's lisping Cressida and Donald Wolfit's Ulysses (Stratford, 1936), until Michael Macowan's modern-dress version at the Westminster (1938), with the Ulysses of Robert Speaight. John Byron was Troilus (Open Air, 1946), and Paul Scofield and Laurence Harvey in, respectively, the Stratford revivals of 1948 and 1954. Tyrone Guthrie practically satirized the satire in his celebrated Old Vic production (1956) with its Hohenzollern Greeks undermined by faction, its Ruritanian Trojans undermined by frivolity, and the poetry sadly wasted.

The most important productions of our day were at Statford (1960, by John Barton and Peter Hall) and the Aldwych (1962, Peter Hall alone). The play was presented in a symbolic cockpit (as a critic described it): on this white-sanded, shallow octagonal platform, before an abstract torrid backcloth, love and chivalry were grated to dusty nothing. John Barton directed other RSC treatments (1968–9, 1976–7).

Most American productions have been amateur ones in the universities. Professional versions in New York (1932; Otis Skinner as Thersites, 1955; and 1975, with the same actress playing Cressida, Cassandra and Helen) had little popular response. At Stratford, Connecticut (1957), the play was set during the period of the American Civil War, with the Trojans played as the Confederacy.

In 1949 Luchino Visconti directed the play in the Boboli Gardens at Florence, with half the characters on horseback.

In other terms

Sir William Walton's opera *Troilus and Cressida* (1954), after Chaucer's poem rather than Shakespeare's play.

Chief characters

Hector Chivalrous paladin of the Trojans, but futile in argument (II.2).

Troilus Twenty-two years old. The longest part, and far from a simple hero. Against ending the war (II.2); passionately hurt by Cressida. Ulysses says of him (IV.5), "His heart and hand both open and both free;/For what he has he gives, what thinks he shows." Ion Swinley** (Old Vic, 1923), Paul Scofield*** (Stratford, 1948).

Paris The Trojan prince whose seizure of Helen began the Trojan war. "Well may we fight for her whom we know well/The world's large spaces cannot parallel" (II.2).

Pandarus Cressida's uncle and matchmaker. Early exuberance declining to utter hopelessness at the very end of the play (V.10). Max Adrian*** (Stratford, 1962).

Agamemnon "Great commander, nerve and bone of Greece" (I.3).

Menelaus Helen's cuckolded husband.

Achilles Despicably arrogant Greek champion; treacherously murders the unarmed Hector (V.8).

Ajax Although the Homeric hero becomes a "beef-witted" block, he has a telling couplet (V.9) when he hears that Achilles has slain Hector: "If it be so, yet bragless let it be;/Great Hector was as good a man as he."

Ulysses, Prince of Ithaca. He has the wise speeches on Degree (I.3) and Time (III.3). Donald Wolfit*** (Stratford, 1936); Robert Speaight*** (Westminster, 1938).

Nestor "Most reverend, for thy stretch'd out life," says Ulysses (I.3).

Diomedes The Greek "sweet guardian" of Cressida.

Thersites Rancid camp-follower of the Greeks. "Core of envy . . . Crusty batch of nature" (V.1). William Poel (1912) saw him as a jester and cast for the part a Scots-accented actress, Elspeth Keith. He has sometimes been a scrubby journalist. "Still wars and lechery! Nothing else holds fashion" (V.2).

Cressida At the heart of the play. A searching portrait of a woman who, though dismissed by Ulysses as a "daughter of the game", does know her frailty. "I have a kind of self resides with you;/But an unkind self that itself will leave/To be another's fool" (III.2). "The error of our eye directs our mind" (V.2). She has the superb lines, "Prophet may you be" (III.2). Edith Evans*** (King's Hall, Covent Garden, 1912; Stratford, 1913), Pamela Brown** (Stratford, 1936), Dorothy Tutin*** (Stratford, 1960; Aldwych, 1962).

Andromache Hector's wife. A pallid remembrance of Calphurnia (*Julius Caesar*), V.3.

Helen Her scene (III.1) offers no reason why the Trojan war should have lasted so long, or why, in the words of Troilus (not Marlowe here), she is "a pearl whose price hath launch'd above a thousand ships" (II.2).

Cassandra The prophetess of Troy must not be underplayed. Her entry, "raving", at II.2, should be genuinely exciting.

ALL'S WELL
THAT ENDS WELL

1602–3

King of France	*Countess of Rousillon*, Bertram's
Duke of Florence	mother
Bertram, young Count of	*Helena*, a gentlewoman protected
Rousillon	by the Countess
Lafeu, an old lord	*A Widow* of Florence
Parolles, a follower of Bertram	*Diana*, the Widow's daughter
Two French Lords, named *Dumain*,	*Violenta* (non-speaking) and
serving with Bertram	*Mariana*, the Widow's
Renaldo, steward, *Lavache*, a	neighbours and friends
clown, *A Page*, servants to the	Lords, Officers, Soldiers, etc.,
Countess of Rousillon	French and Florentine

Scene: Rousillon, Paris, Florence, Marseilles

Synopsis

Helena, an orphan, loves Bertram, son of the dowager Countess of Rousillon, who has brought her up. When the haughty young man goes as a ward to the French King, Helena – whose father had been a celebrated physician – follows him, hoping that she may cure the King of a painful illness. She does so (Act II) with one of her father's remedies; and being offered her choice of husband from the gentlemen at court, chooses Bertram. Snobbishly, he objects – "A poor physician's daughter my wife!" – but forced by the King, agrees to the match. Immediately afterwards he runs away to Florence as a volunteer in the Tuscan wars – the Florentines against the Sienese – with a cowardly braggart, Parolles, as his companion.

Back at Rousillon (Act III) Helena learns that Bertram will take her as his wife when she has got from his finger a prized heirloom-ring and borne him a child. She goes, in pilgrim's dress, to Florence, where Bertram is seeking to seduce a widow's daughter, Diana. Helena persuades Diana to yield to him but to ask for his ring and to make an assignation which she, Helena, will keep.

Meanwhile, the fellow-officers of Parolles (Act IV) trick him into exposing his cowardice. Diana, having got Bertram's ring, duly arranges a midnight meeting with him; hidden by darkness, Helena takes Diana's place and gives Bertram as a keepsake a ring she had received from the King of France. Hearing that Helena is dead, Bertram returns to Rousillon, where his mother and the old lord, Lafeu, also believe the story.

Lafeu (Act V) arranges a match between his daughter and Bertram, who prepares to give to her the ring from Helena. When the King recognizes it he orders Bertram's arrest. Diana, newly arrived, accuses Bertram of seducing her; when he denies it, the King orders her to prison as well, but her mother, the widow, produces "bail", Helena herself, who is to have Bertram's child. "All yet seems well", says the King comfortably, "and if it end so meet/The bitter past, more welcome is the sweet."

In performance

All's Well That Ends Well, based on a story by Boccaccio in the *Decameron,* has not been a popular play, largely because Helena (though Granville Barker approved) can come through as an unlikeably persistent opportunist. Actresses and directors can overcome this: we accept her single-mindedness for the sake of some gravely haunting verse. The couplets in II.1 cannot be glibly dismissed; in performance they have a curious spirit of incantation. Though the dark comedy may be "a mingled yarn, good and ill together", it can grow on readers of the text and listeners in the theatre: unadorned productions so far have been scarce.

There was no theatrical success until the mid-eighteenth century (1741, Goodman's Fields; 1742, Drury Lane, with Peg Woffington as Helena). Thereafter various revivals emphasized the romance less than the comedy: Parolles, a favourite part of Henry Woodward, was always prominent. John Philip Kemble restored the balance when he played Bertram (1794) at Drury Lane, with Mrs Jordan as Helena; but this did not go very well. By 1832 the comedy was actually being played at Covent Garden as an opera (sub-title, *Love's Labour's Won*), with a sheaf of songs from elsewhere in Shakespeare and an added masque. Twenty years later Phelps did the Folio text at Sadler's Wells.

The play slept for over half a century, until Frank Benson, immediately after receiving his knighthood at Drury Lane, appeared as Parolles at Stratford in tercentenary year (1916). William Poel directed an eccentric "vocal recital" (Ethical Church, Bayswater, 1920), with a uniformed nurse wheeling on the King in a bath-chair, and Edith Evans and Winifred Oughton as the brothers Dumain. In 1922 Bridges-Adams's Stratford production pushed the play, as he said, an inch or two towards Cinderella. The young Laurence Olivier was a glossy Parolles in Barry Jackson's modern-dress version (Birmingham Repertory, 1927); Iden Payne had a dull Stratford revival (1935); and in 1940 (Vaudeville) Robert Atkins – probably with the title in mind – bravely directed the piece for three weeks of matinées, during heavy daylight air raids, with Catherine Lacey as Helena and Ernest Milton as the King.

Since then, *All's Well That Ends Well* has gradually had more attention: Old Vic (1953), a production ruined by the clowning of the King into senile hypochondria; Stratford (1955) in Louis Treize costume; Stratford (1959) in a sometimes inconsequential fantastication by Tyrone Guthrie (from which he cut the clown Lavache); Stratford again (1967; Aldwych, 1968), directed sensitively by John Barton, and in London with Lynn Farleigh's transforming Helena; and Greenwich (1975), a straight modern-dress performance under Jonathan Miller.

Tyrone Guthrie staged his version first at Stratford, Ontario (1953), with Alec Guinness as the King, Irene Worth as Helena; and David Jones directed the play there (1971), with Martha Henry. Nancy Wickwire was Helena in the New York Shakespeare Festival (1959); Barbara Barrie in 1966.

Chief characters

King of France His autumnally wistful regal dignity must not be dispersed in the kind of fooling that shattered an Old Vic revival (1953). He is generous and grateful. Ernest Milton** (Vaudeville, 1940).

Duke of Florence Insignificant in the text. Tyrone Guthrie

(Stratford, Ontario, 1953; Stratford-upon-Avon, 1959) used a little scene (III.3) as the basis of a ten-minute comic and totally superfluous interlude.

Bertram One of Shakespeare's weaker (and snobbish) young men. There has been much special pleading for him – a suggestion that he has been corrupted by Parolles – but any actor has some trouble in commending him to us. "War is no strife/To the dark house and the detested wife" (II.3).

Lafeu A sage old lord with a daughter, Maudlin, who is mentioned in the text but unseen in the theatre.

Parolles A hollow, parasitic coward, thoroughly exposed in the blindfold scene where he betrays his own side, and has lines famous in their context (IV.3), "Who cannot be crush'd with a plot?" and "Simply the thing I am/Shall make me live."

Lavache An inferior clown; played at Stratford (1955) as a dwarf. Guthrie cut him altogether from Canadian and English revivals.

Countess of Rousillon. The finest Shakespearian *grande dame*, acted beautifully by Edith Evans*** in the Edwardian manner (Stratford, 1959).

Helena Heroine, opportunist, or both. Rouses mixed feelings, though she says good things: "Twere all one/That I should love a bright particular star/And think to wed it, he is so above me" (I.1); "My friends were poor, but honest" (I.3); should be barefooted in the pilgrim scene (III.5), but seldom is. Lynn Farleigh*** (Aldwych, 1968).

Widow The useful hostess of Florence, whose daughter, Diana, aids Helena's plan.

Diana The widow's daughter. Replies unanswerably and mockingly to Bertram's first refusal to yield his ring (IV.2):

> Mine honour's such a ring;
> My chastity's the jewel of our house ...
> Which were the greatest obloquy i'th' world
> In me to lose.

A gentleman Met in Marseilles (V.1). He is described, agreeably, in the Folio as "A Gentle Astringer" (falconer).

MEASURE FOR MEASURE

1604

Vincentio, Duke of Vienna	*Pompey*, a clown and servant to
Angelo, the Deputy	Mistress Overdone
Escalus, an ancient lord	*Abhorson*, an executioner
Claudio, a young gentleman	*Barnardine*, a dissolute prisoner
Lucio, a fantastic	*Isabella*, Claudio's sister
Two Other Gentlemen	*Mariana*, formerly betrothed to
Varrius, a gentleman, servant to	Angelo
the Duke	*Juliet*, beloved of Claudio
Provost	*Francisca*, a nun
Thomas, Peter, two friars	*Mistress Overdone*, a bawd
A Justice	Lords, Officers, Citizen, Boy,
Elbow, a simple constable	Attendants
Froth, a foolish gentleman	

Scene: Vienna

Synopsis

Vincentio, Duke of Vienna, resolving on the enforcement of the city's ignored laws against immorality, proclaims his departure to Poland; actually he remains, disguised as a friar, to see what his Deputy, the severe Angelo (whose "blood is very snow-broth") will do. One of Angelo's first acts is to imprison Claudio for getting his betrothed, Juliet, with child, an offence that carries the death penalty.

Isabella, Claudio's sister, a potential novice in a religious order, comes (Act II) to plead with Angelo; he invites her to return next day, and when she does, tells her that if she will be his mistress, her brother can be pardoned. Horrified, she sees her brother (Act III) who entreats her to agree. She refuses; but the disguised Duke/Friar suggests that she should give way, and that Mariana, once Angelo's spurned love, should take her place at night.

Mariana (Act IV) accepts the plan; Angelo, faithlessly, has ordered Claudio's death which is prevented by the Duke/Friar and the Provost. The Duke returns as himself (Act V). In a complex scene Angelo, after compulsorily wedding Mariana, is pardoned, Claudio will marry Juliet, and the Duke confesses his own love for Isabella.

In performance

"Haste still pays haste, and leisure answers leisure;/Like doth quit like, and Measure still for Measure" (V.1). Here Shakespeare, who got much of his material from an unacted drama in two parts (*Promos and Cassandra* by George Whetstone, set in Hungary), wrote an intricate tragi-comedy about justice and mercy. It is an examination of moral values that has become something of a chameleon-play in our time, principally because the enigmatic Duke of Vienna (Vincentio), who in disguise watches the behaviour of his Deputy, can be interpreted in so many ways. We have seen him as divine power personified, as a sinister hypocrite, as a complacent statesman and as a master-intriguer; the play has appeared as an allegory, an attack on dictatorship and a sociological exercise.

Whichever the choice, and in spite of its shameless use of the "bed-trick" whereby one girl takes the place of another, *Measure for Measure*, written with absorbing strength and eloquence, can usually hold the stage; one absurd revival (Stratford, 1974) did turn the Duke into a vulgar sham. Isabella, setting honour above her brother's life, is not an easy heroine; it has been proposed plausibly that in her notorious line, "More than our brother is our chastity" (II.4), she is speaking in terms of her religious order. The comedy rests principally on Lucio, a libertine "fantastic", whose morals are as deplorable as his insolence is amusing, and Pompey, a cheerful ruffian in both Vienna's sultry days and its sultrier nights before "the unfolding star calls up the shepherd".

After the customary free versions, Shakespeare's text was revived at Drury Lane (1738) with James Quin as the Duke, Mrs Susannah Cibber as Isabella (a part Peg Woffington would also play, and, later, Mary Ann Yates). The great Isabella was Sarah Siddons (between 1783 and 1811), using all her passionate emotional integrity; John Philip Kemble often acted the Duke with her. In spite of intermittent revivals – e.g. Adelaide Neilson's Isabella at the Haymarket, 1876 and 1878 – the play was not for Victorians, who suspected its morality. Oscar Asche and his wife, Lily Brayton, were Angelo and Isabella (Adelphi, 1906); William Poel (first in 1893) treated *Measure for Measure* less strangely than some of his productions. Between the wars Baliol Holloway appeared, in various years, as Lucio (Stratford, 1922), the Duke and Angelo; and Randle Ayrton was a grittily impressive Duke at Stratford (1931), during the cinema-stage "interregnum" between the two theatres (see p. 175).

Tyrone Guthrie, who had a particular feeling for the piece (interpreted diversely), directed a Vic/Wells revival (1933), with Charles Laughton's Angelo, the unarguable success of his Shakespearian career, and Flora Robson as Isabella. Guthrie came back on other occasions, notably at the Old Vic (1937; Emlyn Williams as Angelo, with Marie Ney), at Stratford, Ontario (1954), and at Bristol Old Vic (1966). Peter Brook (Stratford-upon-Avon, 1950; John Gielgud as a man in torment, and the youthful Barbara Jefford's Isabella) insisted on a daring pause when Isabella knelt to plead for Angelo's life: a silence that lasted originally for thirty-five seconds, and now and then as long as two minutes. Judi Dench was Isabella at Stratford (1962); Dilys Hamlett at the Old Vic (1963), the company's last play before the National Theatre took over; and Paola Dionisotti at Stratford (1978). Jonathan Miller directed (in modern dress) at Greenwich in 1975, and Peter Gill, straightforwardly, at the Riverside Studios, Hammersmith (1979), with the Isabella of Helen Mirren.

Peter Brook directed the play in what has been called "the mosque-like ruin" of his Théâtre Bouffes-du-Nord, Paris (1978).

In other terms

Kate Nelligan, in an otherwise indifferently spoken version (BBC television, 1979), was a moving Isabella who from her habit seemed to have been admitted prematurely to the sisterhood.

Chief characters

Vincentio, the Duke Chooses to wander, disguised, in his Vienna much as Haroun al Raschid did in the streets of Baghdad. A long part (fifth longest in the plays; 835 lines, including "Be absolute for death", III.1); directors during the last thirty years have experimented with it – none more radically than Tyrone Guthrie. At Bristol Old Vic (1966) Vincentio, as Power Divine, showed the stigmata to the Provost (IV.2): "Here is the hand and seal of the Duke." Though Shakespeare clearly intended the last scene with Isabella, "Give me your hand and say you will be mine", as a conventional wrapping-up of the plot, directors are apt to impose a superfluous significance: we cannot be sure now whether Isabella will accept or not. Joseph O'Conor*** (Greenwich, 1975).

Angelo The puritan who falls was acted definitively by Charles Laughton*** (Vic/Wells, 1933), a shuddering glance at a cankered mind.

Escalus The "ancient lord" is one of Shakespeare's expressions of experienced wisdom.

Claudio Comes out sharply in his fear of death, "Ay, but to die, and go we know not where" (III.1).

Lucio The "fantastic" who has, reluctantly, to marry Kate Keepdown.

Elbow A faint glimmer of Dogberry (*Much Ado About Nothing*).

Pompey Cannot restrain his natural exuberance, even in gaol where (IV.3) he evokes the procession of prisoners (Rash, Caper, Deepvow and the rest); and becomes assistant to the executioner, Abhorson ("Can you cut off a man's head?" the Provost asks him, IV.2).

Barnardine Most independent of prisoners, he "will not die today for any man's persuasion" (IV.3).

Isabella A testing part ("a thing enskied and sainted") that can be potently affecting. Her plea for mercy (II.2) outmatches Portia's. Sarah Siddons*** (1783), Barbara Jefford*** (Stratford, 1950; Old Vic, 1957), Sinead Cusack** (Aldwych, 1979).

Mariana Romantically "of the moated grange", she will be Angelo's wife. She has in her first scene (IV.1) a tempting line for actresses, the simple "I have sat here all day."

Juliet Shakespeare this time uses the name for Claudio's unlucky betrothed.

Francisca A nun with nine lines. Memorable only because Ellen Terry played the part for one performance (with Oscar Asche, Adelphi, 1906) to mark her stage jubilee.

Mistress Overdone The Viennese bawd whose name says all.

OTHELLO, THE MOOR OF VENICE

1604

Duke of Venice	before Othello
Brabantio, a Venetian Senator, Desdemona's father	*Clown*, servant to Othello
Gratiano, Brabantio's brother	*Desdemona*, Brabantio's daughter and Othello's wife
Lodovico, Brabantio's kinsman	*Emilia*, Iago's wife
Othello, the Moor, in the service of Venice	*Bianca*, a courtesan, in love with Cassio
Cassio, his honourable Lieutenant	Senators, Gentlemen of Cyprus,
Iago, his Ancient, a villain	Sailors, Officers, Messenger,
Roderigo, a fooled Venetian gentleman	Musicians, Heralds, Attendants, etc.
Montano, Governor of Cyprus	

Scene: Venice, Cyprus

Synopsis

Iago, ensign to the Moorish general Othello, in the service of the Venetian republic, is a man inwardly malevolent and envious, outwardly an honest soldier. Resolved, for his own reasons, to revenge himself upon Othello, he begins one midnight in Venice by getting Roderigo – Desdemona's foolish suitor – to rouse her father with the news that Othello has stolen her. Brabantio at once accuses Othello at the Duke's hastily convened council which is considering a threatened Turkish attack on Cyprus; but the Moor's tale of his wooing, and Desdemona's testimony, persuade all the senators except Brabantio himself. Othello is despatched to govern Cyprus, and he goes with his new lieutenant Cassio (of whom Iago is feverishly jealous), Desdemona following them with Iago and his wife Emilia.

The Turkish fleet has been dispersed in a tempest by the time (Act II) the travellers reach Cyprus. (Roderigo, still pursuing Desdemona, is also there.) On a night of celebration Cassio, who at Iago's prompting has drunk unwisely, is involved in a brawl and disgraced ("Never more be officer of mine," says Othello).

At Iago's suggestion (Act III) Cassio implores Desdemona to plead his cause; Othello, already distressed by Iago's hints at infidelity, grows progressively inflamed. Iago makes diabolical play with a handkerchief (Othello's gift) that Desdemona has dropped and that he ensures Cassio will unwittingly find.

Presently (Act IV), when Othello is overwhelmed by the falsehood that Desdemona is untrue, Iago arranges other "proof". Othello swears to kill her; and envoys from Venice, who have come to recall him, leaving Cassio as governor, are horrified to see him strike his wife. Iago (Act V) urges Roderigo to murder Cassio, and when the effort fails, stabs the dupe to death. Othello smothers Desdemona in her bed; Emilia, rousing the citadel, tells the truth about Iago, confirmed when in desperation he kills her. Whereupon Othello stabs himself, Iago is borne off to torture, and Cassio rules in Cyprus.

In performance

Iago, Othello's "ancient", or ensign, says, "I do hate him as I do hell pains" (I.1). This is the tragedy of a "free and open nature" (also, surprisingly, Iago's phrase) wrecked by an apparently honest soldier. For all his anxiously sought reasons, his resentment at Cassio's appointment over him, and the utterly implausible suggestion that Othello has seduced Emilia (I.3), Iago is a man in love with evil for its own sake. The First Folio cast list describes him simply as 'a villain'. He has a ready imagination: directors ought not to cut his first urging of Roderigo to call aloud "with like timorous action and dire yell/As when, by night and negligence, the fire/Is spied in populous cities.' We know at once that nothing will change the mind behind the mask. The tragedy of Othello is its inevitability, beginning with Cassio's humiliation and continuing to the deaths of Desdemona and the Moor. On the way the fooled Roderigo must die, and, at length, Iago's own wife; but we can say (with Albany at the end of *King Lear*), "That's but a trifle."

Here, then, is the villain. Othello, the victim, shattered as much by his loss of faith in an ideal as by sheer jealousy, is a wonderfully planned part, a man caught – as it has been said – at the meeting-point of two cultural and spiritual traditions. The actor needs temperament and voice: one quality alone will not serve. There are scenes when Othello is possessed by a barbaric ancestry; but for the famous speeches – "Most potent, grave, and reverend signiors" (I.3), "O, now for ever/Farewell the tranquil mind" (III.3), "Never, Iago" (III.3), "It is the cause", "Behold, I have a weapon", and "Soft you; a word or two before you go" (all V.2) – we should have a fitting splendour; towards the end, the arched fury of the breaking wave.

In the text, the time scheme of *Othello* is impossible; still, in performance no one questions it. The tragedy, suggested by an Italian tale in the *Hecatommithi* of Cinthio, has been played steadily since 1604 when we suppose the "grievèd Moor" was Burbage. Margaret Hughes, presumed to have been Desdemona in Thomas Killigrew's company (Vere Street, Clare Market, December 1660), could have been the first professional actress on the English stage: "Here comes the lady; let her witness it."

Revisers have left the play alone. Down the centuries there have always been leading players for Othello and Iago, sometimes alternating incautiously. Betterton ("When he wept his tears broke from him perforce") was Othello during the Restoration and afterwards; James Quin, white-attired, imposing, slow, and not very tender, played at intervals between 1722 and 1751.

David Garrick (more assured as Iago) was too violent, but his rival, silver-tongued Spranger Barry, became the day's most feeling Othello, profoundly distressed. John Philip Kemble needed emotional authority. Edmund Kean (from 1814) gave one of his lightning-flash portraits, kindling in the third act and with a final speech (said Hazlitt) like "the sound of years of departed happiness." Macready (whose Iago could be darkly smouldering) seemed relatively overstudied.

Samuel Phelps was better as Othello, Charles Fechter as Iago. Henry Irving, lachrymose and restless, threw Othello away, but not his sardonic, irregular Iago, during his alternation with the American Edwin Booth. Forbes-Robertson (Lyric, 1902), chivalrous always, never a man for the "steep-down gulfs of liquid fire", was too gentle in a multilated text. Though critics praised Matheson Lang (New, 1920) for Shakespearian excellence at matinées, his public preferred him at night in *Carnival*, a facile modern treatment of the Othello theme. Wilfrid Walter (Stratford, 1930) looked, and sometimes sounded, superb, with George Hayes as his demi-devil Iago; Paul Robeson's Negro Othello (Savoy, 1930) ebbed into monotony; and Tyrone Guthrie failed in a Freudian attempt (Old Vic, 1938) to show that Iago (Laurence Olivier) was attracted to Othello (Ralph Richardson) homosexually.

The next quarter-century brought a few debated performances. Frederick Valk, a thunderously passionate Czech (Old Vic company at New, 1942) mauled the verse but worked closely with his Iago (Bernard Miles), a coarse, chilling fox. Godfrey Tearle, who had been Othello as far back as 1921 (Royal Court), was nobly commanding (Stratford, 1948) but failed to blaze. Orson Welles (St James's, 1951) was unresourceful; and John Gielgud (Stratford, 1961) had to dissipate his glorious speech in a tiresomely scenic Zeffirelli production. Three years later (National at Old Vic, 1964) the Othello of his age proved to be Laurence Olivier, with his wind-tossed harmonies, bursts of barbaric music, and the volcanic temperament of a full Negro. One of two valuable performances in a very different mould was Paul Scofield's for the National company in the Olivier Theatre (1980), an entirely straight production by Peter Hall. Gravely dignified in mind and breeding, Scofield had at the last a sudden agonized fury at "Whip me, ye devils!" when Othello saw too clearly and too late. Donald Sinden (Stratford/Aldwych, 1979–80) was similarly eloquent, affecting and truthful, and overcame one perilous eccentricity in direction.

American stage history, from New York (1751), is governed by two men: Edwin Forrest's massive-bull Othello (1826 to 1871); and, between 1860 and 1891, America's greatest player, the intellectual Edwin Booth. He acted both parts, more surely his Machiavellian Iago, plausible, precisely enunciated, and with frightening inner fires. Paul Robeson had a long New York run, 1943–4; by 1959, when he came across to Stratford–upon–Avon, his voice had become an oddly distant bass rumble.

Italy bred two celebrated Othellos, the sensual, tempestuous Tommaso Salvini, a marvellous tragic actor (New York, 1873; London, 1875), and the savage Sicilian, Giovanni Grasso (London, 1910). Salvini was criticized for his treatment of Othello's death and the fierce hacking at his throat. Edmund Kean in the same scene had been applauded. Leigh Hunt said of him ("piercing himself to the heart with a poignard"): "Can you not mark the frozen shudder as the steel enters his frame? . . . Death by a heart wound is instantaneous. Thus does he portray it; he literally dies standing."

In other terms

Films: 1955 (finished 1952), directed by Orson Welles (Welles as Othello); 1955, directed by Sergei Yutkevitch (largely shot in the Crimea); 1965, National Theatre production (Olivier as Othello, Frank Finlay as Iago), directed by Stuart Burge. Opera: *Otello* (Rossini, 1816); *Otello* (Verdi, 1887). Verdi was seventy-four when he composed his magnificent opera to the libretto Arrigo Boito based upon Shakespeare.

Chief characters

Othello One of the most taxing parts in the Folio. An Othello must be more than simply passionate or (the usual simplification) soldierly. He shuld be a majestic speaker, and we must always be aware of the racial depths. Cassio speaks his epitaph: "For he was great of heart". Edmund Kean*** (from 1814); Laurence Olivier*** (National at Old Vic, 1964); Paul Scofield*** (National at Olivier Theatre, 1980).

Iago The longest part (1,070 lines). "Honest Iago" speaks for himself in I.1: "For necessity of present life,/I must show out a flag and sign of love,/Which is indeed but sign." He is an affirmation of evil for its own sake; behind him is the midnight, and he brings chaos with him. "The pity of it, Iago!" says Othello (IV.1), but Iago has never known pity. Edwin Booth*** (from 1860); Bernard Miles*** (Old Vic at New, 1942).

Cassio The Moor's "honourable lieutenant", impulsive and weak. Iago: "He hath a daily beauty in his life/That makes me ugly" (V.1).

Roderigo Iago's foolish dupe, whom the Folio calls "a gull'd Venetian gentleman". Still vainly pursuing, he is killed (V.1) with "O damn'd Iago! O inhuman dog!" as his last words. He should be played with discretion – not, as frequently, turned into an Andrew Aguecheek.

Montano Former Governor of Cyprus, injured by Cassio in a brawl (II.3).

Brabantio Desdemona's father. Othello, in Iago's net, may remember Brabantio's last couplet – as we can be sure Iago does – "Look to her, Moor, if thou hast eyes to see;/She has deceived her father, and may thee' (I.3). We hear in V.2 of his grieving death.

Lodovico The Venetian envoy, Brabantio's kinsman, who is present (IV.1) when Othello strikes Desdemona. "My lord, this would not be believ'd in Venice,/Though I should swear I saw't."

Gratiano Brabantio's brother and Desdemona's uncle appears (V.1) just in time to know of Roderigo's death; in the next scene he says of Brabantio that Desdemona's marriage was "mortal to him, and pure grief/Shore his old thread atwain." In the play's final speech Lodovico says: "Gratiano, keep the house,/And seize upon the fortunes of the Moor,/For they succeed on you."

Desdemona Has been played too often as a wilting lily. But her marriage was courageous; and we should not be allowed to forget her response to Brabantio (I.3), "My noble father,/I do perceive here a divided duty."

Emilia Iago's wife, Desdemona's attendant and confidante. Anxious to please her husband, she gives him the fatal handkerchief (III.3). "Have we not affections,/Desires for sport and frailty, as men have?" (IV.3). Elizabeth Spriggs*** (Stratford, 1971).

Bianca Cassio's Cypriot courtesan, impudent and brave.

KING LEAR

1605

Lear, King of Britain	*Lear's Fool*
King of France	*Oswald*, Goneril's steward
Duke of Burgundy	*A Captain*, employed by Edmund
Duke of Cornwall	*Gentleman* attendant on Cordelia
Duke of Albany	*A Herald*
Earl of Kent	*Goneril*, wife to Duke of Albany
Earl of Gloucester	*Regan*, wife to Duke of Cornwall
Edgar, Gloucester's son	*Cordelia*, who becomes Queen of
Edmund, bastard son to Gloucester	France
Curan, a courtier	Knights attending on Lear,
Old Man, tenant to Gloucester	Officers, Messengers, Soldiers,
Doctor	Attendants, Servants to Cornwall

Scene: Britain

Synopsis

Lear, King of Britain, aged and choleric, has resolved to divide his realm between his three daughters. Though Goneril (married to the gentle Albany) and Regan (cruel Cornwall's wife) extravagantly declare their love for him, the youngest, Cordelia, disdaining this, says simply: "I cannot heave/My heart into my mouth." Wrathfully, Lear disinherits her, banishing Kent who has spoken on her behalf; but the King of France takes her, dowerless, as his Queen. Lear then gives her share to her sisters, proposing to live with Goneril and Regan alternately with his retinue of a hundred knights.

Edmund, Gloucester's bastard son, foments discord between his legitimate brother Edgar and their father. Kent, disguised, returns to serve his master Lear. Goneril receives Lear with contempt; invoking a curse upon her (I.4), he leaves for Regan. At the same time (Act II) Regan and Cornwall reach Gloucester's castle, whence Edgar has fled. Regan proves to be even harsher than Goneril; believing madness will supervene, Lear goes out with his Fool into the night storm on the heath, where the loyal Kent finds him. Gloucester, braving the anger of the two sisters and Cornwall, gets shelter for them in a hovel (Edgar is there, disguised as a half-witted "Poor Tom") and urges Kent to take the endangered King to Dover ("There is a litter ready; lay him in 't"). Returning to his castle, Gloucester is reviled and savagely blinded by Cornwall, who is then slain by a servant.

Edgar, still as "Poor Tom" and unknown to his blinded father, sets off with him towards Dover. There is a strange meeting (Act IV) between the mad King and the blind man. Soon afterwards Cordelia, who has come from France, is reunited with the enfeebled Lear. Captured (Act V) in a battle which the French forces have lost, they are sent to prison where by Edmund's instructions they are to be murdered. But Edmund – who has been deceiving both the infatuated Goneril and Regan – is killed by Edgar (as a nameless knight) in single combat. Goneril has poisoned Regan; she now stabs herself. Cordelia has been hanged in prison; Lear bears her in, "dead in his arms", and within minutes he himself has died. "The wonder is he hath endur'd so long." Edgar, at Albany's wish, will look to the state; but Kent will follow Lear: "My master calls me; I must not say no."

In performance

King Lear, dawn-in-Britain tragedy of retribution, is an anguished, storm-ridden journey of the mind and spirit. With many of the most searching passages in Shakespeare, it has still to be for some listeners an acquired taste in the theatre, though no one now will talk, as Charles Lamb did, of "An old man tottering about the stage with a walking-stick, turned out of doors by his daughters on a rainy night. . . . The Lear of Shakespeare cannot be acted." During the last half-century the great play has been a normal part of the repertory, though no one has succeeded without reservation as the wilful patriarch driven to madness.

Among the sources for his tragedy of "unaccommodated man" (III.4), Shakespeare worked most directly from an old chronicle drama published in 1605. The true *King Lear* fared unhappily from 1681 when it fell into the hands of Nahum Tate, who produced a ridiculous mutilation, with Edgar and Cordelia as lovers, the Fool eliminated, and a happy ending ("Old Kent throws in his hearty wishes too"). Yet, for a century and a half, Tate's was practically the only version that audiences would accept, though one by David Garrick (with Tate's plot retained, but much of the original verse restored) was familiar at Drury Lane – and Garrick himself devotedly acknowledged – for thirty-odd years from 1756.

In the course of two revivals by Robert Elliston, with Edmund Kean as Lear (1823 and 1826), more of the original returned; but it was left to William Charles Macready (Covent Garden, 1838) to bring back an abridged Shakespearian text, with the Fool assigned to an actress, Priscilla Horton. Once the changes had been made, *King Lear* – shortened according to managerial taste – remained Shakespeare's (Samuel Phelps gave the Fool to an actor at Sadler's Wells, 1845). In England until 1928, and in spite of several renowned players, only Macready's Lear (1838) and Ellen Terry's Cordelia (with Henry Irving, 1892) were really eminent.

Ernest Milton, his Lear cut to the brains, was powerfully individual (Old Vic, 1928; Jean Forbes-Robertson as Cordelia); John Gielgud, larch rather than oak, had a first clear look at the part (Old Vic, 1931); Randle Ayrton (Stratford, 1931, and on Komisarjevsky's variously levelled staircase-set, 1936) abounded in pathos, especially at "We two alone will sing like birds i'th'cage" (V.3); William Devlin, in his early twenties (Westminster, 1934; Old Vic, 1936) was an Olympian figure who needed only a more flexible voice; and Gielgud again (Old Vic, 1940; a production supervised by Granville-Barker) had grown masterfully.

Donald Wolfit (Scala, 1944) had played Lear earlier without marked response; but the critic James Agate now became as much of a cheer-leader for Wolfit as Hazlitt had been for Kean's Othello. Unarguably affecting, especially in the hovel scene, III.6 ("The little dogs and all... see they bark at me"), the performance did suffer from a creeping monotony of intonation, and a small band of listeners preferred Wolfit as the unexampled Kent he had acted to Ayrton at Stratford (1936). Laurence Olivier's Lear (Old Vic at New, 1946) was closely considered; Gielgud (Stratford, 1950) returned with undimmed impact, especially in the colloquy with Gloucester (IV.6) and the Recognition (IV.7);

Michael Redgrave (Stratford, 1953) had a massive quietness.

A sequence of later performances included Gielgud's final portrait (Palace, 1955), ruined by the caprices of Japanese décor. Charles Laughton (Stratford, 1959) added little. Paul Scofield, in a pitilessly Brechtian production by Peter Brook (Stratford/Aldwych, 1962), resembled for a moment an ancient sea captain commanding the bridge of his vessel, defying the cosmic fates as he drove, unmanned, towards death. Robert Eddison (Actors' Company, and in New York, 1973) is remembered for his extreme pathos in the last scene; and Donald Sinden (Stratford, 1976; a director-marred production) and Anthony Quayle (Old Vic, 1978), for their steady understanding.

In America, where the Shakespeare text did not return until Macready visited New York (1844), the most famous nineteenth-century Lears were Edwin Forrest (only twenty when he essayed it first in 1826), Edwin Booth (1875), and John E. McCullough (1877). In the twentieth century: Robert Mantell (1905), Louis Calhern (1940), and at Stratford, Connecticut (1963, 1965), the exceptional Morris Carnovsky.

Ludwig Devrient (with "one of the noblest old man's heads I have seen", wrote a contemporary) was an admired German Lear in the early nineteenth century.

In other terms

Films: 1970, directed by Grigori Kozintsev, with Yuri Yarvet as Lear; 1971 (shot in Denmark, 1969–70), directed by Peter Brook, with Paul Scofield as Lear. Play: *Lear* by Edward Bond (Royal Court, 1971).

Chief characters

Lear, King of Britain (752 lines in the full text). A mighty part, though it can often fare better in the imagination than in performance. William Charles Macready*** (e.g. Covent Garden, 1838), Randle Ayrton*** (Stratford, 1931, 1936), Donald Wolfit*** (notably Scala, 1944), John Gielgud*** (notably Old Vic, 1940), Paul Scofield*** (Stratford/Aldwych, 1962).

King of France Cordelia's romantic rescuer in the first act does not reappear. In IV.3 the French army has arrived, we hear that he has gone back suddenly and left behind him one of Shakespeare's faintest personages, the Marshal of France ("Monsieur La Far") of whom we are told no more.

Duke of Cornwall Regan's abominable husband, who blinds Gloucester ("Turn out that eyeless villain", III.7) and is, rightly, slain.

Duke of Albany Goneril's gentle husband proves his mettle in the final scenes.

Earl of Kent The most loyal of Lear's followers, who will not long outlive his master: "I have a journey, sir, shortly to go" (V.3). Donald Wolfit*** (Stratford, 1936).

Earl of Gloucester The blinding scene is as intolerable as anything in the Folio: Lilian Baylis, at the Old Vic, would have it played immediately after the interval, so that the more sensitive in the audience could avoid it. One of the themes of the play is sight and blindness.

Edgar The actor needs to give a protean performance ("Poor Tom"; peasant; Edmund's challenger at blazingly theatrical passage, V.3). Speaks the lines (V.2): "Men must endure/Their going hence, even as their coming hither:/Ripeness is all."

Edmund Gloucester's bastard son, the play's Iago. "A most toad-spotted traitor" (V.3). "Yet Edmund was belov'd," he says with almost his last breath.

Fool Lost to the theatre for a century and a half. Then restored, in Macready's 1838 revival, by an actress. Lear's personified conscience. Alec Guinness*** (Old Vic at New, 1946).

Oswald Goneril's steward, whose death (IV.6) is fitting. The young Gordon Craig acted the part with Irving.

Goneril Possibly, though it is a hard choice, marginally the less repellent of the elder daughters; the subject of Lear's curse (I.4).

Regan "Go thrust him out at gates," she says of blinded Gloucester (III.7), "and let him smell his way to Dover." Her body and that of Goneril should be on the stage at the last. It is a piece of tragic symmetry, sometimes forgotten, that the play begins with an old man and his three daughters, and ends with them, now all dead.

Cordelia "Her voice was ever soft, gentle and low – an excellent thing in woman" (V.3). Ellen Terry*** (Lyceum, 1892), Peggy Ashcroft*** (Stratford, 1950).

MACBETH

1606

Duncan, King of Scotland	*A Sergeant*
Malcolm and *Donalbain*, his sons	*A Porter*
	An Old Man
Macbeth and *Banquo*, Generals of the King's army	*An English Doctor*
	A Scots Doctor
Macduff, Lennox, Ross, Menteith, Angus, Caithness, Noblemen of Scotland	*Lady Macbeth*
	Lady Macduff
	Gentlewoman attending on Lady Macbeth
Fleance, son to Banquo	*The Weird Sisters*
Siward, Earl of Northumberland, General of the English forces	*Hecate*
	Ghost of Banquo, Apparitions,
Young Siward, his son	Lords, Gentlemen, Officers,
Seyton, an officer attending on Macbeth	Soldiers, Murderers, Attendants,
	Messengers
Boy, son to Macduff	

Scene: Scotland and England

Synopsis

Upon a "blasted heath" near Forres, three Witches, Weird Sisters, meeting the King of Scotland's generals, Macbeth and Banquo, hail Macbeth in a triple prophecy, ending with the promise of kingship. Banquo is told that he "shall get kings, though thou be none". After King Duncan has made him Thane of Cawdor (as the Witches promised), Macbeth knows that he and his unflinching wife are ambitious for the greater honour. She drives him forward; and that night he murders the sleeping King, their guest at the castle of Inverness. In the daybreak (Act II) Macduff and Lennox discover the murder, assumed to be by the King's sons, Malcom and Donalbain, who fly for safety. Macbeth goes to Forres to be crowned. Remembering the Witches' prophecies, he has Banquo killed (Act III), though the boy

Fleance escapes; that night Banquo's ghost appears to Macbeth at a state banquet.

Macbeth goes (Act IV) to the Witches' "pit of Acheron". There he is told that he must beware of Macduff, that he is to fear no man born of woman, and that he will remain unvanquished until Birnam Wood has come to Dunsinane. Macduff, meanwhile, has joined Malcolm in England, where he hears that in Fife the tyrant has had his family murdered. Revenge will follow. In the castle of Dunsinane (Act V) Lady Macbeth, burdened by guilt, reveals much during her sleepwalking ("Infected minds," says the doctor, "to their deep pillows will discharge their secrets"). Malcolm's invading army advances under the shelter of branches from Birnam Wood; Macbeth, who has just learned of his wife's suicide ("She should have died hereafter"), hears that Birnam Wood is indeed coming towards Dunsinane. Trusting desperately to a charmed life that "must not yield to one of woman born", he faces in battle Macduff, who cries to him: "Let the angel whom thou still hast serv'd/Tell thee Macduff was from his mother's womb/Untimely ripp'd." In combat Macbeth is slain; and Malcolm is hailed as King of Scotland.

In performance

This is one of the shortest and certainly the most concentrated of the plays – Macbeth himself speaks nearly one-third of the lines – and it should be acted, if possible, without an interval: a plan more frequent now, though only half a century ago there might be more than twenty scene breaks, as well as three long intervals, during a single evening. That is fatal, for the tragedy of vaulting ambition and overpowering conscience needs to move inexorably and swiftly from the salute on the heath to the last desperate defiance: "Lay on, Macduff;/And damn'd be he that first cries 'Hold enough!'"

It is probable that the surviving play is an abridged text for a Court performance in the summer of 1606 before James I (who is neatly flattered by the "King's Evil" speech in IV.3), but in the excitement of the theatre any oddities and ambiguities during the first part of the received text can slip by without comment.

The tragedy is an astonishing portrait of two creatures, one beset by imagination, the other not, but both possessed by the powers of evil. Macbeth at first is urged forward by his determined wife; then, on the throne, their deed behind them and conscience environing them, he becomes the stronger of the two: "I am in blood/Stepp'd in so far that, should I wade no more,/Returning were as tedious as go o'er." It is there, in mid-tragedy, that Lady Macbeth says – with what longing we realize – "You lack the season of all natures, sleep." We do not meet her again until in the distress of her sleepwalking (V.1), she speaks what she should not: "Heaven knows what she has known."

This is a play of the darkness that goes with "the instruments of darkness": we think of it in "thick night". "Stars, hide your fires;/Let not light see my black and deep desires." Here is the world Shakespeare had written of in a passage from The Rape of Lucrece: "O comfort-killing night, image of hell!/Dim register and notary of shame!" The verse of Macbeth can hang like sable banners on the outward walls.

Based freely on Holinshed's Chronicles, the play has grown to a legend in the theatre, where disasters are said to attend it. Undeniably its record is strange; Sybil Thorndike and Lewis Casson (at the Princes revival of 1926, when she was Lady Macbeth and he was Banquo) sought to exorcize the spirits of evil by reading together the 90th Psalm, "Thou shalt not be afraid for any terror by night".

This aside, it is curious that so few of the many performances in stage history are laurelled: *Macbeth* has been a challenge seldom taken to the full. During the Restoration Sir William Davenant's weird "improvement", with its *divertissements* of dancing and singing Witches, kept the stage, and indeed did so until 1744. David Garrick (though he retained the musical Witches) got back more of the play and appeared himself in the red coat of a British officer, with powdered wig. He, and later John Philip Kemble, were particulary redoubtable Macbeths, Kemble the slower (he could be said to have usurped the time of night). But history is just as much concerned with Hannah Pritchard's Lady Macbeth (1748–68) and above all with Sarah Siddons, whose performances (between 1785 and 1817) of a woman intensely resolved ("Give *me* the daggers"), dignified, and at length infinitely piteous in remorse, established the part on a height that hardly any later actress would reach. Edmund Kean appeared as a chieftain turned moral coward and crumbling ruin.

Still, Macready (from 1820; especially in later years, to his retirement in 1851) was the Macbeth of the nineteenth century, a great general devil-ridden by his imagination. Other actors were Samuel Phelps who at Sadler's Wells cut the remnants of the Davenant text; Henry Irving (notably 1888, 1895), whose Lady Macbeth, Ellen Terry, proved to be more kindling than he was; Beerbohm Tree (1911); the resonant American, James K. Hackett, in blood-red hair and beard (Aldwych, 1920); and Eric Maturin, glumly, in modern dress ("This *blasted* heath!") at the Court, 1928. John Gielgud (Old Vic, 1930) used a voice like the springing into light of a chain of hilltop beacons, fire answering fire; Komisarjevsky's production, with George Hayes (Stratford, 1933) was textually capricious and set in scrolled aluminium screens; Charles Laughton (Sadler's Wells, 1934) saw Macbeth as a pathological subject; and Laurence Olivier (Old Vic, 1937) showed what might come.

Gielgud returned (Piccadilly, 1942) in a grandly spoken performance of a sombre, lonely usurper; but there was no other Macbeth for history (possibly Donald Wolfit, though inspiration was intermittent) until Olivier's second study (Stratford, 1955) grew to its ultimate agonizing despair in beleaguered Dunsinane. Among others on various stages were Michael Hordern, Eric Porter, Paul Scofield, Alec Guinness, Nicol Williamson and Albert Finney. The most discussed, and sometimes over-praised, revival of its period, Trevor Nunn's in the sparest of settings (Stratford, 1976; Warehouse, London, 1977–8), rested on one uncanny performance, the Lady Macbeth of Judi Dench, unwavering in purpose and so hypnotic in her opening speech that one Shakespearian scholar claimed to have seen the "spirits that tend on mortal thoughts". Ian McKellen was Macbeth.

In North America (first performances, 1759) some of the most historic players were Edwin Forrest (from 1828), Charlotte Cushman, profoundly expressive (1840s), and Edwin Booth. In the present century, Robert Mantell, E.H. Sothern and Julia Marlowe, James K. Hackett, Maurice Evans and Judith Anderson (long run at the National Theatre, 1941). Orson Welles (1936) staged the tragedy – known as "the Voodoo *Macbeth*" – in Harlem, set atmospherically in nineteenth-century Haiti with a Negro cast. Stratford, Ontario: 1962, 1971.

In other terms

Opera: Verdi's *Macbetto* (1847). Films: *Macbeth* (1948), directed by Orson Welles (with himself as Macbeth); *Kumonosu-Djo: The Castle of the Spider's Web* or, in an English-titled issue, *The Throne of Blood* (1957), Japanese version directed by Akira Kurosawa, set in mediaeval Japan ("hardly any words, and none of them by Shakespeare", said Sir Peter Hall, calling it the most successful Shakespeare film yet made); *Macbeth* (1960), directed by George Schaefer, with Maurice Evans and Judith Anderson; 1971, directed by Roman Polanski, with Jon Finch and Francesca Annis as the Macbeths.

Chief characters

Duncan, King of Scotland His age (he is usually played as an ancient) must be left to actor and director. But in the theatre the *Macbeth* cast is growing younger with the years. Eric Maxon* (Stratford, 1933).

Malcolm Has a long and false self-accusation in the English scene that here clogs the action (IV.3).

Macbeth Haunted and possessed, he dwindles from "Bellona's bridegroom lapp'd in proof" (I.2) to the gaunt, famished wolf of Dunsinane. Early in the play – and one is reminded of Iago's appearance in *Othello* after "Chaos is come again" – Macbeth reaches the palace at Forres (I.4) and hears Duncan's memory of the executed Thane of Cawdor: "He was a gentleman on whom I built/An absolute trust." Surprisingly few actors have been able, memorably, to plot the graph of Macbeth's rise and fall or to sustain the brooding verse (e.g. "Come seeling night", III.2). William Charles Macready*** (between 1820 and 1851), John Gielgud*** (Piccadilly, 1942), Laurence Olivier*** (Stratford, 1955).

Banquo Worthy general and (III.4) menacing ghost.

Macduff The avenger. In IV.3, after the tale of his wife and children's murder, he uses the phrase "one fell swoop", which (though it has waned to a cliché) should not be thrown away.

Ross The bringer of news, good (I.3) and ill (IV.3).

Lennox Enters Inverness with Macduff (II.2) after a night that has been unruly but in which the Macbeths have heard only the owls scream and the crickets cry.

Siward, Earl of Northumberland Lives for the epitaph to his son, "God's soldier be he!" (V.8).

Seyton Loyal to the end, he is to Macbeth as Catesby to Richard III.

A porter (II.3) He admits Macduff and Lennox to Inverness Castle after the "unruly" night. He need not be a figure of low comedy. His references to an "equivocator" may be to the trial of Henry Garnet, the Jesuit hanged for high treason in May 1606.

Lady Macbeth Although the ambition-obsessed wife has two superb key scenes (the "Letter", I.5; the Sleepwalking, V.1), the part is sometimes overestimated. A very few actresses have transformed it: such names as Hannah Pritchard, Helen Faucit, Ellen Terry, Barbara Jefford, besides those we choose now – Sarah Siddons*** (1785–1817), Sybil Thorndike*** (Princes, 1926), Judi Dench*** (Stratford/Warehouse, 1976–8).

Lady Macduff In the scene of her murder (IV.2) she has to have a plausible Young Macduff ("Poor prattler, how thou talk'st!")

The Weird Sisters (or Witches). "You should be women,/And yet your beards forbid me to interpret/That you are so." For a long time played by men. Directors are still seeking to vary them;

above all, they should remember John Masefield's phrase, "Satan's kingdom does not laugh." Elizabeth Spriggs, Rosamund Greenwood, Yvonne Bryceland*** (National, 1978).

Hecate The Witches' "mistress of your charms,/The close contriver of all harms" is generally regarded as an un-Shakespearian interpolation. Once familiar, and then for a long time ignored, these couplets have been returning (III.5, IV.1).

ANTONY AND CLEOPATRA

1606–7

Mark Antony, Octavius Caesar and *M. Aemilius Lepidus*, triumvirs	*Silius*, an officer in the army of Ventidius
Sextus Pompeius	*Euphronius*, an ambassador from Antony to Caesar
Domitius Enobarbus, Ventidius, Eros, Scarus, Dercetas, Demetrius, Philo, friends to Antony	*Alexas, Mardian, Seleucus, Diomedes*, attendants on Cleopatra
Maecenas, Agrippa, Dolabella, Proculeius, Thyreus, Gallus, friends to Caesar	*A soothsayer*
	A clown
	Cleopatra, Queen of Egypt
Menas, Menecrates, Varrius, friends to Pompey	*Octavia*, Caesar's sister and wife to Antony
Taurus, Lieutenant-General to Caesar	*Charmian, Iras*, ladies attending on Cleopatra
Canidius, Lieutenant-General to Antony	Officers, Soldiers, Messengers and Attendants

Scene: the Roman Empire

Synopsis

Mark Antony is one of the triumvirs, the three joint rulers of the Roman world. Cleopatra, in her Alexandrian palace, is Queen of Egypt. They are infatuated with each other; but Antony leaves Alexandria for Rome when he hears that Fulvia, his wife, has died, and that Sextus Pompeius (Pompey), son of Pompey the Great, has risen against Octavius Caesar.

In Rome (Act II) Antony patches up a quarrel by agreeing to marry Caesar's sister, Octavia; the triumvirs attend a friendly feast in Pompey's galley. Still, Antony will not relinquish Cleopatra; Caesar will not keep the peace with Pompey. Ultimately (Act III), Caesar opposes Antony at Actium, and in the sea-battle Cleopatra's squadron flies. Antony is defeated. He wins a first day of land fighting (Act IV), but on a second day – the enemy's "preparation is by sea" – the Egyptian fleet surrenders.

After hearing a false report of Cleopatra's death, and falling on his sword, Antony is borne, mortally wounded, to Cleopatra in her "monument" (or mausoleum). There he dies. Rather than be taken to Rome as a captive, she has herself arrayed (Act V) in the royal robes and crown of Egypt and dies from the bite of an asp brought to her by a peasant. So she is found with her waiting-women dead beside her; and Caesar orders, "She shall be buried by her Antony;/No grave upon the earth shall clip in it/A pair so famous."

In performance

The scene is described embracingly as "the Roman Empire", and the play is imperial. None has more verbal glory, even though its central narrative can be expressed in a line or two from the opening speech. There the inconsiderable Philo (who fades into the dark) says of Antony: "You shall see in him/The triple pillar of the world transformed/Into a strumpet's fool." True, but the ordering of the tragedy is magnificent, and Antony at the last (IV.15) is mourned as no man has been in the world's drama: "The crown o'th'earth doth melt.../There is nothing left remarkable/Beneath the visiting moon." The speaker is the Egyptian queen of whom Enobarbus had said in the most quoted speech of all (II.2): "Age cannot wither her, nor custom stale/Her infinite variety."

Soon after Antony's death, Cleopatra herself has gone, with Charmian, to speak her epitaph (V.2): "Now boast thee, death, in thy possession lies/A lass unparallel'd." Whatever Antony and Cleopatra were, they are transfigured in a play of forty-two scenes – several very short – that surges across "the wide arch of the rang'd empire". Here is the flexibility of Shakespeare's theatre (the earliest peformances were at the Blackfriars). In a swift progress Ventidius and the Roman forces should be appearing at one side of the stage upon a plain in Syria, while Enobarbus and Menas on the other are moving towards a cabin in Pompey's galley. Today the tragedy has its problems. The lovers are hard to cast. Moreover (though this is no longer the trouble it used to be) a director obsessed by spectacle is doomed. The splendour is in the language and the speed.

Shakespeare's main source was North's text of Plutarch's *Lives*. For two hundred years little happened to *Antony and Cleopatra* in London; Dryden's adaptation, *All For Love* (Drury Lane, 1678), held the stage for a century. Garrick used a much altered version of Shakespeare (himself as Antony, Mrs Yates as Cleopatra) that ran for only six nights in 1759. John Philip Kemble (1813) mingled Dryden and Shakespeare in transient chaos; and no one else during the century was helpful. When Tree, changing the order of the early scenes, revived the play at His Majesty's (1906), it appeared almost furtively – in spite of Constance Collier's imperious Cleopatra – among a mass of scenic effects including a procession through the streets of Alexandria with Cleopatra as the goddess Isis.

Robert Atkins (Old Vic, 1922) typically let the play speak for itself on a bare stage, as judicious directors have done since. Dorothy Green, who acted often with Benson, as well as with Bridges-Adams at Stratford (1927), and with Gielgud (Old Vic, 1930), was the Cleopatra of her time – "Royal Egypt", and not an operatic contralto. The worst production between the wars was Komisarjevsky's (New, 1936), in retrospect a catalogue of disaster, with a charming but unintelligible Russian comedienne as Cleopatra and a variety of insensitive changes. (Even so, the small-part performances of Margaret Rawlings as Charmian and George Hayes as Soothsayer and Clown were gratefully acknowledged.)

Edith Evans twice played Cleopatra with only mild success (1925, Old Vic, to Baliol Holloway; 1946, Piccadilly, to Godfrey Tearle). Vivien Leigh (St James's, 1951, with Laurence Olivier) was intelligent, low-keyed and small in scale. On the whole, the most realistic postwar performances were those of Michael Redgrave and the beautifully sensitive Peggy Ashcroft (Stratford and Princes', 1953), Barbara Jefford (Old Vic, 1978), and Glenda

Jackson and Alan Howard (Stratford/Aldwych, 1978–9). Peter Brook, with extreme clarity, directed the last of these with an uncut text and set it austerely in a glazed pavilion.

Rose Eytinge's revival (Broadway Theatre, 1877) was the richest of the nineteenth century in New York. Later, there were performances as misguided as Tallulah Bankhead's (1937) – "She barged down the Nile and sank," said John Mason Brown – and as properly balanced as Katharine Cornell's (1947), with the experienced Antony of Godfrey Tearle. Maggie Smith and Keith Baxter led the Stratford, Ontario, cast in 1976.

Chief characters

Mark Antony Though his vigour remains, he is a great soldier in his autumn; "Beguil'd ... to the very heart of loss" (IV.12). Michael Redgrave*** (Stratford and Princes', 1953).

Octavius Caesar Standing marmoreally for Rome, he is usually played ice-cold; he had unexpected warmth in Peter Brook's Stratford/Aldwych productions (1978–9). Maurice Evans** (Old Vic, 1934).

Lepidus As we see in *Julius Caesar*, the weakest of the triumvirate, or "three world-sharers". He gets rapidly drunk in Pompey's galley (II.7). Soon Caesar deposes and imprisons him (III.5, 6).

Pompey (Sextus Pompeius) "Rich in his father's honour, creeps apace/Into the hearts of such as have not thrived/Upon the present state" (I.3). Pompey the Great's younger son, he concludes a treaty with the triumvirs at Misenum, but in III.4 and 5 we hear of Caesar's resumed war against him and of his death.

Enobarbus The blunt soldier who from being Antony's dearest friend, deserts his cause and dies of a broken heart. He speaks the renowned description (transmuted from the prose of North's *Plutarch*) of Cleopatra upon the river Cydnus: "The barge she sat in, like a burnish'd throne,/Burned on the water" (II.2). Randle Ayrton*** (Stratford, 1931 and 1935).

Eros Antony's attendant who commits suicide rather than obey Antony's command to kill him. "Thus do I escape the sorrow/Of Antony's death" (IV.14).

Thyreus Caesar's messenger to Cleopatra is whipped at the order of Antony, who has seen him kissing the Queen's hand (III.13).

Euphronius Antony's schoolmaster, sent as ambassador to Caesar (III.12). A passing figure, he dwells for ever in the four lines beginning "Such as I am, I come from Antony." Robert Eddison* (Old Vic, 1977).

A Soothsayer In a few revivals there has been an unwisely economical habit of coupling him with Euphronius. They could hardly be less alike.

A Clown If the country fellow who brings the asps to Cleopatra (V.2) is played too broadly, he will endanger the transcendent scene that follows. The repetition of "worm" is perilous, even though Cleopatra herself does give the cue, "Hast thou the pretty worm of Nilus there?" The man should be quiet and strange; one of the few actors to deal with him was George Hayes** (New, 1936).

Cleopatra, Queen of Egypt, "whose every passion fully strives/To make itself ... fair and admir'd" (I.1). Few actresses have fully realized the long adagio of her end ("My desolation does begin to make/A better life"). Dorothy Green*** (particularly Old Vic, 1930), Peggy Ashcroft*** (Stratford and Princes', 1953), Barbara Jefford*** (Old Vic, 1978).

Octavia Caesar's sister, Antony's wife: "the piece of virtue,

which is set/Between us as the cement of our love" (III.2).
Charmian Waiting-woman to Cleopatra, she has the great farewell, "Now boast thee, death" (V.2). Margaret Rawlings** (New, 1936).
Iras Cleopatra's second waiting-woman, she hardly speaks (nineteen lines to Charmian's eighty-four), but when she does it can be memorable: "Finish, good lady; the bright day is done,/And we are for the dark" (V.2). She dies, as Enobarbus does in an earlier scene, of a broken heart.

TIMON OF ATHENS

1607–8

Timon, an Athenian nobleman	*Poet, Painter, Jeweller, Merchant,*
Lucius, Lucullus and *Sempronius*,	*Mercer*
flattering lords	*An old Athenian*
Ventidius, one of Timon's false	*Three strangers*
friends	*A page*
Alcibiades, an Athenian	*A fool*
commander	*Phrynia, Timandra*, mistresses to
Apemantus, a churlish philosopher	Alcibiades
Flavius, Timon's steward	*Cupid, Amazons*, in the Masque
Flaminius, Lucilius, Servilius,	Lords, Senators, Officers,
Timon's servants	Soldiers, Servants, Thieves and
Caphis, Philotus, Titus, Hortensius,	Attendants
servants to Timon's creditors	

Scene: Athens and the neighbouring woods

Synopsis

Timon, a noble Athenian and the most bountiful of men, is the prey of parasites, false friends, whom the professional misanthrope Apemantus despises. Only Flavius, his steward, realizes that – though "to Lacedaemon did [his] land extend" – Timon's money has almost gone.

When (Act II) his creditors ask for payment, he gets nothing but excuses from those he has helped so generously. Belatedly embittered (Act III) he invites all his "friends" to a mock banquet at which he spurns them by throwing lukewarm water in their faces. Cursing Athens (Act IV), he leaves the city for a cave in the woods by the seashore where he dwells as a misanthrope. While digging for roots he discovers gold; some of it he gives to an Athenian commander, Alcibiades, who having been unjustly banished, is now returning to avenge himself on the city. Much of the treasure goes to Flavius who has loyally sought out his master. ("Hate all," says Timon to him, "curse all; show charity to none", IV.3).

Finally (Act V) Timon drives off other former parasites, as well as the Athenian senators. Later, one of the soldiers of Alcibiades finds a tomb by the shore, "upon the very hem o'the'sea", and brings Timon's epitaph ("Here lie I, Timon; who, alive, all living men did hate") to the conquering general. Alcibiades prepares to enter Athens, promising to "use the olive with my sword".

In performance

Shakespeare detested, and must have suffered from, ingratitude; and *Timon of Athens* is his single-minded cry against it. In his apparently ceaseless magnanimity, Timon is at first the victim of every sycophant. "I am wealthy to my friends," he says, but when he is brought too late to realize that his money has gone ("'Tis deepest winter in Lord Timon's purse"), he turns a scorching hatred upon the world that deceived him. Though the play has a strangely unfinished, unrevised quality, Timon's language in his later misanthropy is sovereign, music borne to us uncannily through the storm, both on the page and – given an actor to speak it – on the stage. This is rare, for the play, hard to animate theatrically, has never been a favourite and its record is uneventful.

The sources were a brief digression in Plutarch, Painter's *The Palace of Pleasure*, and a dialogue by Lucian, *Timon; or, The Misanthrope*. For two centuries adaptors and revisers were at work. Thomas Shadwell, in his long-approved *The History of Timon of Athens, the Man Hater* (1678) added a "love interest" and two women called Evandra and Melissa. Richard Cumberland, in a more ephemeral version (1771), supplied Timon with a daughter, Evanthe, whom just before his death he gives to Alcibiades. Shakespeare's text, with a few of Cumberland's additions but no women at all, came to Drury Lane (1816), fortified by the inspiration of Edmund Kean. Samuel Phelps, acting Timon himself, brought back the full Shakespearian tragedy (1851 and 1856).

Thereafter, minor revivals aside, a gulf opened until Robert Atkins directed (and played) at the Old Vic in 1922. Wilfrid Walter, pictorially and resoundingly, was Timon for Bridges-Adams at Stratford (1928); Nugent Monck (Westminster, 1935) directed a cut version with Ernest Milton at his most mannered, and incidental music by twenty-one-year-old Benjamin Britten. At Birmingham Repertory (1947), Barry Jackson presented his own modern-dress arrangement of a play that, so he said provocatively, "has a good deal in common with contemporary Birmingham". Tyrone Guthrie (André Morell as Timon) added much exaggerated low comedy (Old Vic, 1952); in 1956, also at the Old Vic, Ralph Richardson seemed to be baffled.

There have been two exceptional revivals, one in Stratford, one in France. In the first (1965) Paul Scofield acted and spoke superbly, especially during the curse (IV.1) – thunder buffeting from crag to crag and ending in the full diapason. Peter Brook (1974) urged the play forward with a tingling impulse in the battered majesty of his Théâtre des Bouffes-du-Nord. The banquet for the sycophants that in other productions had often dwindled to unworthy farce here seemed to rise in a cloud of fury from a circle of cushions.

Michael Langham directed the tragedy in modern dress at Stratford, Ontario (1963) and brought it over to the Chichester Festival Theatre in the following year.

Chief characters

Timon The betrayed patron turned misanthrope; victim of his own indiscriminate generosity ("Methinks I could deal kingdoms to my friends/And ne'er be weary", I.2). The only fully realized character, he commands the play until he makes "his everlasting mansion/Upon the beachèd verge of the salt flood" (V.1). Paul Scofield*** (Stratford, 1965).

Apemantus A professional cynic who, in the woods (IV.3), is out-cursed by Timon.

Lucius One of the false friends. In Michael Langham's production (Stratford, Ontario, 1963) he denied the request of Timon's messenger for a loan (III.2) while he was receiving a massage and pedicure in a steam-bath. Probably the director was inspired by the messenger's early phrase, "I have sweat to see his honour."

Alcibiades The general, outlawed by Athens, who returns to take the city. A part curiously undeveloped.

Flavius The honest, loyally undemanding steward. "All save thee", says Timon (IV.3), "I fell with curses."

Poet In "a thing slipp'd idly from me" (I.1) he offers an allegory of the play to come.

Phrynia and **Timandra** The only women, mistresses of Alcibiades. The note of their single scene (IV.3) is: "Give us some gold, good Timon. Hast thou more?"

CORIOLANUS

1607–8

Caius Marcius, afterwards Caius Marcius Coriolanus	*Conspirators* with Aufidius
	Adrian, a Volscian
Titus Lartius and *Cominius*, Generals against the Volscians	*A citizen of Antium*
	Two Volscian guards
Menenius Agrippa, friend to Coriolanus	*Volumnia*, mother to Coriolanus
	Virgilia, wife to Coriolanus
Sicinius Velutus and *Junius Brutus*, Tribunes of the People	*Valeria*, friend to Virgilia
	Gentlewoman attending on Virgilia
Young Marcius, son to Coriolanus	Roman and Volscian Senators,
A Roman herald	Patricians, Aediles, Lictors,
Nicanor, a Roman	Soldiers, Citizens, Messengers,
Tullus Aufidius, General of the Volscians	Servants to Aufidius, and other Attendants
Lieutenant to Aufidius	

Scene: Rome and the neighbourhood, Corioli and the neighbourhood, Antium. Period: 490 BC

Synopsis

Caius Marcius, arrogant patrician, loathes the common people, the hungry plebeians of Rome, who return his hate. He shows so much personal bravery in the defeat of the Volscians, led by Tullus Aufidius, that he is given the name of Coriolanus (from the town of Corioli, the Volscian stronghold) and, in Rome, is chosen as candidate for the consulship (Act II). Detesting the obligatory display of humility in public, he carries it out with contempt, though the Tribunes of the People are in venomous opposition.

Accusing him (Act III) of being a traitor to the Roman people, they urge the plebeians to demand his death. At length he goes into exile ("There is a world elsewhere") and seeks his enemy Aufidius who, at Antium (Act IV), is planning a fresh attack. News of this deeply disturbs the Roman citizens; Coriolanus, advancing as a general of the Volscians, remains obdurate until (Act V) he yields to the pleading of his mother, wife and son, and prepares to make a treaty of peace. Aufidius, who has been bitterly jealous, charges him before the Volscian Senate with betraying the cause, and he is stabbed to death. "Struck with sorrow", Aufidius orders the body to be taken up: "He shall have a noble memory."

In performance

The play is about the clash of a proud, obstinate autocrat, his mother's son, with the Roman plebeians ("mutable, rank-scented") led by malevolent tribunes. It is also a narrative of destructive envy. The play does not grow with ease, but once its complex battle scenes outside Corioli are over, it does roll forward in a slow, cold and splendid tide.

Coriolanus is founded on North's *Plutarch*. Though there were two early variations (1681 and 1719), its eighteenth-century record was overshadowed by a mosaic-play formed from Shakespeare and (a new work) Thomson's *Coriolanus*, first with alterations by the actor, Thomas Sheridan (1754), and later by John Philip Kemble (Drury Lane, 1789). Kemble and Sarah Siddons, then at their meridian, appeared very often as Coriolanus and Volumnia. Julian Charles Young, writing of a later performance, described Mrs Siddons at the entry of Coriolanus in triumph: "She towered above all around, and rolled, almost reeled across the stage; her very soul, as it were, dilating and rioting in its exultation." Edmund Kean was a disappointment; Macready (notably Covent Garden, 1838) had the mind and the manner; Phelps (from 1848) established the play in the Sadler's Wells repertory; and Frank Benson and Genevieve Ward appeared together many times (from Comedy Theatre, 1901) as Coriolanus (acted by Benson previously) and Volumnia. Henry Irving and Ellen Terry (Lyceum, 1901) were thoroughly miscast; Coriolanus, Irving said, was "not worth a damn."

Among many later actors were Ion Swinley (Old Vic, 1924); the flamboyant Irishman, Anew McMaster, in gale force (Stratford, 1933); and Laurence Olivier (Old Vic, 1938), with his ominous growl on the word *'mildly'* (III.2), when entreated to "answer mildly" on going to the Forum to face the tribunes. Sybil Thorndike played Volumnia. Elsewhere were Alec Clunes (Stratford, 1939), John Clements (Old Vic at New, 1948), Ian Richardson (Stratford, 1967), Ian Hogg (Stratford, 1972), and Nicol Williamson (Aldwych, 1973). Strongest were Olivier's second Coriolanus (Stratford, 1959, devastating in arrogance and irony); and Alan Howard's first (Stratford/Aldwych, 1977–8). The National Theatre (Old Vic, 1971) presented a not particularly stimulating production by Manfred Wekwerth and Joachim Tenschert, described glumly as "a reassessment" of the tragedy "viewed through Brechtian glasses, re-ground by experience."

In 1767 the play arrived in North America (Philadelphia), where the most renowned Coriolanus would be Edwin Forrest (New York, from 1831), a largely external performance; John Edward McCullough (New York, 1878) used a sustained attack. A few actors this century included Erford Gage (1938), Robert Ryan (1954) and Robert Burr (1965).

In the spring of 1934, when various French anti-republican groups were seeking a revolution, the Comédie Française was persuaded to stage a version freely translated and adapted to the politics of the hour. It led to fierce demonstrations, in the theatre and out, but no revolution.

110

In other terms

Günter Grass's sardonic *The Plebeians Rehearse the Uprising* (1966), about Berthold Brecht rehearsing his adaptation, *Coriolan*, was done at the Aldwych (1970). John Osborne "reworked" Shakespeare in *A Place Called Rome* (published 1973). Beethoven's well-known overture *Coriolan* was written for *Coriolanus*, a play (1802) by the Austrian playwright, von Collin (1771–1811).

Chief characters

Caius Marcius Coriolanus Here, an exacting part, is the disdainful egoist who speaks for what John Masefield described as "the clash of the aristocratic temper with the world"; who is driven from his city by mob law; who later "does sit in gold, his eye/Red as 'twould burn Rome" (V.1); and who yields in the end, as he has always done, to his mother's plea. Laurence Olivier*** (Old Vic, 1938; Stratford, 1959); Alan Howard*** (Stratford/Aldwych, 1977–8).

Cominius Roman general against the Volscians, who after the attack on Corioli bestows on Marcius the name of Coriolanus. Speaking before the Senate (II.2), he narrates the life of Coriolanus and how at sixteen, after the fight against Tarquin, he was "brow-bound with the oak". John Wyse* (Stratford, 1933).

Menenius Agrippa The old patrician, brave and garrulous, the devoted friend of Coriolanus, who tells the story of the Belly and its Members – a parable of Senate and People – to the mutinous crowd in I.1, and whom Coriolanus ("This man was my beloved in Rome") refuses to hear as the Volscian army advances. Michael Hordern*** (Stratford, 1952).

Sicinius Velutus and **Junius Brutus** Tribunes of the People. "The tongues o'th' common mouth," exclaims Coriolanus (III.1); "I do despise them,/For they do prank them in authority,/Against all noble sufferance." The tribunes, usually acted as lamentable demagogues, return his bitterness.

Tullus Aufidius The Volscian leader who after swearing revenge on Coriolanus (I.10), welcomes him as an exile to Antium (IV.5), is possessed with envy, and calls at last for his death (V.6). Albert Finney* (Birmingham Repertory, 1956).

Volumnia The archetypal Roman matriarch (Swinburne named her "Volumnia Victrix") who sways her son from his purpose when Rome seems lost. The First Citizen says of Coriolanus in the play's opening scene that his exploits had been to please his mother. Sarah Siddons*** (1789 and later); Genevieve Ward*** (particularly Comedy Theatre, 1901); Sybil Thorndike*** (Old Vic, 1938).

Virgilia Wife to Coriolanus. "My gracious silence" (II.1).

Valeria The Roman lady who flashes into an early domestic interlude (I.3). In the Supplication scene with Volumnia and Virgilia (V.3) she receives from Coriolanus a salute that often, and wrongly, has been cut: "The moon of Rome, chaste as the icicle/That's curdied by the frost from purest snow,/And hangs on Dian's temple." Yvonne Coulette** (Stratford/Aldwych, 1977–8).

PERICLES,
PRINCE OF TYRE

1607–8

Gower, as Chorus	*Boult*, his servant
Antiochus, King of Antioch	*The daughter of Antiochus*
Pericles, Prince of Tyre	*Dionyza*, wife to Cleon
Helicanus, Escanes, Lords of Tyre	*Thaisa*, daughter to Simonides
Simonides, King of Pentapolis	*Marina*, daughter to Pericles and
Cleon, Governor of Tarsus	Thaisa
Lysimachus, Governor of Mytilene	*Lychorida*, Marina's nurse
Cerimon, a lord of Ephesus	*A bawd*
Thaliard, a lord of Antioch	*Diana*, the goddess of chastity
Philemon, servant to Cerimon	Marshal, Lords, Ladies, Knights,
Leonine, servant to Dionyza	Gentlemen, Sailors, Pirates,
A pander	Fishermen and Messengers

Scene: Dispersedly, in various Mediterranean countries

Synopsis

Throughout, John Gower, the mediaeval poet, acts as Chorus. His *Confessio Amantis* (1385–93), in which he retells the story of Apollonius of Tyre, was one of Shakespeare's main sources.

Pericles solves the riddle propounded by Antiochus, King of Antioch, to all his daughter's suitors. The answer, which no one has found (death is the penalty of failure), is that father and daughter have had an incestuous relationship. When Pericles shows that he knows the meaning, and Antiochus is suspiciously hospitable, the young Prince realizes that he must escape; back in Tyre he leaves Helicanus to govern in his absence and sets off for Tarsus (or Tharsus) where he relieves the famine-stricken city.

Still pursued by a minion of Antiochus, he puts again to sea (Act II), only to be wrecked on the shores of Pentapolis; there the King is celebrating with a tournament the birthday of his daughter Thaisa. Pericles wins, and he and Thaisa are betrothed. They expect ultimately to go to Tyre (where Pericles will now be safe), but in a great sea-storm (Act III) Thaisa, after giving birth to a daughter, Marina, is thought to be dead and is thrown overboard in a waterproof chest, with a letter. When it comes to land in Ephesus the noble Cerimon ("'Tis known I ever have studied physic") revives Thaisa who, believing herself to be the only survivor, becomes a priestess of Diana's temple. Pericles, meantime, returns to Tyre, entrusting the infant Marina to the care of Cleon, Governor of Tarsus, and his wife Dionyza.

Some fourteen years pass. Pericles is in Tyre; Marina has grown up in Tarsus. Dionyza, jealous of a girl who overshadows her own daughter, is about to have her murdered; then pirates kidnap Marina (Act IV) and take her to a brothel in Mytilene. When Dionyza and Cleon tell Pericles his daughter is dead, he vows (says Gower) "Never to wash his face or cut his hairs." In Mytilene Marina, whose purity bewilders her employers and startles the Governor, Lysimachus, manages to leave the brothel and work in an "honest house." Pericles, in utter dejection, chances to visit the city; Lysimachus (Act V) sends for Marina to comfort the stranger, and there, in his anchored ship, Pericles realizes that this is his daughter. In a dream Diana urges him to go to her temple at Ephesus, where presently he relates his tale to the priestess. She is Thaisa; and all griefs are over. Marina and Lysimachus (to whom she is now betrothed) will rule in Tyre, and Pericles and Thaisa spend the rest of their lives in Pentapolis.

In performance

"From ashes ancient Gower is come" – a phoenix-figure on whose version of an old plot Shakespeare – and possibly that shadowy figure, George Wilkins – based a picaresque romance. It delighted Jacobeans with its wandering narrative, its music and its masquing, and was the envy of other dramatists, soured as Ben Jonson was (he called *Pericles* "some mouldy tale") by another man's success. Gower, courier in his rough couplets, leads us on the oldest of pleasures, the telling of a story. *Pericles* is little more than a fantastic and beguiling stage exploit, beginning with a blunt record of events and then, as Shakespeare takes over, adding the bounty of sometimes major verse to "glad" the ear. Directors have talked about neo-Platonic allegories; *Pericles* is not material for such an exercise as that.

In his share Shakespeare is both remembering some of his old ideas and looking forward to later work. His rambling narrative, from which the sound of the sea is never far distant, can hold us from the riddle, and the appearance of the unnamed daughter of Antiochus, through shipwreck and wooing, storm and loss, to the final reunion of Pericles and Thaisa in Diana's temple. The Levantine tour drifts us from Antioch to Tyre, to Tarsus, to Pentapolis, to the gale-swept Mediterranean, to Mytilene and to Ephesus. The prince gains a king's daughter. He calls, in grand Shakespearian phrase, upon "the god of this great vast" to "rebuke these surges/Which wash both heaven and hell" (III.1). A princess rises, alive, from a wave-tossed chest. Her daughter's innocence shines through the murk of a brothel. The "goddess argentine" summons Pericles to "do upon mine altar sacrifice", and there before him is a wife miraculously restored.

It is a great moment when Shakespeare's unmistakable voice enters with the third-act storm; but we ought in the theatre to have everything that has happened earlier. The play is a sequence of romantic episodes, a serial always to be continued. So applauded (and mocked) in its own day, *Pericles* did not appear in the First Folio, possibly because the received text was known to be corrupt. (Oddly, it was the first Shakespeare play staged at the Restoration, with Thomas Betterton, then twenty-five, as Pericles.) Though the general opinion is that Shakespeare wrote the last three acts and barely touched the first two by another hand (maybe George Wilkins), there is a second and comparably credible view. This is that of two "pirate" reporters trying to recreate from memory a largely Shakespearian text; the first had only a blurred recollection and the second knew the last three acts well.

In 1738 the play suffered from a feeble adaptation by George Lillo, called *Marina*. Indeed, until a pictorial revival by Samuel Phelps (Sadler's Wells, 1854), it had no real look. Silence after this until old John Coleman's legendary and preposterous adventure (Stratford, 1900), a *Pericles* eccentrically hashed, much of the original (in Coleman's own words) expunged, eradicated, eliminated and omitted, and a good deal of rubbish added. Robert Atkins put back Shakespeare (Old Vic, 1921); and he directed the play again, with loving simplicity, at the Open Air Theatre, Regent's Park (1939); here Robert Eddison's romantic, lyrical

Prince grew as the play did. Nugent Monck disposed of it all in ninety minutes at Stratford (1947), with the first act cut and Paul Scofield as Pericles, a part he acted once more, now in a full production by John Harrison, at the Rudolf Steiner Hall, London (1950). Richard Pasco gave his gentle truth to Pericles at the Birmingham Repertory (1954); a strained Stratford revival (1958) turned Gower to a calypso-singer; and in 1969, also at Stratford, Ian Richardson – who looked at the last as if he had risen from a mosaic in the cathedral of Torcello – played Pericles with a shining imagination. Derek Jacobi (Her Majesty's, 1973) was at the centre of a production planted in the brothel throughout; and a small-scale treatment (Other Place, Stratford, 1979; Warehouse, London, 1980) had Peter McEnery as the Prince. Stratford, Ontario, 1973–4: Nicholas Pennell as Pericles.

In other terms

The Painfull Adventures of Pericles, Prince of Tyre (1608), generally supposed to have been based on the play, with one or two additions from the story in Laurence Twine's *The Patterne of Paynfull Adventures* (1576).

Chief characters

Pericles, Prince of Tyre The wanderer who lives through many hazards, and whose recognition scene with Marina (V.1) is affectingly reminiscent of Lear and Cordelia. Robert Eddison*** (Open Air, 1939). Ian Richardson*** (Stratford, 1969).

Antiochus Evil author of the riddle Pericles solves (I.1).

Simonides Thaisa's benevolently playful father.

Cleon The Governor of Tarsus whose first scene (I.4) is sincerity in distress. Later he is punished for his wife's crime. Gower's last chorus (V.2) explains how the wrathful citizens burn Cleon and Dionyza in their palace.

Lysimachus The Governor of Mytilene rapidly overcome by Marina. But there should be credit to an unnamed lord (V.1) who first suggests that Marina would "win some words" of the silent Pericles.

Cerimon A lord of Ephesus with medical knowledge. It would be agreeable to think that Shakespeare intended Thaisa's restorer to be a compliment to his Stratford son-in-law, Dr John Hall.

A pander, Boult, a bawd The deplorable and baffled staff of the Mytilene brothel in Act IV.

Dionyza Cleon's wife. Though she becomes a paltry villainess, we may think of her as she is seen first, in the "misery of Tarsus" (I.4) that Pericles relieves. Cathleen Nesbitt** (Open Air, 1939).

Thaisa (pronounced Ty-eesa). Daughter of Simonides of Pentapolis. Cast into the sea after childbirth, apparently dead, revived by a noble physician, and later Diana's priestess.

Marina Daughter of Pericles. One of the enchanting lost girls of Shakespeare's final period. (The speed with which she gets from shore to ship at Mytilene, V.1, is reason enough for her to say she has "been gazed on like a comet".) Marina should not be doubled with Thaisa, as some directors attempt, for (so it is with Sebastian and Viola in *Twelfth Night*) we lose the effect of the key moment of reunion: here, certainly, Marina's "My heart leaps to be gone into my mother's bosom." Still, Susan Fleetwood*** managed it at Stratford (1969) with a rare, healing joy.

Gower, the Chorus He has been played in our time by a handsome actress, as an avuncular ancient, as a coloured calypso-singer, and a kind of Welsh bard.

CYMBELINE

1609

Cymbeline, King of Britain	*A Roman captain*
Cloten, son to the Queen by a former husband	*Two British captains*
	Pisanio, servant to Posthumus
Posthumus Leonatus, a gentleman, Imogen's husband	*Cornelius*, a physician
	Two Lords of Cymbeline's court
Belarius, a banished lord, disguised under the name of *Morgan*	*Two gentlemen* of the court
	Two gaolers
Guiderius and *Arviragus*, Cymbeline's sons, disguised under the names of *Polydore* and *Cadwal* and supposed sons to Belarius	*The Queen*, Cymbeline's second wife
	Imogen, Cymbeline's daughter by his former Queen
	Helen, a lady attending on Imogen
Philario, Italian friend to Posthumus	*Apparitions:* Jupiter and the Leonati
Iachimo, friend to Philario	Lords, Ladies, Roman Senators, Tribunes, a Soothsayer, a Dutch Gentleman, a Spanish Gentleman, Musicians, Officers, Captains, Soldiers, Messengers, Attendants
A French gentleman, friend to Philario	
Caius Lucius, General of the Roman forces	

Scene: Britain; Italy

Synopsis

Cymbeline, king of Britain, has an evil second wife who wishes to see her own oafish son, Cloten, wedded to Cymbeline's daughter, Imogen. But Imogen, against her father's will, has married Posthumus Leonatus, who is banished; before parting he gives a bracelet to Imogen. Iachimo, in Rome, boasts to the angry Posthumus that Imogen is corruptible; later, in Britain, he arranges to be secreted in a trunk in her bed-chamber, and when she is asleep (Act II) he emerges and steals her bracelet. Posthumus, persuaded, vows to be revenged on Imogen. Writing to her to meet him at Milford Haven, he orders his servant, Pisanio, to kill her on the journey.

Rome demands from Britain tribute that the King (Act III) refuses. Pisanio, faithful to the bewildered Imogen, tells her to disguise herself as a boy and seek the invading Roman general. Losing herself in Wales, she is sheltered, under the name of Fidele, by a long-banished lord, Belarius, who calls himself Morgan, and two youths who are actually sons of the king (and Imogen's brothers), stolen in infancy and brought up in a mountain cave. In sickness, Imogen/Fidele takes a sleeping drug that gives the appearance of death.

Cloten, in the clothes of Posthumus, has followed her with evil intent, but one of the youths meets and kills him (Act IV). Returning, the brothers and Belarius find "Fidele" apparently dead; when she wakes, alone, she mistake Cloten's headless body for her husband's. Profoundly grieved, she joins the Roman general, whose forces are ready to attack Cymbeline.

The courage of Belarius and the princes win the battle for

Britain ("This was a strange chance/A narrow lane, an old man, and two boys", V.3). All come at length before the king, and swiftly, one revelation growing from another, the plot is resolved: happiness for everyone except the Queen (who has died); Cymbeline's magnanimous submission to Rome; and even pardon for Iachimo, who has fought with the Romans. Imogen and Posthumus are reunited.

In performance

"A father cruel and a step-dame false;/A foolish suitor to a wedded lady/That hath her husband banish'd." That is Imogen speaking in I.6. Already the plot of *Cymbeline* is coiling itself: an intricacy that mingles *The Decameron* with Holinshed and the fairy-tale of Snow White, and Renaissance Italy with the classical Rome of Caesar Augustus – a pattern which the rashly dogmatic critic, Samuel Johnson, described as "unresisting imbecility". The play, flowering again and again into the loveliest of Shakespeare's late verse, has suffered from the convolutions of a narrative that actually, as Sir Arthur Quiller-Couch made clear in a famous essay, is a miracle of technique. Not all of its people rise easily from the text. Neither the much-troubled Cymbeline nor his evil Queen is a personage; Posthumus is usually functional; Cloten is a blown-up Thurio (*Two Gentlemen of Verona*). Still, in the theatre, two parts – Imogen, the princess who is the nonpareil of Shakespeare's women, and (in a much lesser degree) Machiavellian Iachimo, the "slight thing of Italy" – are parts intensely rewarding.

Throughout, the text yields gold: "A mole, cinque-spotted, like the crimson drops/I'th' bottom of a cowslip" (II.2); the aubade ordered improbably by Cloten, "Hark! hark! the lark at heaven's gate sings" (II.3); "Neptune's park, ribb'd and pal'd in/With rocks unscalable and roaring waters" (III.1); "I'th' world's volume/Our Britain seems as of it, but not in't;/In a great pool a swan's nest" (III.4); the dirge, "Fear no more the heat o'th' sun" (IV.2); "As small a drop of pity as a wren's eye" (IV.2); "Hang there like fruit, my soul,/Till the tree die" (V.5); "The benediction of these covering heavens/Fall on their heads like dew, for they are worthy/To inlay heaven with stars" (V.5).

Though set among the tragedies, *Cymbeline* is a romance; it would have suited audiences at the candle-lit Blackfriars Theatre which Shakespeare's company, the King's Men, used from 1608. The inevitable supplanting play during the Restoration was called *The Injured Princess; or, The Fatal Wager*, written by Thomas D'Urfey, and revived as late as 1738. Covent Garden used Shakespeare's text (1746); and David Garrick's acting (from 1761 at Drury Lane, in a version slightly altered) could transform Posthumus. John Philip Kemble also played Posthumus, first in 1785, and then (in 1787) with his elder sister Sarah Siddons as a celebrated Imogen. Helen Faucit, between 1837 and 1865, was the crown of nineteenth-century Imogens until Ellen Terry's creation (Lyceum, 1896), with Irving indifferently as Iachimo, "a statue of romantic melancholy", said Shaw. Sybil Thorndike, who had been an Old Vic Imogen (1918) came back to her at the New in 1923, a year when Barry Jackson, at the Birmingham Repertory, began the fashion for modern-dress Shakespeare. Imogen since then has had four extremely distinguished actresses, all at Stratford: Peggy Ashcroft (1957), Vanessa Redgrave (1962), Susan Fleetwood (1974) and Judi Dench (1979). The best Iachimos have also been at Stratford: Eric Porter (1962) and, supremely, Ian Richardson (1974).

In other terms

Bernard Shaw, who considered the last act to be "a tedious string of unsurprising dénouements sugared with insincere sentimentality after a ludicrous stage battle", rewrote the last act himself (1936) as *Cymbeline Refinished*, a superfluous and flippant exercise that was performed at the Embassy Theatre (1937) at the end of an otherwise Shakespearian text.

Chief characters

Cymbeline, vacillating King of Britain. One of the lesser title roles. No one in the First Folio is more progressively puzzled than he is during Act V.

Cloten The Queen's dire son has one happy moment, his defiance of Caius Lucius (III.1). Otherwise, he is rejected by Imogen (II.3), listens to music that he detests (II.3), and is decapitated in conflict with Guiderius (IV.2). The key to the pronunciation of his name, sometimes botched, is the line in IV.2, "I have sent Cloten's clotpoll down the stream."

Posthumus Imogen's husband has a long part, but it is generally unrewarding.

Belarius (alias Morgan). The grand old man of wild Wales has something of the firm-set oaken quality of Kent (*King Lear*).

Guiderius and **Arviragus** (Polydore and Cadwal). The two "princely boys" who speak the dirge, "Fear no more the heat o'th'sun/Nor the furious winter's rages" (IV.2). They speak it because Guiderius (Polydore) cannot sing ("I'll weep, and word it with thee") – a line that brings us close to one of Shakespeare's boy players.

Iachimo "Slight thing of Italy" (also "bold Iachimo, Sienna's brother"), a natural conspirer who needs a hypnotic utterance to express such language as "the crickets sing" (II.2). Ian Richardson*** (Stratford/Aldwych, 1974).

Pisanio Another example of personified loyalty.

Soothsayer His name is Philarmonus; and he has his moment (V.5) when he interprets the "tablet" left on the breast of Posthumus after the vision of Jupiter.

A Gaoler A few minutes of determined black comedy; but with the celebrated phrase, "O, the charity of a penny cord! It sums up thousands in a trice" (V.4).

Queen Cymbeline's wife. The nameless Queen has one speech out of character when she defies Rome (III.1). Elsewhere she is an evil stepmother of fairy-tale. Her end, "with horror, madly dying, like her life", is reported in V.5.

Imogen Cymbeline's daughter. The soul of beauty, honour and faith. Probably her name, before a compositor got it wrong, was Innogen (signifying innocence). Four variously remarkable performances at Stratford within little more than twenty years: Peggy Ashcroft*** (1957), Vanessa Redgrave*** (1962), Susan Fleetwood*** (1974) and Judi Dench*** (1979).

Apparitions There has been much debate about the scene in V.4: first, the entrance of the Leonati, ghosts of the father, mother and brothers of Posthumus, then the descent of Jupiter, "in thunder and lightning, sitting upon an eagle and hurling a thunderbolt". Granville-Barker was contemptuous of the rhyming; other critics have called it an important theophany. Written as the kind of masque expected at the Blackfriars Theatre, it serves its purpose impressively enough on today's stage.

THE WINTER'S TALE

1611

Leontes, King of Sicilia	*A mariner*
Mamillius, his son, the young Prince of Sicilia	*A gaoler*
Camillo, Antigonus, Cleomenes, Dion, lords of Sicilia	*Hermione*, Queen to Leontes
	Perdita, daughter of Leontes and Hermione
Polixenes, King of Bohemia	*Paulina*, wife to Antigonus
Florizel, his son, Prince of Bohemia	*Emilia*, a lady attending on the Queen
Archidamus, a lord of Bohemia	*Mopsa* and *Dorcas*, shepherdesses
Old shepherd, reputed father of Perdita	*Time*, as Chorus
Clown, his son	Other Lords, Gentlemen, Ladies, Officers, Servants, Shepherds, Shepherdesses
Autolycus, a rogue	

Scene: Sicilia and Bohemia

Synopsis

Leontes, King of Sicilia, grows so wildly and unreasonably jealous of Polixenes, King of Bohemia, for nine months a visitor at his court, that he believes his wife Hermione has been unfaithful and that her unborn child is not his own. Through Camillo, a Sicilian lord, he seeks to poison his guest, but Camillo warns Polixenes and they depart at once for Bohemia.

Leontes (Act II) orders his wife to be imprisoned and their elder child Mamillius removed from her. In prison she gives birth to a daughter; when Paulina brings the babe to Leontes, hoping to soothe him, he commands her husband Antigonus to abandon the "bastard by Polixenes" in some desert place.

At the trial of Hermione (Act III) a message from the Delphic oracle declares the Queen's innocence; Leontes, refusing to credit it, hears immediately of the death of young Mamillius. Hermione faints and is carried out; presently Paulina tells Leontes that his Queen is dead and he vows life-long mourning. Antigonus, meantime, has left the babe on the Bohemian shore, with the name he gives her (Perdita) and gold in a bundle. Then he vanishes for ever ("Exit, pursued by a bear"). A shepherd and his son find the child.

Sixteen years pass. In Bohemia (Act IV) Florizel, the King's son, is in love with Perdita, brought up as a shepherdess. At the sheep-shearing feast a disguised Polixenes (who is with Camillo) reveals himself, threatening to disinherit his son and to put Perdita to death if they do not leave each other. Camillo tells them to go to Leontes in Sicilia, but he also tells Polixenes, hoping there may be a reconciliation.

All (including Shepherd and Clown, with their proofs of Perdita's discovery long ago) leave, variously, for Sicilia, and there (Act V) Leontes and Polixenes are reconciled; so is Polixenes to Florizel and Perdita. They go to Paulina's chapel to see a remarkable "statue" of Hermione; kissing it, Leontes finds that, after the gulf of years, his wife – long cared for by Paulina – is still alive.

In performance

Some titles and names are fated in print (e.g. "Thorndyke" for Thorndike, "Schofield" for Scofield), but possibly none more than *The Winter's Tale* which again and again is given the indefinite article – no doubt a recollection of Mamillius when he says "a sad tale's best for winter". The play, which has been called a cycle of life, death and resurrection, is among the later romances of Shakespeare's autumn, and it has to be treated as *Cymbeline* is, with no grumbling about the unlikelihood of the narrative. Largely, Shakespeare based it, with his own enrichment, upon Robert Greene's romance of *Pandosto* (1588), which in 1607 had been reprinted as *Dorastus and Fawnia*. (Yet the changes are radical, and Paulina, Antigonus and Autolycus are Shakespeare's own: so, too, is the bear.)

Briefly, it is a Janus-play of winter and spring, a Sicilia of the passions contrasted with those scenes from a Bohemian world that are direct from rural Warwickshire.

The early verse dialogue can be abnormally packed and knotted; still, what is difficult in the text can come over in the theatre if it is swiftly spoken: the play must never be allowed to drag its feet. It is the third of Shakespeare's main treatments of jealousy, a sin that could obsess him. In *The Merry Wives of Windsor* Ford is farcical; in *Othello* jealousy is the cause of high tragedy; Leontes, in *The Winter's Tale*, seized by a destroying yellow fever, is spared after a passage of sixteen years from the first terrifying attack that takes him to the rim of madness, perhaps over it. The plot is in three movements: the King's fury; the flowered idyll of the Bohemian pastoral, lit by the speeches of Perdita and the songs of Autolycus; and finally the grave beauty of peace and reconciliation.

The Winter's Tale does not appear to have been staged for over a century before 1741, when there were productions at Goodman's Fields and (with Hannah Pritchard as Paulina) at Covent Garden. Garrick's abridgment, *Florizel and Perdita* (Drury Lane, 1756), was founded on the fourth and fifth acts, all else condensed into a 150-line prologue by Garrick, himself as Leontes: this served until the beginning of the nineteenth century, when Kemble (Leontes) brought back most of the original to Drury Lane (1802) and Sarah Siddons was Hermione. The century's truest Leontes was Macready, who from 1823 often played a part temperamentally suited to him. Charles Kean's accustomed archaeological pageantry (Princess's, 1856; Bohemia changed to Bithynia) is recalled because Ellen Terry, at nine years old, had her first speaking part, Mamillius.

Mary Anderson captivatingly doubled Hermione and, especially, Perdita (Lyceum, 1887); Ellen Terry, at her professional jubilee, was Hermione for Tree (His Majesty's, 1906); and in 1912 (Savoy) Granville Barker, cutting only six lines, directed his apron-stage revival, with Henry Ainley and Lillah McCarthy. Rehearsing his company almost to weariness, he urged them until his sensitive ear was satisfied, to speak rapidly but to remember the musical structure of the verse: all must be quick, continuous, intimate, vital. That would remain the definitive production until (after several other revivals) Peter Brook's at the Phoenix in 1951, uncompromising in its restraint except for the blizzard through which Time emerged as Chorus. John Gielgud's voice in the remorse of "Stars, stars, and all eyes else dead coals!" (V.1) rings from half a century's acted Shakespeare. Judi Dench's doubling of Hermione and Perdita (1969) was the most distinguished personal feat in any Stratford revival of the play since the war.

Henry Daniell (Leontes), Eva Le Gallienne (Hermione) and Florence Reed (Paulina) had a popular triumph in a Theatre Guild revival in New York (1945–6). Christopher Plummer was Leontes at Stratford, Ontario (1958).

In other terms

Film: *The Winter's Tale* (1966), directed by Frank Dunlop. Music: setting for "When daffodils begin to peer" by John Ireland.

Chief characters

Leontes, King of Sicilia Morbidly irrational, he brings disaster upon himself. But it is his memory of Hermione (V.1) and his reunion (V.3) that stay with us when the play is done. William Charles Macready*** (especially Covent Garden, 1837, with Helen Faucit's Hermione), John Gielgud*** (Phoenix, 1951).

Mamillius The young prince who tells his own winter's tale ("There was a man ... dwelt by a churchyard", II.1). Ellen Terry's début (Princess's, 1856) when she tripped over her go-cart.

Camillo Important in the movement of the plot (I.4, IV.4).

Antigonus Paulina's husband, who brings the infant Perdita to the Bohemian coast ("Blossom, speed thee well"), and who is killed by a bear as the Clown describes in III.3.

Polixenes, King of Bohemia Wronged guest and stern parent.

Florizel An impetuous prince for a fairy-tale. "When you do dance," he says to Perdita (IV.4), "I wish you/A wave o'th'sea, that you might ever do/Nothing but that." Gyles Isham* (Stratford, 1931).

Shepherd and **Clown** They are from the inner sheepfolds of Warwickshire Arden and should be so performed. Paul Scofield's Clown** (Stratford, 1948), the subject of a painting by Laura Knight, was vastly and rustically endearing.

Autolycus The "snapper-up of unconsidered trifles" (IV.3) is a vagrant rich in ballads, songs and snatches; a rogue, sharp of mind and eye, who in his time has served the prince. He can affect a patronizing hauteur in the meeting with Shepherd and Clown. Some comedians, given an inch, will turn the part into what has been called "a gallimaufry of gambols". Among the best in remembrance, certainly the most persuasive, was Donald Wolfit*** (Stratford, 1937) with his long peering nose.

Time, as Chorus, carries us forward sixteen years. Now he is usually a person with an hour-glass. Charles Kean (Princess's, 1856) supplied a classical allegory. After the discovery of Selene, or Luna, in her car, accompanied by the stars (personified by living figures), she gradually sank into the ocean. Time appeared as a classical figure surmounting the globe. When he had spoken, Phoebus (according to John William Cole, Kean's recorder) "rose with surpassing brilliancy in the chariot of the Sun, encircled by a blaze of light which filled every portion of the theatre."

Third Gentleman Paulina's steward in an hour of fleeting splendour (V.2); he reports to a pair of other gentlemen events that Shakespeare failed to show in action. Granville Barker (Savoy, 1912) realized the theatrical possibilities of the scene.

Hermione The Emperor of Russia's daughter. A heroine of patient nobility. After her eloquence at the trial and her collapse on hearing of the prince's death, she speaks no word until her "statue" takes life at the end of the play: "You gods, look down." Mary Anderson*** (Lyceum, 1887), Judi Dench*** (Stratford, 1969).

Perdita Shakespeare's Bohemian girl. Princess in a shepherd's cottage, she strews the verse with flowers ("Daffodils that come before the swallow dares", IV.4). Though it is as challenging in V.3 as it is to double the Thaisa and Marina of *Pericles*, Judi Dench*** (Stratford, 1969) managed it with the unforced art Mary Anderson*** had shown over eighty years earlier at the Lyceum.

Paulina Wife of Antigonus. Candid and courageous, the heart of common sense. "I pray you, do not push me. I'll be gone" (II.3). Dorothy Green** (Old Vic, 1936), Flora Robson*** (Phoenix, 1951).

THE TEMPEST

1611

Alonso, King of Naples	*Trinculo*, a jester
Sebastian, his brother	*Stephano*, a drunken butler
Prospero, rightful Duke of Milan	*Master of a ship*
Antonio, his brother, usurping Duke of Milan	*Boatswain*
	Mariners
Ferdinand, son of the King of Naples	*Miranda*, Prospero's daughter
	Ariel, an airy spirit
Gonzalo, an honest old counsellor	*Iris, Ceres, Juno, Nymphs, Reapers,*
Adrian, Francisco, lords	spirits
Caliban, a savage and deformed slave	Other Spirits attending on Prospero

Scene: A ship at sea, afterwards an uninhabited island

Synopsis

Twelve years before the play begins, Antonio, helped by the King of Naples, Alonso, usurped his brother Prospero's dukedom of Milan and put Prospero and his child Miranda to sea in a rotten boat. They reached a far-off island where Prospero resorted to the books on magic that a loyal lord, Gonzalo, had sent with him. He freed Ariel, an "airy spirit" whom the dead witch, Sycorax, had imprisoned in a cloven pine, and he attempted to educate the witch's son, the deformed Caliban. When Caliban sought to rape Miranda, Prospero made him into a slave.

Prospero tells the story to his daughter just after the raising of a magical storm that has cast upon the island Alonso and Antonio with Alonso's son Ferdinand, his brother Sebastian, and attendant lords. Ariel leads Ferdinand to Prospero's cell; there the youth falls in love with Miranda, and Prospero sets him to the hardest of menial tasks. The King (Act II) believes that Ferdinand is drowned; Antonio and Sebastian plan to murder Alonso, but thanks to the invisible Ariel, the deed is prevented. Stephano and Trinculo, Alonso's butler and jester, are involved drunkenly with Caliban.

Aided by Ariel (Act III) Prospero uses his magic art to baffle the royal party. Agreeing to the betrothal of Miranda and Ferdinand, he summons a masque for them (Act IV). Later (Act V) he decides to abandon his revenge, to forgive his enemies, and break his magic staff. Then he reveals himself, demands back his dukedom, shows Ferdinand at chess with Miranda, sets Ariel free, and speaks a wistful epilogue before sailing home.

Shakespeare has obeyed the "unities" here: the action of *The Tempest* passes on a single day and in the same place.

In performance

"The isle is full of noises,/Sounds, and sweet airs, that give delight and hurt not." That, unexpectedly, is Caliban (III.2) during an adventure of the spirit that was Shakespeare's last unaided play. The isle, like Alonso's daughter and offstage Queen, Claribel of Tunis, is ten leagues beyond man's life, a meeting-ground of elemental forces. It was once fashionable to suggest that Prospero could be Shakespeare, and that the breaking of his staff and the burial of his magic book symbolized a farewell to the theatre. But there are opinions for all tastes: one, rather dreary, is that the piece is a study in colonialism (an idea treated without luck in a London revival). It is simpler to regard *The Tempest* as a haunted poem inspired vaguely by many sources – folk-tales, romantic comedies, and some of the pamphlets about the wreck in Bermuda ("the still-vexed Bermoothes" of the text) of a ship from an English fleet that had sailed for Virginia in 1609.

The play is Prospero's. Though its other people – except for Ariel and Caliban, who stand for the spirit and the flesh – are relatively conventional, it can be strong magic both in the text and the better stage performances. True, not many revivals have been more than intermittently right, and some writers hold that theatrically the poem is inaccessible.

During the Restoration, Davenant and Dryden (1677) devised an unfortunate perversion, *The Tempest; or, the Enchanted Island*, that contained, among its characters, "Hippolito, one that never saw Woman, right Heir of the Dukedom of Mantua; Miranda and Dorinda, daughters to Prospero, that never saw Man; Caliban and Sycorax, his sister, two Monsters of the Isle; Milcha, a female spirit". It was all extremely silly, but much loved for nearly a century, a period during which there were adaptations of the adaptation, one (with Purcell's music) by Thomas Shadwell. For a long period from 1757 Garrick regularly returned Shakespeare's text to Drury Lane, yet the Davenant–Dryden muddle, readjusted, continued to keep its hold, under Kemble, for several years from 1789.

Macready, as we would expect, reverted to Shakespeare (Covent Garden, 1838), playing Prospero himself, with Priscilla Horton as Ariel. Afterwards, Phelps and Charles Kean treated the poem in their familiar ways: the first, solid and straightforward; the second burying the verse in spectacular effects and "scenic appliances" (the masque was like an uninhibited harvest festival). Beerbohm Tree (His Majesty's, 1904) was as scenically unrestrained as Kean, playing Caliban himself in a production, with actor-managerial transpositions, that A.B. Walkley of *The Times* called *The Girl from Prospero's Island*. Between the wars (1919–39) *The Tempest* survived most reasonably in a Robert Atkins production (Old Vic, 1924), with Ion Swinley as Prospero; under Bridges-Adams (Stratford, 1934, with its great galleon in distress); and again under Atkins (Open Air, 1936 and 1937), Swinley once more in Prospero's "beating mind". Elsa Lanchester's silver Ariel, all spirit, was the one relief of Tyrone Guthrie's sparse Vic/Wells revival (1934).

During the ensuing years John Gielgud acted Prospero three

times (Old Vic, 1940; Stratford and Drury Lane, 1957; and Old Vic, for National company, 1974). On the third occasion he was an El Greco figure. Michael Redgrave (Stratford, 1951) resembled one of Blake's prophets, and in the Ariel of Alan Badel – though less memorable, maybe, than Elsa Lanchester's – it was as if a Donatello figure, given quivering life, moved through the island air and rode on the "curl'd clouds".

New York: 1916, 1945 (directed by Margaret Webster, with Arnold Moss as Prospero), 1974 (Prospero, Sam Waterston). Stratford, Ontario: 1962.

In other terms

Opera: *Der Sturm* (1956) by the Swiss composer, Frank Martin.
Poetry: W.H. Auden's sequence of poems, *The Sea and the Mirror*.
Music: Dramatic Fantasia (1830) by Hector Berlioz; incidental music (1872) by Arthur Sullivan; Fantasy (1873) by Tchaikovsky.
Film: by Derek Jarman (1980).

Chief characters

Alonso, King of Naples Except for one outburst of grief for Ferdinand, this is a grey, subdued part.

Sebastian His brother; a serviceable minor villain.

Prospero controls the play as he controls the island. A man of potent eloquence who is tedious in the theatre only when his actor is: the opening exposition, as much for the audience as for Miranda, can be troublesome. But the great speeches, "Our revels now are ended" (IV.1) and "Ye elves" (V.1), are unfailing when uttered in such voices as Ion Swinley's*** (Open Air, 1936), John Gielgud's*** (Old Vic, 1974) and Paul Scofield's*** (Leeds Playhouse and Wyndham's, 1974–5). Prospero is a powerful magician, not a tired schoolmaster.

Antonio Prospero's usurper and Sebastian's fellow-cynic.

Ferdinand "I might call him / A thing divine," says Miranda (I.2), "for nothing natural / I ever saw so noble."

Gonzalo The good old lord who imagines an earthly paradise (II.1) is among Shakespeare's wise veterans. "O rejoice/Beyond a common joy, and set it down/With gold on lasting pillars" (V.1).

Caliban "Hag-born = not honour'd with a human shape". Yet this son of Sycorax has a sudden touching awareness at "the isle is full of noises" (III.2). Robert Atkins*** (many times, e.g. Open Air, 1933) was masterly in his groping for speech.

Trinculo Part of the obligatory fooling.

Stephano The drunken butler.

Francisco An otherwise insignificant lord, who describes Ferdinand in the water after the wreck, "Sir, he may live" (II.1).

Miranda A girl of about fifteen, she is a rare portrait of innocence. "O brave new world/That has such people in 't" (V.1).

Ariel "On the bat's back I do fly/After summer merrily" (V.1). The "airy spirit" has been imagined in many ways, none more persuasively than Elsa Lanchester's*** silver flash in the sunlight (Sadler's Wells, 1934). Some Prosperos do not look at their Ariel but use the reading, "I *think* thee, Ariel; come" (IV.1).

Iris, Ceres, Juno Their betrothal masque (IV.1) is tranquil and underrated; directors are given to incomprehensible experiments with it. The goddesses have appeared in the shape of tottering "corn-dollies", amorphous figures (one Stratford designer called them "ethereal marionettes"). Sometimes the measured verse has been blurred in offstage delivery.

HENRY VIII

1612–13

King Henry the Eighth	Queen Katharine
Cardinal Wolsey	*Three gentlemen*
Cardinal Campeius	*Dr Butts*, physician to the King
Capucius, Ambassador from	*Garter King-at-Arms*
Emperor Charles V	*Surveyor to the Duke of Buckingham*
Cranmer, Archbishop of	*Brandon*, and a *Sergeant-at-arms*
Canterbury	*Doorkeeper of the Council Chamber*
Duke of Norfolk	*Porter*, and his *Man*
Duke of Buckingham	*Page to Gardiner*
Duke of Suffolk	*A Crier*
Earl of Surrey	*Queen Katharine*, King Henry's
Lord Chamberlain	wife, afterwards divorced
Lord Chancellor	*Anne Bullen*, her Maid of Honour,
Gardiner, Bishop of Winchester	later Queen
Bishop of Lincoln	*An old lady*, friend to Anne Bullen
Lord Abergavenny	*Patience*, Queen Katharine's
Lord Sands	woman
Sir Henry Guildford	Lord Mayor, Aldermen, Lords
Sir Thomas Lovell	and Ladies in the Dumb Shows;
Sir Anthony Denny	Woman attending upon the
Sir Nicholas Vaux	Queen; Secretaries to Wolsey;
Cromwell, in Wolsey's service	Scribes, Officers, Guards, and
Griffith, gentleman-usher to	other Attendants; Spirits

Scene: London, Westminster, Kimbolton. Henry VIII ruled from 1509 to 1547. In 1509 he married, as the first of six wives, his elder brother's widow, Katharine of Aragon.

Synopsis

Henry VIII dances with Anne Bullen at Cardinal Wolsey's London mansion, York Place. The Duke of Buckingham (Act II) is condemned to execution on a charge of high treason raised by Wolsey. At the inquiry into Henry's marriage, Queen Katharine (also worked against by Wolsey) leaves the court at Blackfriars to "appeal unto the Pope". Wolsey's efforts to stop the King from marrying Anne are discovered, and more evidence of intrigue that will lead to his dismissal and the loss of his possession.

Secretly, the King marries Anne who (Act IV) is crowned Queen. Katharine (who has heard of the death of her enemy, Wolsey) dies at Kimbolton in Huntingdonshire. Gardiner, malicious Bishop of Winchester, tries to bring down Cranmer, the new Archbishop of Canterbury (Act V), but the King intervenes. The play ends with Cranmer, as godfather of Anne's child, Princess Elizabeth, prophesying at her christening that she will be "A pattern to all princes ..."

In performance

We have to ask whether Shakespeare wrote the play alone, or whether much of it is John Fletcher's (and, if so, which scenes are Shakespeare's). Though no one can answer with any certainty, collaboration is plausible. A loose chronicle rather than a play tautly contrived, it is so actable that the theatre has responded eagerly: only specialists will spend time in separating Hand A from Hand B.

Primarily a play of farewells – to the world, to life, to greatness – it has an October sense, a pervading melancholy that is set off by its ceremonial which, if instructions are obeyed, has more pomp than anything else in Shakespeare (no wonder that Charles Kean rose to it). *Henry VIII*, often used as a pageant for a celebration, has also been a play for a disaster. Fire, caused by the discharge of "chambers", or stage cannon, at Henry's entry to Wolsey's masque, destroyed the first Globe Theatre on Bankside, Southwark, during a performance on June 29, 1613.

Shakespeare and/or Fletcher drew on the chronicles of Edward Halle and Raphael Holinshed. At the Restoration and after, Thomas Betterton enjoyed playing the King and did so until 1709, the year before he died. The eighteenth century would have such actresses as Hannah Pritchard and the imperative Sarah Siddons ("Lord Cardinal, to you I speak") as Katharine. Mrs Siddons, appearing with her brother John Philip Kemble (Wolsey), was in fullest grandeur many times between 1788 and 1816. Wolsey had become the principal male part, acted during the nineteenth century by Macready, Charles Kean (who had a moving barge and a historical panorama of London in a Princess's scenic orgy), and Henry Irving, whose Lyceum production (January 1892, with Ellen Terry as Katharine) was even more extravagant than Kean's. Tree's revival (His Majesty's, 1910–12), also ostentatiously caparisoned, dialogue cut for the pageant's sake, ended with Anne's coronation; Tree himself was a hard, brooding Wolsey (and in New York, 1916). Sybil Thorndike was a magnificent Katharine (Empire, 1925; few people noticed a youth, Laurence Olivier, as First Serving Man).

In Tyrone Guthrie's production (Sadler's Wells, 1933) Henry became for a while the main character because Charles Laughton, in a popular film, had recently acted him as a gross sensualist. On the stage Laughton's husky sibilance could not recreate his former vitality, and the night belonged to Flora Robson as Katharine. The most satisfying later productions were Guthrie's at Stratford (1949), which in spite of an overplus of "business", did quicken the sprawling pageant; Michael Benthall's (Old Vic, 1953 and 1958), each keeping a balance between processional play and personal drama, and in 1958 with John Gielgud and Edith Evans as Wolsey and Katharine; and Trevor Nunn's (Stratford/Aldwych, 1969–70), mildly Brechtian, with Donald Sinden's Holbein Henry in strong, relishing charge.

New York: 1946, directed by Margaret Webster, with Eva Le Gallienne (Katharine) and Walter Hampden (Wolsey).

Chief characters

Henry VIII Shakespeare manages to be as tactful as possible; and several actors have filled out the part. Paul Rogers*** (Old Vic, 1953), Donald Sinden*** (Stratford/Aldwych, 1969–70).
Cardinal Wolsey The "scarlet sin". Beginning sourly, exorbitant in arrogance, he falls (III.2) "like a bright exhalation in the evening." His farewell elegy, with its drooping cadences, may be Fletcherian.
Cranmer, Archbishop of Canterbury. At the centre of Act V, where Henry saves him from the malice of Gardiner, and he speaks the christening eulogy on the child who one day will be Queen Elizabeth I (V.1).

Duke of Buckingham First vigorous, then submissive. His farewell, "All good people" (II.1), before "this long divorce of steel", has long been a show-piece. Johnston Forbes-Robertson*** (Lyceum, 1892); Ion Swinley*** (Old Vic, 1924).

Cromwell In Wolsey's service; afterwards the King's. A loyally sympathetic listener in III.2.

Griffith Katharine's gentleman-usher at Kimbolton. "Such an honest chronicler as Griffith" (IV.2).

Queen Katharine A woman of unremitting courage and regality, both at the trial and in her fading. "Though unqueened, yet like/A queen, and daughter to a king, inter me." The angelic vision she sees in IV.2 can worry directors. Sarah Siddons*** (Drury Lane, 1788; Covent Garden, 1806), Sybil Thorndike*** (Empire, 1925), Peggy Ashcroft*** (Stratford/Aldwych, 1969–70).

Anne Bullen "I would not be a queen" (II.3). "No, we'll no Bullens," says Wolsey (III.2). But she will be crowned in pomp (IV.1).

An old lady Her brief scene with Anne (II.3) is a small, shrewd and racy masterpiece. Athene Seyler*** (Sadler's Wells, 1933).

THE TWO NOBLE KINSMEN

1613–14

Theseus, Duke of Athens	baboon
Pirithous, his friend	*A schoolmaster*
Palamon and *Arcite*,	*A taborer*
cousins from Thebes;	*Hymen*, god of marriage
the two noble kinsmen	*Hippolyta*, Queen of the Amazons
Artesius, an Athenian soldier	and then wife of Theseus
Valerius, a Theban	*Emilia*, her sister
A herald	*The gaoler's daughter*
A boy	*Three queens*, widows of Kings
A gentleman	killed in the siege of Thebes
Six knights assisting Palamon and	*Nell* and four other country
Arcite	wenches
Gaoler	*A woman*, Emilia's servant
Wooer of gaoler's daughter	Nymphs, Attendants,
Two friends of gaoler	Countrymen, Garland-bearer,
Gaoler's brother	Hunters, Maids, Executioner,
A doctor	Guard of soldiers
Six countrymen, one dressed as a	

Scene: Athens, Thebes, country near Athens

Synopsis

Three mourning queens urge Theseus, Duke of Athens – at his celebration of marriage to Hippolyta – to attack Creon, King of Thebes, who slew their husbands; Theseus agrees to wage war. Palamon and Arcite, Creon's nephews, two noble kinsmen, fight for Thebes, but Theseus captures and imprisons them. From the window of their prison (Act II) they see Emilia, sister of Hippolyta, and both fall in love with her. Arcite, released but banished from Athens, goes disguised into Emilia's service. The gaoler's daughter, passionately infatuated with Palamon, enables him to escape and later goes mad for his loss (Act III). The two kinsmen meet and fight with each other; sparing them on the intercession of Emilia (who cannot say whom she loves) and Hippolyta, Theseus orders them to return in a month and fight again; the winner will have Emilia, the loser will be executed. To restore the sanity of the gaoler's daughter (Act IV), a wooer is advised to impersonate Palamon.

The month passes. Arcite (Act V) prays to Mars and Palamon to Venus for success, and Emilia prays at Diana's altar. Arcite wins the combat but later, falling from his horse, he is mortally wounded. With his last breath he gives Emilia, and with her all the world's joy, to Palamon (who is saved from execution). The gaoler's daughter has recovered and is about to marry.

In performance

There is now general agreement that this romance, deriving from Chaucer's *Knight's Tale*, was a Shakespeare–Fletcher partnership. Shakespeare – though the play did not get into the Folio of 1623 – is usually allowed the whole of Act I, the first scene of Act III, and the whole of Act V except the second scene. The unloved sub-plot of the gaoler's daughter is assigned to Fletcher, but how much each dramatist edited the other none can speculate. Jacobean theatre taste is mirrored in the incidental pageantry.

The few revivals of a piece seldom performed in three centuries have strengthened belief in its theatrical power, if not in the consistent quality of its verse.

Davenant adapted the play as *The Rivals* (1664), removing the gaoler's daughter. Between 1667 and 1928 no more was heard: then Andrew Leigh put on the true text at the Old Vic, with Ernest Milton and Eric Portman as Palamon and Arcite, and Jean Forbes-Robertson as the gaoler's daughter. Richard Digby Day adapted the text for an imaginatively simple Open Air Theatre revival in Regent's Park (1974).

Chief characters

Theseus, Duke of Athens. "The all-noble Theseus" (I.3) describes him.

Hippolyta "Most dreaded Amazonian.../That equally canst poise sternness with pity.../Dear glass of ladies" (I.1).

Emilia Cannot make up her mind between Palamon and Arcite, and she does not grow in ours, though Arcite's May-morning speech (III.1) is an enchantment. "What a mere child is fancy", she says in IV.2, "that having two fair gauds of equal sweetness,/ Cannot distinguish, but must cry for both!"

Palamon "Melancholy becomes him nobly" (V.3).

Arcite (pronounced "Ar-sight"). "Mercy and manly courage are bedfellows in his visage" (V.3). In V.1 he has the glorious invocations to Mars.

The Gaoler's Daughter In her love for Palamon, a nymphomaniac. It is a glum sub-plot, though playgoers, in general, are less sensitive than they were.

The Three Queens Their first-act appeal to Theseus is profoundly dignified and touching. Later, the Third Queen speaks the couplet (I.5) transmuted from Chaucer: "This world's a city full of straying streets,/And death's the market-place, where each one meets."

THE POEMS AND
SONNETS

The Poems

Venus and Adonis, called by Shakespeare "the first heir of my invention" – that is, his first published work or his first poem – was published and printed in London (1593) by Richard Field from Stratford-upon-Avon, and dedicated to Henry Wriothesley, third Earl of Southampton (1573–1624). It was often reprinted. Written ornately, and under the influences of the Latin poet Ovid, the 1,194 lines of the narrative are in a verse form rhymed like this, a six-line stanza in which a quatrain is followed by a couplet:

> Lo, here the gentle lark, weary of rest,
> From his moist cabinet mounts up on high,
> And wakes the morning, from whose silver breast
> The sun ariseth in his majesty:
> Who doth the world so gloriously behold
> That cedar-tops and hills seem burnish'd gold.

[lines 853–8]

Venus, relentless goddess of love, is determined to woo the reluctant Adonis by any possible means. When he leaves her to go hunting, he is killed by a vicious boar. A flower ("a purple flow'r ... check'red with white", line 1,168) grows to his memory where his blood has fallen.

The Rape of Lucrece (1594), printed and published by Field and dedicated to the Earl of Southampton, was also popular and often reprinted. Here, in 1,855 lines, the form of a narrative slower, more rhetorical and more discursive than *Venus and Adonis* is a seven-line stanza of iambic pentameters (rhyme royal), as in

> Without the bed her other fair hand was,
> On the green coverlet, whose perfect white
> Show'd like an April daisy on the grass,
> With pearly sweat, resembling dew of night.
> Her eyes, like marigolds, had sheath'd their light,
> And canopied in darkness sweetly lay,
> Till they might open to adorn the day.

[lines 393–9]

The Roman Sextus Tarquinius steals at night to the bedroom of Lucrece (Lucretia), chaste wife of Collatinus, and in spite of her anguished appeals, rapes her. Next day, after urging that she must be revenged, she stabs herself to death. Her body is borne through Rome; Tarquin is banished.

Dr Caroline Spurgeon (see page 164) once noted the strange back-eddy of the river Avon beneath an arch of Clopton Bridge at Stratford, and recalled a passage in *Lucrece:*

> As through an arch the violent roaring tide
> Outruns the eye that doth behold his haste,
> Yet in the eddy boundeth in his pride
> Back to the strait that forc'd him on so fast ...

[lines 1,667–70]

The French dramatist, André Obey, wrote *Le Viol de Lucrèce* (1931) for Jacques Copeau's Compagnie des Quinze at the Vieux-Colombier, Paris. It was staged in London, at the Arts Theatre, in June that year. (Obey, in 1932, also modernized *Venus et Adonis* for the Paris company.) Thornton Wilder adapted *Le Viol de Lucrèce* as *Lucrece,* and with music by Deems Taylor, it was staged on Broadway, 1932. Colin Chandler directed a London production (1948) at the Boltons Theatre, Kensington.

Benjamin Britten loosely based his *Rape of Lucretia* (1946) on Shakespeare's narrative.

The Phoenix and The Turtle, a haunting allegorical elegy of sixty-seven lines, was first ascribed to Shakespeare when it appeared, untitled, among commendatory poems attached to a long poem by Robert Chester, *Love's Martyr; or, Rosalin's Complaint* (1601). After the birds have been summoned to mourning, there is an anthem for the phoenix and the turtle-dove, and the poem's last fifteen lines are a lament for the dead, or "threnos", composed by Reason, which begins:

> Beauty, truth, and rarity,
> Grace in all simplicity,
> Here enclos'd in cinders lie.

The Passionate Pilgrim, published by the not-too-reputable William Jaggard (1599) as "by W. Shakespeare", is a miscellany of poems by various hands, of which only five are certainly Shakespeare's. These are corrupt versions of the 138th and 144th Sonnets, and versions of parts of three scenes from *Love's Labour's Lost* (IV.3, 56–69; IV.2, 100–13; V.3, 101–20). Shakespeare's name was removed from the title page of an edition in 1612.

A Lover's Complaint, a pastoral in the seven-line "rhyme royal" stanza, was published with the Sonnets in 1609. It is indifferent work of highly doubtful authenticity.

The Sonnets

Shakespeare wrote 154 sonnets (fourteen-line lyrics). Except for two (138, 144), first seen in altered versions in a miscellany called *The Passionate Pilgrim* (1599), they were originally published in a quarto of 1609 ("never before imprinted") and had obviously not been read by the author in proof. The critic Inga-Stina Ewbank has described them concisely as "a practically true record of two different love relationships, with the fluctuations of mind and mood involved in each".

As early as 1598, Francis Meres, a schoolmaster, critic and divine (1565–1647), referred in a collection of miscellaneous essays, *Palladis Tamia,* to Shakespeare's "sug[a]red sonnets among his private friends". The sonnet-form was particularly fashionable during the early 1590s (its vogue had begun with Sir Philip Sidney's *Astrophel and Stella* in 1591). Hence the belief that Shakespeare, who liked to introduce sonnets into his plays – *Love's Labour's Lost,* for one – was writing his sequence at that time. The Canadian-born critic and adventurous researcher, Dr Leslie Hotson (b.1897) has suggested moving back to 1588–9 by interpreting a line in Sonnet 107, "The mortal moon hath her eclipse endured", as a reference to the crescent formation of the Spanish Armada which sailed towards England in the summer of 1588; but Hotson is in a minority.

We do not know with certainty to whom the sonnets are addressed. Indeed, though some critics are more sanguine than others, we cannot be sure about any of the principal characters in the story, the Poet, the Poet's Friend, the Dark Lady, or the dedicatee, "Mr W.H.". It has been suggested that the sonnets are only a literary exercise; few now would take this negative view. It seems that the chief claimants to be the youth to whom they are addressed are either Henry Wriothesley, third Earl of Southampton (1573–1624), dedicatee of *Venus and Adonis* and *The Rape of Lucrece,* or William Herbert, third Earl of Pembroke (1580–1630), dedicatee – with his brother Philip – of the First Folio of 1623.

Either of these could be the "Mr W.H." of the 1609 quarto, edited by Thomas Thorpe, which is dedicated as follows:

TO. THE. ONLIE. BEGETTER. OF.
THESE.INSUING. SONNETS.
MR. W. H. ALL. HAPPINESSE.
AND. THAT. ETERNITIE.
PROMISED.
BY.
OUR. EVER-LIVING. POET.
WISHETH.
THE. WELL-WISHING.
ADVENTURER. IN.
SETTING.
FORTH.
T.T.

Much rests on the interpretation of the word "begetter": if this is taken to be "inspirer", then Mr W.H. and the youth of the sonnets are the same man. Southampton was Shakespeare's early patron; the sonnet-story can parallel various circumstances in his career. Those who favour him say that to conceal his identity, Thorpe reversed Henry Wriothesley's initials. Those against the claim ask why no one after 1594 mentions that Southampton had apparently any sustained interest in Shakespeare; moreover, he is not named in the dedication of the First Folio.

Adherents of William Herbert, who became third Earl of Pembroke in 1601, speak of the production of Shakespeare's first plays (written between 1589 and 1592) by the company known as Pembroke's Men under the patronage of William Herbert's father. Young William Herbert, it is said, would have been more likely than the older Southampton to be the "sweet boy", the "lovely boy", of the sonnets: his supporters suggest that Shakespeare addressed the sequence to him in 1595. There have been several other candidates, none persuasive.

The dark temptress of the sonnets has become known as the Dark Lady. She could be, but improbably, Mary Fitton (c.1578–1647), one of Queen Elizabeth's maids of honour, and mistress of William Herbert; but Dr A.L. Rowse (b.1903), the historian, firmly believes her to be the half-Italian Emilia Lanier (c.1569–1645), English-born daughter of Baptista Bassano, a musician, and wife of a composer, Alphonso Lanier. Dr Rowse holds that the sonnets, addressed to Southampton, reached their publisher, Thorpe, through Sir William Harvey (Mr W.H.), who was the young widowed third husband of Southampton's mother and who had not long married again.

The first 126 sonnet-letters are addressed by the poet to his friend, a handsome young nobleman. Sonnets 127–52 (the so-called "vituperative" sonnets) are about the faithless Dark Lady: the last two, 153–4, are very ordinary versions of an epigram to Cupid, a theme from the Greek Anthology. Numbers 1–17 urge the fair youth to marry and to preserve his beauty in a child. Presently the Poet's association with him becomes a close friendship which has its ardours and endurances, including the Friend's entanglement with the Poet's mistress (the Dark Lady) and the dangerous rivalry of another poet: this could be such a person as George Chapman (c.1560–1634), dramatist and translator of Homer, or Christopher Marlowe (A.L. Rowse's favoured candidate), or, for that matter, many poets of the time.

Mostly, the sonnets are works of great beauty, designed in a rhyming pattern of three four-line groups with a last clinching couplet: only a few vary from the norm. Scores of phrases are famous out of context: for example:

> When forty winters shall besiege thy brow,
> And dig deep trenches in thy beauty's field,
> Thy youth's proud livery, so gaz'd on now,
> Will be a tatter'd weed of small worth held.   [2]

> Thou art thy mother's glass, and she in thee
> Calls back the lovely April of her prime.   [3]

> And summer's green all girded up in sheaves
> Borne on the bier with white and bristly beard.   [12]

> And your true rights be term'd a poet's rage
> And stretchèd metre of an antique song.   [17]

> Devouring Time, blunt thou the lion's paws.   [19]

> A woman's face, with Nature's own hand painted,
> Hast thou, the Master Mistress of my passion.   [20]

>   My love is as fair
> As any mother's child, though not so bright
> As those gold candles fix'd in heaven's air.   [21]

> My glass shall not persuade me I am old
> So long as youth and thou are of one date.   [22]

> The painful warrior famousèd for fight,
> After a thousand victories once foil'd,
> Is from the book of honour razèd quite,
> And all the rest forgot for which he toil'd.   [25]

> When to the sessions of sweet silent thought
> I summon up remembrance of things past,
> I sigh the lack of many a thing I sought,
> And with old woes new wail my dear time's waste.   [30]

> Full many a glorious morning have I seen
> Flatter the mountain-tops with sovereign eye.   [33]

> Why didst thou promise such a beauteous day,
> And make me travel forth without my cloak . . .?   [34]

> No more be griev'd at that which thou hast done;
> Roses have thorns, and silver fountains mud.   [35]

> Like stones of worth they thinly placèd are,
> Or captain jewels in the carcanet.   [52]

> What is your substance, whereof are you made,
> That millions of strange shadows on you tend?   [53]

> Not marble nor the gilded monuments
> Of princes shall outlive this pow'rful rhyme;
> But you shall shine more bright in these contents
> Than unswept stone, besmear'd with sluttish time.   [55]

> Like as the waves make towards the pebbled shore,
> So do our minutes hasten to their end.   [60]

Beated and chopt with tann'd antiquity. [62]

Since brass, nor stone, nor earth, nor boundless sea,
But sad mortality o'ersways their power,
How with this rage shall beauty hold a plea,
Whose action is no stronger than a flower? [65]

Tir'd with all these, for restful death I cry. [66]

Bare ruin'd choirs where late the sweet birds sang. [73]

Was it the proud full sail of his great verse . . .? [86]

From you have I been absent in the spring,
When proud-pied April, dress'd in all his trim,
Hath put a spirit of youth in every thing. [98]

                              Three winters cold
Have from the forests shook three summers' pride. [104]

And beauty making beautiful old rhyme. [106]

Incertainties now crown themselves assur'd,
And peace proclaims olives of endless age. [107]

Love's not Time's fool, though rosy lip and cheeks
Within his bending sickle's compass come. [116]

In the old age black was not counted fair
Or if it were, it bore not beauty's name. [127]

Th'expense of spirit in a waste of shame
Is lust in action. [129]

Finally, here is the complete 18th sonnet:

Shall I compare thee to a summer's day?
Thou art more lovely and more temperate.
Rough winds do shake the darling buds of May,
And summer's lease hath all too short a date;
Sometime too hot the eye of heaven shines,
And often is his gold complexion dimm'd;
And every fair from fair some time declines,
By chance, or nature's changing course, untrimm'd;
But thy eternal summer shall not fade
Nor lose possession of that fair thou ow'st;
Nor shall Death brag thou wand'rest in his shade
When in eternal lines to time thou grow'st.
   So long as men can breathe or eyes can see,
   So long lives this, and this gives life to thee.

THE APOCRYPHA

Though various plays (known as the Apocrypha), not included in the First Folio, have been attributed to Shakespeare, only *Pericles* and *The Two Noble Kinsmen* can be considered as his work in any substantial part. It is believed now that he wrote one of the additions – Hand D, in the surviving incomplete manuscript – to a play called *Sir Thomas More*, written by various authors for the Admiral's Men at a date conjectured as about 1593 or 1601. Sir Edmund Tilney, Master of the Revels, required the revisions. That presumed to be by Shakespeare consists of 147 lines in which More, Sheriff of London, is pacifying the rioting anti-alien apprentices on May Day in 1517. The play – which eventually failed to pass the censor – was staged in June 1954 at the Theatre Centre, London. A critic noticed a phrase (not in the "Hand D" addition): "This tide of rage that with the eddy strives" (I.3: see *The Rape of Lucrece*, p. 128).

Other plays in the Apocrypha – the dates are those of the earliest editions – have included *Arden of Feversham* (1592), revived on various occasions during the last half-century, *Locrine*★ (1595), *the Reign of King Edward III* (1596), *Mucedorus* (1598), *Sir John Oldcastle*★ (1600), *Thomas, Lord Cromwell*★ (1602), *The London Prodigal*★ (1605), *The Puritan*★ (1607), *A Yorkshire Tragedy*★ (1608), *The Merry Devil of Edmonton* (1608), *Fair Em* (undated; second edition 1631) and *The Birth of Merlin* (quarto edition, 1662). Those marked with an asterisk were added in 1664 to the second issue of the Third Folio. The only one that might be partly Shakespearian is *Edward III*, a favourite with William Poel (see p. 159). The silliest, betrayed by its title, is *A Pleasant Comedy of Fair Em, the Miller's Daughter of Manchester, with the love of William the Conqueror*. The second scene ("Manchester; the interior of a mill") begins with the miller addressing Em:

> Come, daughter, we must learn to shake off pomp,
> To leave the state that erst beseemed a knight
> And gentleman of no mean descent,
> To undertake this homely miller's trade;
> Thus must we mask to save our wretched lives,
> Threatened by conquest of this hapless isle.

The plays contain some agreeable stage directions, e.g., in *Locrine*, "Enter Humber alone, his hair hanging over his shoulders, his arms all bloody, and a dart in one hand"; in *The Birth of Merlin*, "Thunder and lightning; two Dragons appear, a White and a Red, they fight a while, and pause"; and, in *The Merry Devil of Edmonton*, "The chime goes, in which time Fabell is oft seen to stare about him, and hold up his hands."

There is also a lost play, *Cardenio*, which the King's Men acted in 1613 and was entered in the Stationers' Register forty years later as "The History of Cardenio by Mr Fletcher and Shakespeare". The dramatist, Lewis Theobald (1688–1744) – the name is pronounced "Tibbald" – claimed in 1727 that a play which he had edited, *The Double Falsehood*, was by Shakespeare and founded on the story, by Cervantes, of Cardenio and Lucinda in *Don Quixote* (of which an English version had appeared in 1612). Theobald said that he had revised and adapted the piece from an old manuscript.

BIOGRAPHIES

Abbreviations
CH, Companion of Honour. GBE (Knight or Dame), Grand Cross of the Order of the British Empire. DBE, Dame Commander of the Order of the British Empire. CBE, Commander of the Order of the British Empire. OBE, Officer of the Order of the British Empire.

The symbol ▷ indicates that the person before whose name it appears has a separate biographical entry.

*(**) Stars indicate exceptional performances.

For the plays in which the characters mentioned occur, see list at end of biographies (pp. 170–71).

Achurch, Janet (1864–1916) Fair, blue-eyed, intense, she was briefly with ▷Frank Benson's touring company (1885). Her Lady Macbeth is pictured in a Benson memorial window at the Royal Shakespeare Picture Gallery, Stratford. Later the Ibsen actress of her time. Admired by ▷Shaw, though he disliked her Cleopatra (Manchester and London, 1897).

Adams, Maude (1872–1953) Much-admired American actress of "soft, elusive charm" (Brooks Atkinson), she appeared occasionally in Shakespeare, as Juliet (1899), Rosalind, and – when she returned to the stage in 1931, after thirteen years' absence – as Portia, to ▷Otis Skinner's Shylock, in an unexciting production that did not reach New York.

Agate, James (1877–1947) For more than twenty years drama critic of *The Sunday Times*, author of many books on the stage and of a voluminous nine-volume journal, *Ego* (published between 1935 and 1948), which may outlive his often observant, sometimes capricious, criticism. The best of his work on Shakespeare is in *Brief Chronicles* (1943).

Ainley, Henry (1879–1945) Began with ▷Benson in the provinces, 1899. Wayward and romantically leonine, with a noble voice, he is remembered for many parts, principally in the fury of Leontes for ▷Granville Barker (Savoy, 1912). Illness caused his retirement from the stage (1932).

Aldridge, Ira (1807–67) An American Negro, who used to be known as "the African Roscius", he played in England some of the great tragic parts, notably Othello. He was Aaron (London, 1852) in a much-altered text of *Titus Andronicus*. Naturalized Englishman, 1863.

Alexander, George (1858–1918) Conspicuously handsome, he acted for some years with ▷Henry Irving at the Lyceum. Later, during twenty-nine years at his own theatre, the St James's, he was among the most quietly dignified players of his period. In Shakespeare, apart from the Lyceum period, he was Orlando (1896) and Benedick (1898), both at the St James's. Knighted, 1911.

Allen, Viola (1867–1948) An American actress from 1882 to 1918, who established herself principally as leading lady of Charles Frohman's Empire Theatre company in New York for five years. Later, 1903–7, she presented and acted in *Twelfth*

Night (Viola), *The Winter's Tale* (one of the few players to double Hermione and Perdita), and *Cymbeline* (Imogen).

Alleyn, Edward (1566–1626) During the 1590s an actor of great power who created Marlowe's Tamburlaine, Faustus and Barabas (*The Jew of Malta*) at the Rose Theatre on Bankside. He founded what is now Dulwich College and died wealthy.

Anderson, Judith (b.1898) Commanding tragic actress, Australian-born, whose career has been mainly American. Shakespeare parts have included Gertrude to ▷John Gielgud's Hamlet (New York, 1936) and Lady Macbeth, not fully persuasive when she played it in London (Old Vic and New Theatre, 1937), though it developed in later years. DBE, 1960.

Anderson, Mary (1859–1940) A beautiful Californian actress who was Juliet at sixteen (in Louisville, Kentucky) and a witty, tender Rosalind (which she brought to Stratford for one performance in 1885). First to double Hermione and Perdita*** (Lyceum, 1887). On her marriage, in 1890, she left the stage and settled in the Worcestershire village of Broadway.

Andrews, Harry (b.1911) Tall, vigorous actor who was in Gielgud companies during the 1930s, the Old Vic company (New Theatre, 1945–9) and various Stratford seasons where his Wolsey (1949), Duke (*Measure for Measure*, 1950), Enobarbus (1953) and Othello (1956) were all strongly realized. CBE, 1966.

Armin, Robert (*c.*1568–1615) Formerly a goldsmith's apprentice, he followed ▷Will Kempe as principal comedian of Shakespeare's company. Hence, possibly, the dramatist's change from broader clowns to such more astringent and complex figures as Touchstone, Feste, Lavache and the Fool. Armin was himself a dramatist.

Asche, Oscar (1871–1936) An Australian who joined ▷Benson (1893), and who became a London actor-manager in, among other plays, *Measure for Measure* (Adelphi, 1906) and *Othello* (His Majesty's 1907). A traditional Shakespearian, massive in aspect, vocally a resounding bass-baritone, he was devoted to stage spectacle.

Ashcroft, Peggy (b.1907) From her first Old Vic season (1932–3) she has grown into a leader of her profession. An actress of unfailing clarity and wisdom, she has been honoured for Juliet*** (New, 1935), Titania*** (Haymarket, 1945), Beatrice*** (Stratford, 1950), Portia*** and Cleopatra*** (Stratford, 1953), Rosalind and Imogen*** (Stratford, 1957), a deeply engaged Margaret of Anjou*** (*Wars of the Roses* trilogy at Stratford, 1963–4), and much else. Since 1968 a director of the Royal Shakespeare Company. For a time married to ▷Theodore Komisarjevsky. DBE, 1956.

Atkins, Robert (1886–1972) Often spoken of as an Elizabethan reborn, he directed, in a method totally straightforward, more Shakespeare than anyone of his day, at the Old Vic, the Open Air Theatre, Regent's Park (where he worked for thirty years), and for two seasons (1944–5) at Stratford. He was also an actor, slow and resolute, known especially in later years (Open Air Theatre) for a Caliban*** in which the monster's intellect dawned like a sullen daybreak, and for a relishing Sir Toby and Bottom. CBE, 1949.

Ayrton, Randle (1869–1940) Masterly in tragedy and comedy, and ▷Benson's stage director before the First World War, he was loved in Stratford, where he played leads for several seasons (especially in the late 1920s and 1930s); cared very little for London success. Independent and acutely professional, a stocky man with a direct, blistering gaze, who never lost the Cheshire vowels in his stinging voice, he could control a theatre. His

Lear***, which he acted for ▷Bridges-Adams, and in 1936 on ▷Komisarjevsky's stage-filling Stratford staircase, was the most majestic of its period. He spoke the last words in the first Shakespeare Memorial Theatre (1925) and the first words (Henry IV's "So shaken as we are, so wan with care"**) in the present theatre on the afternoon of April 23, 1932.

Baddeley, Angela (1904–76) Making her début at the Old Vic when she was eleven, she played in maturity, and with the firmest technique, about a dozen Shakespeare parts between Anne Bullen (Empire, 1925), Juliet's Nurse* (Stratford, 1958) and Regan (Stratford, 1959). Her second husband was the director, ▷Glen Byam Shaw. CBE, 1975.

Badel, Alan (b.1923) Visually and vocally imperative, a graduate of the Birmingham Repertory where he played Richard III (1949), he had some highly adaptable Stratford years, crackling through Justice Shallow** (*Henry IV, Part 2*, 1951), and in the same season realizing Lear's Fool as a timid bird. In 1951 his Ariel was described as "a Donatello figure given radiant life". A Romeo from the right latitude (Old Vic, 1952); unluckier with Hamlet (Stratford, 1956).

Baff, William (b.1931) Versatile American director who has staged *The Tempest* (Stratford, Connecticut, 1960), and, for the San Francisco-based American Conservatory Theatre, 1967–76, *King Lear, Hamlet, The Tempest, The Taming of the Shrew*.

Bankhead, Tallulah (1902–68) Senator's daughter from Alabama who had a tumultuous career on both the London stage (1923–30: "a smouldering young woman with a voice like hot honey and milk"), and later, for more than three decades, in America. Redoubtable when suited, she appeared only once in Shakespeare, an unfortunate *Antony and Cleopatra* (five performances, New York, 1937). John Mason Brown wrote of her: "She barged down the Nile last night – and sank."

Barker, Harley Granville (1877–1946) In middle life a hyphen crept into his name. Half-Scottish, half-Italian; author, actor, director and the most influential Shakespearian of the twentieth-century theatre. Though he ceased to direct after 1914 (when he was thirty-seven), he put his practical wisdom and scholar's insight into five volumes of *Prefaces to Shakespeare* (beginning 1927). His three famous revivals***, demolishing any kind of outworn tradition, were *The Winter's Tale* and *Twelfth Night* (Savoy, 1912) and *A Midsummer Night's Dream* (Savoy, 1914).

Barrault, Jean-Louis (b.1910) Parisian actor and director, close student of mime. Broke with the Comédie Française where he played his first lucid, sensitive Hamlet*** (1942), and for his own company (1946) acted the part in a new text by André Gide. Married to the actress Madeleine Renaud.

Barrett, Wilson (1846–1904) Actor-manager who specialized in florid melodrama, particularly when managing the Princess's Theatre during the 1880s, five years of rant leavened by a competent and typically resonant Hamlet (1884).

Barrie, Barbara (b.1931) Accomplished American actress who has played at Stratford, Connecticut, and in New York, mainly in the comedies. Thus she was Helena (*All's Well That Ends Well*) and Viola (both in the New York Shakespeare Festival, 1966) and Hermia (Stratford, 1958).

Barry, Ann (1734–1801) Originally married to an actor called Dancer, she was ▷Spranger Barry's second wife (1768), as assured in tragedy as in comedy and capable of unusual pathos. Played Rosalind, Imogen, Cordelia, Viola. "She knew not how to insinuate herself into the heart," said a critic. "Her mode was to seize it."

Barry, Elizabeth (1658–1713) The first major British actress, she played opposite ▷Betterton in such parts (of many) as Lady Macbeth, Mistress Page, Queen Katharine and Cordelia in the ▷Nahum Tate version of *King Lear*. Mistress of the Earl of Rochester; at her best in tragedy. "With all her enchantment," Antony Aston wrote in 1753, "this fine creature was not handsome. . . . She was middle-sized, had darkish hair, light eyes, and was indifferent plump."

Barry, Spranger (1719–77) Handsome without effeminacy, tall and silver-voiced, this Irish-born actor was ▷Garrick's rival, especially as Romeo***, which he acted at Covent Garden (1750) while Garrick was in the same part at Drury Lane. Also a Hamlet, Othello and Lear.

Barrymore, Ethel (1879–1959) One of the "royal family" of the American stage, and elder sister of ▷John, she acted Juliet indifferently (1922), but, opposite ▷Walter Hampden (1925), was a good Ophelia and Portia. "You don't have to be bewildered by Shakespeare," she said. "There he is. Leave him alone."

Barrymore, John (1882–1942) At first a sound debonair actor in run-of-the-mill drama, he heightened his work startlingly. He is remembered for his Hamlet*** (New York, 1922; London, 1925) with what Ophelia (III.1) calls "the courtier's, soldier's, scholar's eye, tongue, sword." His career ebbed into failure.

Barton, John (b. 1928) A sensitive and intellectual director who came to Stratford in 1960 from Cambridge, where he was a Fellow of King's College. He has since directed many of the plays freshly with a civilized mind and a faultless ear for the verse (gifts evident in e.g. *Twelfth Night*, 1969). Has a sometimes perilous gift for Shakespearian pastiche that, though it ruined *King John* (1974), was used with unerring adroitness in his conflation of the *Henry VI* trilogy (*The Wars of the Roses*, Stratford, 1963–4).

Baylis, Lilian (1874–1937) Manager of the Old Vic from 1898 to her death. A single-hearted idealist, dumpy, demanding, honest, with an intimidatingly sharp glance, she attracted unfailing loyalty. She is a modern legend of the stage. Her theatre and its history, in particular its later Shakespeare, remain as her memorial. CH, 1929.

Bellamy, George Anne (*c.*1727–88) An Irish-born actress, she would have been called Georgina but the name was misheard at her christening. She played Juliet (to ▷Garrick), Cordelia and Lady Macbeth, Portia and Constance, and appeared to live her turbulent private life in public.

Bennett, Vivienne (1905–78) Trained as a dancer, she became an actress of extreme intelligence, grace and dignity, with a snow-crystal enunciation. She had two Old Vic seasons (1935–6), especially Rumour** (*Henry IV, Part 1*), Desdemona, Ophelia*** (to ▷Maurice Evans), Lady Macbeth and Hermione**. At Stratford (1939) she was Beatrice, Rosalind and Katharina; and in later years, on other stages, she appeared as Paulina and Titania.

Bensley, Robert (1742–1817) A famous late-eighteenth-century Malvolio in London. Charles Lamb said that he looked, spoke and moved "like an old Castilian".

Benson, Frank (Francis Robert) (1858–1939) Much-loved actor-manager in his Shakespeare touring company – for many years a university of the theatre – and from 1886 to 1919, with few breaks, director of the Stratford-upon-Avon "festivals". Visionary and chivalrous leader; on his night he could be a superb actor, as in his Richard II*** (from 1896), though his quality could vary like a fever-chart. His work for the stage has been obscured by silly apocryphal stories (usually about an obsession with sport). Knighted at Theatre Royal, Drury Lane, after playing Julius Caesar during the Shakespeare tercentenary performance, May 1916.

Benthall, Michael (1919–74) Responsively imaginative pictorial director whose work has been underrated. Nine years at the Old Vic, including the complete First Folio sequence (1953–8), which he shared with other directors. CBE, 1960.

Bernhardt, Sarah (1844–1923) The great French actress appeared as Hamlet in London (1899) in the Morand-Schwob translation. Max Beerbohm was scornful; for Maurice Baring it was "the ultimate triumph of intelligence".

Betterton, Thomas (c.1635–1710) Principal actor of the Restoration period. Short-necked, pock-marked and inclined to plumpness, he had high tragic power. Pepys thought his Hamlet*** "beyond imagination". ▷Colley Cibber said: "He made the Ghost equally terrible to the spectators as himself." Applauded also as Lear, Othello, Hotspur. Offstage he was not a particularly appealing figure. Married to ▷Mary Sanderson.

Betty, William Henry West (1791–1874) Described as the Young Roscius, he was a likeable, precocious child from Ulster, who appeared at Covent Garden and Drury Lane during 1804–6 in a variety of adult leading parts (Hamlet and Macbeth among them). For a short period he was a cult – but it is untrue, as it has been said, that the House of Commons was adjourned so that Members could see his Hamlet. The fashion for "Infant Phenomena" – there were others – waned rapidly. Though he went back to the stage after going up to Cambridge, Betty was an average, run-of-the-mill provincial actor until his early retirement.

Bland, Joyce (1906–63) An actress of unforced truth, most of whose work in Shakespeare was during four Stratford seasons, the last in 1939. Juliet (1930) and Hermione (1937) live in the mind.

Bloom, Claire (b.1931) A very young Ophelia at Stratford (1948). Magical in Juliet's early rapture (Old Vic, 1952), she could not take the part into tragedy.

Booth, Barton (1681–1733) ▷Betterton's successor as leading tragedian; celebrated for his stage "attitudes". Aaron Hill, the dramatist, said of this balanced actor that at his most expressive, "the blind might have seen him in his voice, and the deaf have heard him in his visage".

Booth, Edwin (1833–93) Son of ▷Junius Brutus Booth, and head of the later nineteenth-century American stage; a magnificent tragic actor, especially as a patrician and spiritual Hamlet***. Booth, who alternated Othello and Iago with ▷Irving at the Lyceum, London (1881), was a dreamer and a hereditary melancholic.

Booth, Junius Brutus (1796–1852) English-born actor, with a grand swell of voice to suit his physique, he founded the Booth dynasty of the American theatre; a sinister Richard III. Father of ▷Edwin Booth, and of John Wilkes Booth (1839–65) who assassinated Abraham Lincoln in a Washington theatre.

Bourchier, Arthur (1863–1927) One of the founders of the Oxford University Dramatic Society, later a London manager. An uncompromising Henry VIII for ▷Tree (His Majesty's 1910). Vain and irritable, he could be a sound, flamboyant player. His first wife was ▷Violet Vanbrugh.

Bracegirdle, Anne (c.1673–1748) A Restoration actress of much beauty. Beginning as a child (▷Thomas Betterton and his wife adopted her), she later played such Shakespearian parts as Ophelia, Desdemona and Mistress Ford. She retired at thirty-four.

Bradley, A.C. (Andrew Cecil) (1851–1935) Professor of Poetry at Oxford (1901–6) and the author of *Shakespearean Tragedy* (1904), an influential and still exciting analysis of *Hamlet, Othello, King Lear* and *Macbeth.*

Bridges-Adams, W. (William) (1889–1965) Among the most talented and personally modest Shakespeare directors of the twentieth century, he followed ▷Benson at Stratford (1919), working in the old theatre until the fire of 1926, in a cinema during the 'interregnum' (1926–31), and at the present theatre (1932–4). His productions in an unusually full text – he was known as "Unabridges" – were rapid, never exhibitionist, and always unified by the sagacity apparent in his book, *The Irresistible Theatre* (1957) and the selected letters edited by ▷Robert Speaight (1971). CBE, 1960.

Brook, Peter (b.1925) "The youngest earthquake I know," said ▷Sir Barry Jackson in 1946. Since then Brook has become the most important and invigorating director in the international theatre, often contentious but celebrated for such productions as *Love's Labour's Lost* (Stratford, 1946, in Watteau décor), *Measure for Measure* (Stratford, 1950), *The Winter's Tale* (Phoenix, London, 1951), his rediscovery of the least-regarded tragedy, *Titus Andronicus* (Stratford, 1955), the Beckettian *King Lear* (Stratford, 1962), *A Midsummer Night's Dream*, with its circus elements (Stratford, 1970), *Timon of Athens* (at his Paris theatre, the Bouffes-du-Nord, 1974), and *Antony and Cleopatra* (Stratford/Aldwych, 1978–9). CBE, 1965.

Brown, Ivor (1891–1974) Surest and most logical drama critic of his generation, he also edited the *Observer*, 1942–8. His biography, *Shakespeare* (1949), contained an eloquent answer to anti-Stratfordians. CBE, 1957.

Brown, Pamela (1917–75) Though this fine and often curiously enigmatic actress was in Shakespeare too infrequently, she is remembered for her lisping Cressida** at Stratford (1936) when she was eighteen. Other generally acclaimed parts were Ophelia (New, 1944) and Goneril (New, 1946).

Bruce, Brenda (b.1918) Highly professional actress who had done little Shakespeare before joining the RSC in 1964. Splendid Nurse (Stratford, 1980).

Bryant, Michael (b.1928) A good actor, with a method deceptively quiet, he appeared at the National as Jaques** (1979) and Iago (1980).

Burbage, Richard (*c.*1567–1619) Son of the joiner, James Burbage (*c.*1530–97), who in Shoreditch erected the first purpose-built English theatre. Richard created – we must believe remarkably – such characters as Hamlet, Othello and Lear at the Globe on Bankside. He was broad-featured with a high forehead and an authoritative gaze.

Burton, Richard (b.1925) A Welsh actor, familiar in films, who played several parts at Stratford (1951, a slow, absorbed Henry V) and at the Old Vic between 1953 and 1956. There he was a serviceable Hamlet, a part he repeated in New York (1964) – this time in casual modern dress – under ▷John Gielgud's direction. CBE, 1970.

Byam Shaw, Glen *see* **Shaw, Glen Byam**

Byford, Roy (1873–1939) A large and zestful comedian at Stratford for several seasons in the 1920s and 1930s. In the opening productions of the present theatre (1932) he could play Falstaff*** without padding.

Calhern, Louis (1895–1956) American leading actor who, after a long career in a variety of commanding modern parts, had one major Shakespeare attempt, King Lear, New York, 1950.

Call, Edward Payson (b.1928) At American festivals and regional theatres, away from New York, he has directed such plays as *As You Like It* (1966) and *Julius Caesar* (1969) at the Guthrie, Minneapolis; *Troilus and Cressida* (1976), at the Globe, San Diego, California, with a few arguable innovations; and the sequence of *Richard II*, the two *Henry IVs*, and *Henry V*, at Antioch, California.

Campbell, Douglas (b.1922) Burly, Scottish-born actor, son-in-law of ▷Lewis Casson and ▷Sybil Thorndike – his wife is the actress Ann Casson – he has played Falstaff and Macbeth, and directed much Shakespeare, particularly in many seasons at Stratford, Ontario.

Campbell, Mrs Patrick (1865–1940) Though not naturally a Shakespearian, this dark Italianate beauty whom ▷Shaw called "perilously bewitching" acted several of the parts in a tumultuous, idiosyncratic career. They varied between an unlikely Juliet (1895) and a Lady Macbeth (1898), which A.B. Walkley (*The Times*) said had a "mysterious, sensuous charm". Each of these was with ▷Forbes-Robertson. She was Lady Macbeth again (Aldwych, 1920) to the Macbeth of the American, ▷James K. Hackett.

Carey, Denis (b.1909) Director and actor, Irish-born, who has staged acutely several of the plays at Bristol Old Vic and the Old Vic, London (a lyrical *Two Gentlemen of Verona*, 1952), at Stratford-upon-Avon, and the Stratford, Connecticut theatre (of which in 1955 he was first director). Married to the actress Yvonne Coulette.

Carnovsky, Morris (b.1897) An American actor of much sensibility, once a leader of the Theatre Guild in New York. He came notably to Shakespeare in 1956 when he joined the Stratford, Connecticut company, and in ensuing years acted such parts as Shylock (1957), Claudius (1958), and Prospero (1960). His Lear (1963, 1965) had "pathos and majesty, senility and strength, balanced in exactly the right proportions" (▷Robert Speaight).

Cass, Henry (b.1902) Directed the Old Vic company, 1934–6, in seasons that included a *Richard II* and *Hamlet*, each with ▷Maurice Evans.

Casson, Lewis (1875–1969) Welsh-born husband of ▷Dame Sybil Thorndike. A director with an "essentially musical approach", as ▷Robert Speaight put it, influenced by ▷Poel and ▷Granville Barker. Among his productions were *Macbeth* (Princes, 1926) and *Coriolanus* (Old Vic, 1938). An actor of austere honesty as Banquo (1926), Kent (Old Vic, 1940) and much else. Drama Director, Arts Council, 1942–5. Knighted, 1945.

Cellier, Frank (1884–1948) A virile actor of much virtuosity, he played several of the major parts. Remembered for Henry IV (*Henry IV, Part 2*, Court, 1921), a raging Ford (Stratford, 1923), and what was called "a masterly shell" of Quince** (Kingsway, 1923; Drury Lane, 1924).

Chambers, Edmund (1866–1953) Scholar whose *William Shakespeare: A Study of Facts and Problems* (2 vols, 1930) is an impressive compilation, more than a bare repository. Knighted, 1925.

Church, Tony (b.1930) Richly versatile actor, principally with Royal Shakespeare Company, in such parts as King Lear (1974), Ulysses (1976), Armado** (1973, 1975, 1979).

Cibber, Colley (1671–1757) Dramatist, manager, actor, and eventually an inferior Poet Laureate (1730 until death); author of a shrewdly delightful discursive autobiography, *An Apology for the*

Life of Mr Colley Cibber, Comedian (1740). Pale and meagre in aspect, he could play fops with address and had a way with villains (Iago, Richard III). He made the ultra-theatrical version of *Richard III* that held the stage until well into the nineteenth century.

Cibber, Susannah (1714–66) Colley's daughter-in-law and sister of the English composer, Dr Arne. Played Ophelia with ▷Garrick. Unhappily married to the extravagant and ruthless Theophilus Cibber, an actor, as his second wife.

Clive, Kitty (Catherine) (1711–85) A heartily robust Drury Lane comedienne, whose desire to play tragic parts ▷David Garrick wisely repressed. She was Catherine in *Catherine and Petruchio*, Garrick's version of *The Taming of the Shrew*. Hogarth often painted her. "The Comic Muse with her retired," wrote Horace Walpole at her death.

Clunes, Alec (1912–70) Sensitive but resolute actor prominent at the Old Vic during the mid-1930s and at Stratford (1939, 1957). Honoured for eleven years of London management at the Arts Theatre Club. His parts included Coriolanus and Benedick (Stratford, 1939), Hamlet (Arts, 1943), Henry V (Old Vic, 1951), Claudius*** (Phoenix, 1955), Caliban (Stratford and Drury Lane, 1957).

Coleridge, Samuel Taylor (1772–1834) English poet and critic, whose *Biographia Literaria* (1817) and the posthumously published *Literary Remains*, collected in various editions, hold the most valuable Shakespeare criticism of the Romantic period.

Collier, Constance (1878–1955) Actress who used the grand manner and her deep contralto as Cleopatra** (to ▷Tree's Antony) at His Majesty's, 1906. She played much with Tree in London, and as Mistress Ford to his Falstaff in New York (1916). Gertrude to ▷John Barrymore's Hamlet (Haymarket, 1925).

Compton, Fay (1894–1978) Christened Virginia Lilian Emmeline. An admired and beautiful English actress of vast experience, who had no official recognition. She was Ophelia to the Hamlets of ▷John Barrymore (1925), ▷Godfrey Tearle (1931) and ▷John Gielgud (1939). ▷James Agate wrote of the first: "It was fragrant, wistful, and had a child's importunacy unmatched in my time."

Condell, Henry (d.1627) Elizabethan and Jacobean actor – he may have been Horatio in *Hamlet* – who, with ▷John Heminges, sponsored the First Folio of Shakespeare's plays (1623), assembled "without ambition either of self profit or fame; only to keep the memory of so worthy a friend and fellow alive, as was our Shakespeare." In his will Shakespeare left Condell 26s 8d to buy a memorial ring.

Cooke, George Frederick (1756–1812) An actor of bold, rough power, who ruined himself with audiences in London – where he appeared first when forty-four – by his grossly excessive intemperance. He played in America for two years before his death. Cooke had a square, hook-nosed face, wide mouth and glinting eyes set wide apart; his voice was sharp and strong. Renowned as Richard III, Shylock and Iago.

Cornell, Katharine (1898–1974) The nonpareil of American Juliets*** (she first played the part in 1933). Cleopatra in the New York revival, 1947. Her husband was the director Guthrie McClintic (d.1961).

Courtenay, Tom (b.1937) English actor of quietly concentrated personality. He appeared with the Old Vic (1960–1), and his Hamlet (Edinburgh Festival, 1968) was affectingly vulnerable.

Cowl, Jane (1890–1950) American actress, remembered now for her fresh and passionate Juliet (Henry Miller, New York, 1923) in a long-running production that contained fifteen scene-breaks. Her other Shakespeare parts were Cleopatra (Lyceum, New York, 1924) and a Viola (in Andrew Leigh's production, Maxine Elliott, 1930) that was both pictorially and emotionally right.

Craig, Edward Gordon (1872–1966) Son of ▷Ellen Terry and E.W. Godwin, acted for nine years in Irving's Lyceum company. Later became the twentieth century's most debated stage designer, though his influence was felt primarily out of Britain, from which he was long self-exiled. Unbiddable and unpractical, preoccupied with theory and unfair to the actor, Craig was what ▷Granville Barker called "supreme master in a theatre of the clouds". He never ceased to fight against the naturalistic stage, always advocating simplification and symbolic form.

Cronyn, Hume (b.1911) Canadian-born, American-trained actor of redoubtable technique who had done hardly any Shakespeare until he appeared as Hamlet, on tour (1949). Sixteen years later he received an award for his Polonius in the ▷Gielgud production (New York, 1964); next year he was Richard III at Minneapolis, and he has played Shylock and Bottom (1976) at Stratford, Ontario. Married to the actress ▷Jessica Tandy.

Cushman, Charlotte (1816–76) Strange and forcible American actress, mainly a tragedienne. An imperious Lady Macbeth, which she played to ▷Macready (they had a curious personal resemblance) in Philadelphia, 1843. Appeared as several of Shakespeare's women; also in male parts: Romeo to her sister Susan's Juliet (Haymarket, London, 1845), Hamlet and Wolsey.

Daly, Augustin (1839–99) American dramatist and manager, known as much in London as in New York (in each city a theatre bore his name). He was lucky to have in his sumptuous Shakespeare revivals so conspicuous an actress as ▷Ada Rehan: ▷Shaw admired her, but did not spare his wrath for Daly's treatment (London, 1895) of the texts of *The Two Gentlemen of Verona* and *A Midsummer Night's Dream*.

Dane, Clemence (1888–1965) Pseudonym of Winifred Ashton. A former actress and prolific emotional dramatist, her "invention", *Will Shakespeare* (1921), was an honourable failure, with its portrait of Shakespeare less persuasive than an overwhelming Queen Elizabeth. CBE, 1953.

Daneman, Paul (b.1925) An adaptable Shakespearian, with Birmingham Repertory experience (1950–2), he has played a good deal of Shakespeare, notably at the Old Vic (1953–5, 1957–8, 1961–2) where his parts varied between Shallow (*Henry IV, Part 2*), the Bastard* (*King John* 1961) and Richard III.

De Havilland, Olivia (b.1916) Sister of Joan Fontaine, and for many years a prominent Hollywood actress where she developed from such an early part as Hermia in Reinhardt's *A Midsummer Night's Dream* (1935) to a player of proved quality. She was Juliet to ▷Douglas Watson's Romeo, New York, 1951.

Dench, Judi (b.1934) Since her Old Vic Ophelia (1957), this startling actress, short of stature but mesmerically governing, has developed – in both tragedy and comedy – into one of the first classical players of her time. With the Old Vic (an impulsively young Juliet***, 1960), but usually with the RSC at Stratford and the Aldwych (Viola***, 1969, 1970, 1971; Hermione and Perdita***, 1969–70; Beatrice***, 1976–7; an uncanny Lady Macbeth***, 1976–8; Imogen***, 1979). Married to ▷Michael Williams. OBE, 1976.

Denison, Michael (b.1915) Expert and appealing actor, whose Shakespearian work has included the 1955 Stratford season (Lucius in the ▷Brook *Titus Andronicus*, Bertram in *All's Well That Ends Well*); Prospero and Malvolio (Open Air, 1972);

Malvolio (Old Vic, 1978). Married to the actress Dulcie Gray.

Devine, George (1910–66) Acted with ▷Gielgud during the 1930s, and at the Palace Theatre, 1955 (Gloucester and Dogberry). Made some effective Shakespeare productions, but known principally as the man who inspired the English Stage Company (Royal Court from 1956). CBE, 1957.

Devlin, William (b.1911) In his first professional season (1934), aged twenty-two, he brought to the Westminster a King Lear that needed only a more flexible voice. Afterwards, during a heavy Old Vic season (1935–6), he played Richard III and Leontes as well as Lear; he was Aufidius in the ▷Olivier *Coriolanus* (1938). Main postwar work at Bristol Old Vic, though he had other London Old Vic parts, and two years (1954–5) at Stratford.

Dewhurst, Colleen (b.1920) Talented American actress, Canadian-born. She has interspersed her authoritative work in modern plays (particularly O'Neill's) with such Shakespearean performances as Tamora (*Titus Andronicus*, 1956) and Lady Macbeth (1957), Cleopatra (1963), and Gertrude (1972) for the New York Shakespeare Festival.

Donat, Robert (1905–58) A ▷Benson-trained actor, with all the gifts, and a resolute perfectionist, he could have been a great Shakespearian. Unluckily, his career, divided between cinema and theatre, was thwarted by incurable asthma and attendant complications. Good in some complex modern parts, such as the two Camerons in James Bridie's *A Sleeping Clergyman*, he had little classical success. He was beset by vocal worries both in his decorative Romeo (for Old Vic on tour, 1939) and his last Shakespeare part, Benedick (Aldwych, 1946).

Doran, Charles (1877–1964) Reliable Irish actor, in youth trained by ▷Benson, his high period was 1920–9, when he toured as Hamlet, Macbeth, Shylock, Falstaff and much else with his own company. In its time this included the young ▷Ralph Richardson and ▷Donald Woolfitt (as he spelt it then).

Dotrice, Roy (b.1925) A felicitous protean actor, at Stratford played such parts as Caliban and a surprising double of the Duke of Bedford and Edward IV (*The Wars of the Roses*), all in 1963, and Hotspur and a faintly glimmering Shallow (*Henry IV, Part 2*) in 1964.

Dover Wilson, John *see* **Wilson, John Dover**

Dow, Ada (1847–1926) Remembered principally because, in the early 1880s, as sister of the owner of Cincinnati Opera House, she observed the promise of the girl (Sarah Frost), who became ▷Julia Marlowe. Rented a New York apartment, and (in Brooks Atkinson's words) devoted three years to body and mind training "and an unwavering discipline that only a fanatical young lady could have endured". Ultimately, she presented Julia, then nineteen, in *Ingomar*.

Drake, Fabia (b.1904) It is never forgotten in Stratford history how Fabia Drake's flashing speech in the small part of Lady Percy▷ (*Henry IV, Part 1*) animated the first performance at the present theatre (April 23, 1932). She joined the company in the autumn of 1929, playing half a dozen leading parts at three weeks' notice on the North American tour. Among much else at Stratford her Rosalind*** (1932) and, in the ▷Komisarjevsky productions, Portia (1932–3) and Lady Macbeth (1933) were prized.

Drew, John (1853–1927) Known as "the courtliest actor of his day", he was one of a celebrated stage group: Mrs John Drew was his mother, and he was the uncle of Lionel, ▷Ethel and ▷John Barrymore. The most complete of his few Shakespearian parts was Petruchio which he played (under the ▷Daly management) to the full-scale Kate of ▷Ada Rehan; they were in London, 1893.

Dryden, John (1631–1700) The Restoration master of a transient form, the "heroic drama" in rhymed couplets. Better recalled for his Antony-and-Cleopatra tragedy, *All For Love* (1677); less worthily for a glum perversion of *The Tempest* (1667), with Sir William Davenant.

Eddison, Robert (b.1908) A finely graced Shakespearian of splendidly diverse gifts, he has had many of the great parts, among them Hamlet (Bristol Old Vic, 1947; St James's, 1948), Macbeth (Old Vic, 1962), King Lear (with Actors' Company, 1973, also in New York). He gave his untarnished lyric quality to Pericles*** (Open Air, 1939), and his versions of Feste (for Old Vic at New, 1948; and for Prospect at Old Vic***, 1978) could govern the night.

Elliston, Robert (1774–1831) Actor and manager, handsome, elegant and eccentric, as good in tragic roles as in Falstaff. Charles Lamb said: "Wherever Elliston walked, sat, or stood still, there was the theatre."

Evans, Edith (1888–1976) Discovered as an amateur when ▷William Poel cast her as Cressida*** (King's Hall, Covent Garden, 1912; Stratford, 1913), she grew into an actress able to suggest beauty without being, in the conventional sense, beautiful, and fortunate in her gleaming, glissading speech. Shakespearian parts varied between the Rosalind*** of a sophisticated pastoral (Old Vic, 1937; New, 1938), her famous Juliet's Nurse*** (New, 1935), a bulky crone with a life beyond the theatre, and her Countess*** (Stratford, 1959). DBE, 1946.

Evans, Maurice (b.1901) English actor who, after a dazzling Old Vic season (1934–5), when he played Richard II*** and Hamlet in its entirety, went to New York and conquered again as Richard (1937). As a leading classical actor in the United States (of which he became a citizen in 1941) he appeared as Falstaff (*Henry IV, Part 1*), Hamlet, Malvolio and Macbeth.

Eytinge, Rose (1835?–1911) Nineteenth-century American actress, remembered for Ophelia, Desdemona, Lady Macbeth, as well as Beatrice (to ▷Lester Wallack's Benedick), and as Cleopatra (New York, 1877).

Farjeon, Herbert (1887–1945) Versatile and witty English grandson of the American actor Joseph Jefferson, he was respected alike as London drama critic, librettist of intimate revue, and editor of the Nonesuch Shakespeare. Probably his most lasting work on Shakespeare is the posthumous collection of essays, *The Shakespearian Scene* (London, 1949).

Farleigh, Lynn (b.1942) Acted for the RSC the most readily plausible Helena*** (*All's Well That Ends Well*) of her day (Aldwych, 1968).

Faucit, Helen (Helena) (1817–98) For some time ▷Macready's leading lady – the austere tragedian even wrote a poem to her – she gave her beauty and earnestness to such parts as Imogen and Hermione (both Covent Garden, 1837) and Cordelia (Covent Garden, 1838). Though she had officially left the stage, she returned as Beatrice on the opening night of the Shakespeare Memorial Theatre, Stratford (April 23, 1879). She married the author Sir Theodore Martin.

Fechter, Charles (1824–79) London-born of French parents, acted first and effectively in Paris, but spent several years in England. His flaxen-curled, romantic Hamlet (Princess's, 1861) had a tingling intelligence that defied his uncertain accent. Later he managed the Lyceum, and from 1869 ended his career in New York. Temperamental and difficult offstage, he could sway an audience.

Ffrangcon-Davies, Gwen (b.1896) She has played Juliet (Regent, 1924), Titania (Drury Lane, 1924), Lady Macbeth (with ▷John Gielgud, Piccadilly, 1942) and Queen Katharine (Stratford, 1950; Old Vic, 1953). Fragile, intense and able to hint at unearthliness. James Bridie, the dramatist, wrote of her much discussed Lady Macbeth: "She is a Pict . . . a real Highland Lady Macbeth, subtle, hysterical and bloody, and restrained."

Finney, Albert (b.1936) This Lancashire-born actor, stocky and direct, was a youthful plain-soldier Henry V (1957) and a determined Macbeth, each in his early twenties at Birmingham Repertory. He appeared at Stratford (1959) and played Hamlet and Macbeth for the National company. His Hamlet (Old Vic, 1975) was also the first in the new National building (Lyttelton, 1976). Likeable and of great stamina, he does lack the extra imaginative dimension.

Fleetwood, Susan (b.1944) Actress in the Royal Shakespeare Company (1967–9, 1972–5, 1980) and the National Theatre (from 1975), her freshness and unstrained pathos were sovereign. She doubled Marina and Thaisa***, daughter and mother, in the Stratford *Pericles* (1969) and was an enchanted Imogen*** (Stratford/Aldwych, 1974). Also Rosalind*** (Stratford, 1980).

Fletcher, Allen (b.1922) American director, much influenced by ▷Iden Payne, who between 1949 and 1976 directed thirty productions at Ashland, Oregon; on the Elizabethan stage of the Globe, San Diego; and in Stratford, Connecticut. In his *Lear* (with ▷Morris Carnovsky; Stratford, 1963) Goneril and Regan were interpreted from their own point of view, not their father's. His *Coriolanus* (1968) was admirably judged. In San Francisco (1976) he directed *Othello*.

Fletcher, John (1579–1625) Jacobean dramatist of romantic tragi-comedy, often in partnership (e.g. with Francis Beaumont or Philip Massinger). He is believed to have been Shakespeare's collaborator in *Henry VIII*, *The Two Noble Kinsmen* and a lost play, *Cardenio* (1613).

Fontanne, Lynn (b.1892) This exhilarating and superbly professional Broadway actress played little Shakespeare. Even so, the Lunts' *Taming of the Shrew* (Lynn Fontanne, Kate; ▷Alfred Lunt, Petruchio) at the Guild, New York, 1935 – revived at the Alvin, 1940 – was a pleasure described variously as "horseplay in a hayloft" and "a hilarious justification" of the liberties taken with it. At the end they rode off on a chariot into the clouds.

Forbes-Robertson, Jean (1905–62) ▷Sir Johnston's daughter. A grave, wistful, and other-worldly actress, her career faded unhappily when she was in her forties. But she left permanent memories of her Juliet (Old Vic, 1928), Viola** in the "black-and-white" production (New, 1932) and Oberon (Open Air, 1933).

Forbes-Robertson, Johnston (1853–1937) The most mellifluous English verse-speaker of his generation. Tall and ascetic in appearance, and not invariably a stirring actor, he had veracity, authority and a thoughtful sweetness of disposition. Identified especially with Hamlet (Lyceum, 1897), which he acted for his English farewell at Drury Lane (1913): "a sort of Sir Philip Sidney", said the critic, William Archer, who did not mention a certain stained-glass air Forbes-Robertson would never lose. His many parts included Leontes (Lyceum, 1887), Romeo (Lyceum, 1895), Othello (Lyceum, 1902). Knighted, 1913.

Forrest, Edwin (1806–72) American tragedian, strenuous, sombre and proud, a massive figure who appeared as Othello, Lear, Macbeth and Hamlet, and who was idolized by his public. Twice acted in London (1836, 1845). He conceived a violent hatred for ▷Macready that led to a dangerous feud and to the Astor Place riot (New York, 1849), when Macready, after playing Macbeth, had to escape for his life from an infuriated crowd.

Freedman, Gerald (b. 1927) Especially successful in his direction of more than a dozen plays for ▷Joseph Papp's New York Shakespeare Festival (of which he became artistic director, 1967); his work has included such relative rarities as *Titus Andronicus, All's Well That Ends Well, Timon of Athens.* In 1968 he directed Lee J. Cobb as Lear.

French, Leslie (b. 1904) In its mooncast mischief, his Puck*** (Old Vic, 1929; Open Air, many seasons) was definitive. Also played Ariel and Feste.

Garrick, David (1717–79) Only five feet four inches in height, of slight physique, with flexibly expressive features, compelling black eyes and a natural method new in its day, Garrick became his century's noblest actor and one of the most closely charted in stage record. Ready in tragedy and comedy, he excelled as Hamlet, King Lear***, Richard III*** (with which he made his London début in 1741), Macbeth and Benedick. Much of his career (he retired in 1776) was spent as manager of Drury Lane. "An abridgment of all that was pleasant in man," Oliver Goldsmith wrote of him. But also: "On the stage he was natural, simple, affecting, / 'Twas only when he was off, he was acting." Buried in Westminster Abbey.

Gielgud, John (b. 1904) One of the acting dynasty of the Terrys, ▷Ellen's grand-nephew. An actor of natural loftiness, devoted to his craft, Gielgud interprets Shakespeare with mind and nerves, remapping the verse, using his voice like a Stradivarius controlled by a master. He has been called the modern ▷Forbes-Robertson. They are comparable in voice and bearing, but Gielgud has far more passion and theatrical splendour. His supreme parts have been a patrician Hamlet*** (first at Old Vic, 1930), Richard II*** (also Old Vic, 1930), King Lear*** (first at Old Vic, 1931; notably at same theatre, 1940), Macbeth*** (Piccadilly, 1942), Benedick*** (Stratford, 1950; Phoenix, London, 1952; New York, 1959), Leontes*** (Phoenix, 1951), Prospero*** (particularly Old Vic for National company, 1974) and Caesar*** (National, 1977). Only Othello (Stratford, 1961), in an awkward ▷Zeffirelli production, has eluded him. Knighted, 1953. CH, 1977.

Godfrey, Derek (b. 1924) Through his career, with various seasons at the Old Vic and especially Stratford, he has been consistently reliable and intelligent. In his first Vic season (1956) he was a credible Iachimo*. Hector (1960 and 1962), Petruchio (1962) and Jaques** (1980) were among his best Stratford work.

Goring, Marius (b. 1912) A classical player from his early years in the theatre, he has run the Shakespeare gamut from Abhorson (Old Vic, 1933) to Richard III (Stratford, 1953).

Granville Barker, Harley *see* **Barker, Harley Granville**

Green, Dorothy (1886–1961) An admired classical actress with a beautiful contralto speaking voice. In her youth a prominent member of the ▷Benson company (appearing in America, 1913–14), she was known between the wars principally for her four seasons at Stratford and one at the Old Vic (1930–1), with John Gielgud. She acted most of the leading women in Shakespeare: her Cleopatra*** (last seen at the Old Vic, 1930) was famous, "disdaining the sexual pettinesses," said Bridges-Adams, "and showing us the terrifying images of *Vénus entière.*" She directed often.

Greet, Ben (1857–1936) An indifferent actor, but an affectionately regarded manager (never varying the instructions in his early prompt-books), who toured Shakespeare for many years in Britain and the United States, especially in the open air. He directed the still primitive Old Vic, 1914–18. Knighted (Sir Philip Ben Greet), 1929.

Griffith, Hugh (1912–80) Welsh actor of vehement power who had three Stratford seasons (1946, 1951, 1964). In the last of these his Falstaff** (*Henry IV,* both parts) was like a hirsute eagle with bright, darting eyes.

Guinness, Alec (b.1914) An actor of the most telling reserve who, in the 1930s, acted much with ▷Gielgud and at the Old Vic. Suddenly (Old Vic, 1938), at twenty-four, he became Hamlet in ▷Tyrone Guthrie's modern-dress version (with Ophelia's funeral in the rain). Though, because of technical mishaps, early excitement had waned when he played the part again in his own production (New, 1951), he had few other troubles and much achievement: Lear's Fool*** (New, 1946), wry, with a dog's devotion; a delicately judged Menenius (New, 1948); Richard III, and the King in *All's Well That Ends Well* at Stratford, Ontario, 1953. CBE, 1955. Knighted, 1959.

Guthrie, Tyrone (1900–71) An adventurous and greatly loved director, intellectual, independent and international. He always took his own course – unerringly as in *Measure for Measure* (Old Vic and Sadler's Wells, 1933), or *A Midsummer Night's Dream* (Old Vic, 1937); debatably, as in *Troilus and Cressida* (Old Vic, 1956), seen as a struggle between Ruritania and a coalition of Central European Powers, *c.*1913. In *All's Well That Ends Well* (Stratford, 1959) drastic surgery removed the clown Lavache and expanded a ten-line scene with irrelevant comic panoply. Guthrie was the virtual creator of the theatre at Stratford, Ontario. Knighted, 1961.

Hackett, James Henry (1800–71) American character actor, follower and imitator of ▷Kean (as in *Richard III*). Much praised for his contentious and sardonic Falstaff in the *Henry IV* plays and *The Merry Wives of Windsor.*

Hackett, James K. (1869–1926) ▷James Henry Hackett's son by his second wife. A romantic and pictorial actor, he was also Macbeth (New York, 1916; London, 1920, in badly cut text) and Othello (which he brought to Stratford, 1922).

Hall, Peter (b.1930) One of the Cambridge University group so important in British Shakespeare since 1960, he revised the policy of what under his direction (1960–8) became the Royal Shakespeare Theatre, and added a London base at the Aldwych. Made many expert Stratford productions and a few at the National, where in 1973 he succeeded ▷Laurence Olivier as director. "We want to be in a world of experiment," he said at Stratford (1963). CBE, 1963. Knighted, 1978.

Hampden, Walter (1879–1956) Born in New York, toured in England with ▷Benson (for whom he played seventy parts), and became a leading American classical actor. As an actor-manager, played Hamlet – twenty years since his London appearance in the part – Shylock and Othello (all in 1925). Profoundly experienced and basically forthright, he could grow over-analytical.

Hands, Terry (b.1941) Since 1966 this director's amplest work for the Royal Shakespeare Company has been in the histories, especially the trilogy of *Henry VI* (1977). A fussy *Twelfth Night* (1979). Joined ▷Trevor Nunn as RSC's joint artistic director.

Hannen, Nicholas (1881–1972) An actor of quiet aristocratic authority: Buckingham (Sadler's Wells, 1933); Gloucester (Old Vic, 1940), King Henry IV*** (in both parts, Old Vic at New, 1945), Kent (New, 1946). Married to ▷Athene Seyler.

Hardwicke, Cedric (1893–1964) Eminent at Birmingham Repertory, 1922–3; Iachimo in modern-dress (1923). A precise "character" man in London and later in New York, he had one Shakespearian success, Sir Toby** (New, for Old Vic company, 1948). Knighted, 1934.

Harris, Robert (b.1900) A moving and thoughtful Shakespearian who has returned regularly to the plays since his Drury Lane Oberon (1924). Played Hamlet at Old Vic, 1932; Richard II at Stratford, 1947.

Harris, Rosemary (b.1930) English actress respected for her close discernment as Cressida in ▷Guthrie's production (Old Vic, 1956), a tender Ophelia in the National company's opening *Hamlet* (Old Vic, 1963), and much Shakespearian playing in both England and, latterly, America.

Harrison, John (b.1924) Acted at Birmingham Repertory and (1946–7) Stratford; splendid verse-speaker. Directed at Nottingham, Birmingham (e.g. *Troilus and Cressida*), Bristol, and from 1972 Leeds Playhouse. His Leeds production of *The Tempest*, with Paul Scofield's Prospero, had a long London run at Wyndham's, 1975.

Hart, Charles (d.1683) A conscientious Restoration-period actor, especially in heroic tragedy. Played Hotspur, Othello, Brutus. Might have been the illegitimate son of William Hart, son of Joan Hart, Shakespeare's sister

Harvey, John Martin (1863–1944) Always, and in spite of his short stature, an assiduous, sometimes exciting romantic actor, who began with ▷Irving. Later, though as an actor-manager he could not escape identification with his creations in popular melodrama, he was a Richard III and a Petruchio, as well as a touching Hamlet (in several revivals after his first, Lyric, 1905), when he curiously resembled Van Dyck's self-portrait as a young man. Knighted, 1921.

Hayes, George (1888–1967) First worked with ▷Forbes-Robertson and ▷Tree. A magnetic player, inconsistent but astonishing on his night: Aaron*** (Old Vic, 1923); Richard II*** (Stratford, 1928–30); Hamlet, Feste***, Iago (1933); Macbeth (1933 and 1944). His Richard II was triumphant during the Stratford tour of North America in the winter of 1929–30.

Hayes, Helen (b.1900) In her time a leader of the American stage. An immensely generous and receptive actress, she has not done a lot in Shakespeare except Viola (▷Maurice Evans as Malvolio; New York, 1940) when she was less romantic than pathetic in ▷Margaret Webster's inventively baroque production. With Evans she acted (Stratford, Connecticut, 1962), and later toured, in *Shakespeare Revisited: a Programme for Two Players*.

Hazlitt, William (1778–1830) Essayist, and the first major drama critic, a capacity in which, as someone has said, he "invented" his most admired actor, ▷Edmund Kean. Wrote *The Characters of Shakespeare's Plays* (1817).

Helpmann, Robert (b.1909) An Australian who, after an acclaimed London career in ballet, turned to acting and direction. Choreograped *Hamlet* ballet, 1942; played Hamlet (Old Vic at New Theatre, 1944; Stratford, 1948). Directed and appeared at Old Vic during 1950s. Knighted, 1968.

Heminges, John (1556–1630) Actor and business manager in Shakespeare's company. Sponsored with ▷Condell the First Folio of 1623. Shakespeare bequeathed him 26s 8d for a memorial ring.

Henderson, John (1747–85) Actor, poet and musician. A redoubtable late-eighteenth-century Falstaff.

Hepburn, Katharine (b.1909) A gifted American actress. She had a largely Shakespearian decade, with moderate success, when she played Rosalind (New York, 1950), went on an Australian tour with the Old Vic (1955) as Portia, Isabella and Katharina, and had two seasons (1957 and 1960) at Stratford, Connecticut, as Portia, Beatrice, Viola and Cleopatra.

Hiller, Wendy (b.1912) English emotional actress who could express an infinite sorrow in her performance as Hermione (Old Vic, during 1955–6 season when she was also Emilia). Married to the dramatist Ronald Gow. DBE, 1975.

Holloway, Baliol (1883–1967) To read this actor's career is to be made free of the Shakespearian cast lists. In youth a loyal Bensonian, in later years he was familiar at Stratford, and the famous Old Vic season of 1925–6 owed as much to him as to ▷Edith Evans. Though he was inclined to multiply his pauses, his comedy could match his tragedy. Remembered for his Falstaff*** (*The Merry Wives of Windsor*) and his sardonic Richard III***. Proud and latterly neglected, he did not act in the theatre after 1949, a sad loss.

Holm, Ian (b.1931) Between 1958 and 1967 a valuable member of the Royal Shakespeare Company; a restrained Henry V (1964).

Hordern, Michael (b.1911) Though known for his amusing crane-fly studies in nervous agitation, he has been eloquent in such parts as Menenius*** (Stratford, 1952), Macbeth (Old Vic, 1958), Lear (Old Vic, for Nottingham Playhouse company, 1970), John of Gaunt (National at Old Vic, 1972) and Armado (Stratford, 1978). CBE, 1972.

Houseman, John (b.1902) Born Jacques Haussmann in Bucharest, Romania, educated in England, and working mainly in the United States, he has enjoyed a long and varied career as director, writer, producer and actor. He directed Leslie Howard as Hamlet (New York, 1936), produced – with ▷Orson Welles – the New York Mercury Theatre's modern-dress *Julius Caesar* (1937), and directed much Shakespeare in both New York and Stratford, Connecticut, where he served as artistic director from 1956 to 1959. In 1975 he formed a national travelling repertory theatre, The Acting Company, which grew out of his earlier work as director of the drama division of the Juillard School of Performing Arts.

Howard, Alan (b.1937) Among the most scholarly, sensitive and graceful of English classical players, his work in Shakespeare, principally for the RSC (Stratford and Aldwych from 1966), has included Hamlet (1970), the doubling of Theseus and Oberon*** (1970–1, ▷Peter Brook's production), Henry V*** (1975–6), Coriolanus*** (1977–8), Henry VI** (1977–8), Antony (in *Antony and Cleopatra*, (1978–9), Richard II and Richard III (1980).

Hudd, Walter (1898–1963) English actor of needle-point precision (Malvolio, Polonius), who played and directed at Stratford (1946–7), and was with the Old Vic company at the New (1949–50) and at the Vic itself (1959–60).

Hughes, Margaret (d.1719) She was Prince Rupert's mistress. She may also have been the first professional actress on the English stage, as Desdemona in a free version of *Othello* (December 8, 1660) at Vere Street, Clare Market, London. The prologue announced: "No man in gown or page in petticoat, / A woman to my knowledge..."

Hunt, Hugh (b.1911) He had two important periods of direction (Bristol Old Vic, 1945–8; Old Vic, London, 1949–53, seasons that began – when the company was at the New Theatre – with an atmospheric *Love's Labour's Lost****). Later he was first Professor of Drama at the University of Manchester, 1961–73.

Hunt, Leigh (1784–1859) Ranks with ▷Hazlitt as one of the first major English drama critics and, especially, connoisseurs of acting. "To know an actor personally," he said, "appeared to me to be a vice not to be thought of."

Huston, Walter (1884–1950) Canadian-born, this forcible actor and fine technician was on the American stage for more than forty years. He played Othello at Colorado City in 1934 and repeated it three years later in New York (a low-keyed production designed and directed by Robert Edmond Jones).

Hutt, William (b.1920) Canadian classical actor, known principally for his long fruitful association with the Stratford, Ontario, theatre, where he has played Prospero, Richard II, Lear and much else.

Ireland, William (1775–1835) An audacious lawyer's clerk, who forged many "Shakespeare" documents (which were exposed by ▷Edmond Malone). He also wrote what he claimed to be a lost play by Shakespeare, *Vortigern* (1796); it had one disastrous Drury Lane performance.

Irving, H.B. (1870–1919) ▷Henry Irving's elder son. He acted many of his father's parts, suffering inevitably from the comparison, though as Hamlet, for example (London, 1905 and 1917), he was a wise, urgent player in his own right. Married to the actress Dorothea Baird.

Irving, Henry (1838–1905) The late-Victorian actor-manager, born John Henry Brodribb; an extraordinary theatrical figure, the first English actor to be knighted (1895), and one who, in spite of mannerisms of speech and gait, developed a grandeur and hypnotic intensity unexampled in his day. It was said of him that his voice, "muffled-bright", used to fork like lightning through mist. Haunted and haunting (possibly influenced by his early childhood with relations in a then bleakly remote Cornwall), he has always had his detractors; but his twenty years' management of the Lyceum must live in stage history, with such performances as his gentle, immensely sympathetic Hamlet***, a proud Shylock***, Benedick*** (with a quality that ▷Robert Speaight has called "the tang of a patrician amontillado") and Cardinal Wolsey***. ▷Ellen Terry was his leading lady.

Irving, Laurence (1871–1914) ▷Sir Henry Irving's younger son, and possibly a more exciting actor than his brother ▷H.B. Irving. His early Justice Shallow (*Henry IV, Part 2*, Manchester, 1894) and a coldly malign Iago (with ▷Tree, His Majesty's, 1912) were sharply right in their different ways. He was drowned with his wife, the actress Mabel Hackney, when the liner *Empress of Ireland* sank in the Gulf of St Lawrence in 1914.

Jackson, Barry (1879–1961) Enlightened theatre manager and philanthropist, who founded the Birmingham Repertory (1913). During its first fifty years every play in the First Folio, plus *Pericles*, was staged, and many leading players (e.g. ▷Laurence Olivier, ▷Paul Scofield, ▷Margaret Leighton) appeared there in youth. Jackson's bold Shakespearian experiments – in London as well as Birmingham – included the modern-dress *Hamlet* (Kingsway, 1925). Directed Shakespeare Memorial Theatre, 1946–8. Knighted, 1925.

Jackson, Nagle (b.1936) Artistic director (1971–7) of the Ashland Shakespeare Festival, Oregon. Influenced by ▷Iden Payne and ▷Allen Fletcher, he worked on a wide range of plays (including *Pericles* and *Richard II*). He also staged *Richard II* and *King Lear* at Milwaukee.

Jacobi, Derek (b.1938) An actor of compelling sincerity who, after his professional début at Birmingham Repertory Theatre (1960–3), had eight years with the National company at the Old Vic (Laertes in the opening *Hamlet*, 1963). For the Prospect (later the revived Old Vic) company he played Pericles (1973–4, with a season at Her Majesty's), and Hamlet (Old Vic; also, during 1979, at Elsinore).

James, Emrys (b.1930) Mannered but compelling, this Welsh actor has done a lot for the RSC, especially Feste, Iago and (Stratford/Aldwych, 1977–8) Richard of York** in the three parts of *Henry VI*.

Jameson, Pauline (b. 1920) Actress of much grace and presence, whose Shakespearian career has moved between Mistress Page (Stratford, Ontario, 1956) and Regan (for the RSC, 1964–5, and in New York).

Jefford, Barbara (b. 1930) Among the few players of her generation who in power, poise, and depth of voice, have achieved the grand manner. Since 1950, at Stratford, the Old Vic and the National, she has played thirty Shakespearian parts, notably Isabella *** (Stratford, 1950; Old Vic, 1957), Cleopatra *** (especially Old Vic, 1978), Viola and Rosalind. Wife of the actor John Turner.

Johnson, Richard (b. 1927) A classical actor, particularly for the RSC, who has been Romeo and Pericles (Stratford, 1958) and the Antony of *Antony and Cleopatra* (Stratford/Aldwych, 1972–3).

Jones, James Earl (b. 1931) Black American actor of splendid temperament and physique, who has played more than a dozen Shakespeare parts, among them Oberon (1961), Caliban and Morocco (1962), Othello (1964), Macbeth (1966), and King Lear (1973) for the New York Shakespeare Festival. He was again an Othello of size and passion (1971) at the Mark Taper Forum, San Francisco.

Jonson, Ben (1572–1637) His Westminster Abbey tombstone is inscribed "O rare Ben Jonson." Quarrelsome, dogmatic, an unwilling bricklayer turned soldier, and later as a dramatist second only to Shakespeare in the late Elizabethan and Jacobean theatre, his superlative gifts were expressed in such satirical comedies as *Volpone* (1606) and *The Alchemist* (1610), true or wilfully distorting. He wrote the great valediction to Shakespeare, as "Sweet Swan of Avon", that appears in the First Folio.

Jordan, Dorothy (Dorothea) (1762–1816) Her private life was extravagantly scandalous; mistress for twenty years of the Duke of Clarence, later King William IV, she bore him ten children. In public she was a marvellous comedienne (with a laugh like "bubbles of sparking water"). Rosalind and Imogen were among her Drury Lane parts.

Kahn, Michael New York-born director with more than a dozen productions at Stratford, Connecticut, since 1967: among them *Richard II*, *Love's Labour's Lost* (1968), *Othello*, *All's Well That Ends Well* (1970), *Macbeth* (1972), *The Winter's Tale* (1974). Became artistic director at Stratford, 1969.

Keach, Stacy (b.1941) Born at Savannah, Georgia, he has had a packed record, appearing in Shakespeare on many stages and using an exceptional voice and intellect in such parts as Falstaff (both *Henry IV*s, 1968) and Edmund (*King Lear*, also 1968) for the New York Shakespeare Festival; and Hamlet (New Haven, 1971; New York Shakespeare Festival, 1972; Mark Taper Forum, 1974).

Kean, Charles (1811–68) Entirely unlike his father ▷Edmund (who had him educated at Eton), Charles Kean was merely an average actor, though a master of spectacular stage effects and a pedantic antiquarian. He showed these qualities during his Shakespeare revivals at the Princess's, London (1851–9). Married to the actress Ellen Tree.

Kean, Edmund (1787–1833) A tempestuous figure, small in

stature, he could appear larger than life-size while possessing the stage of Drury Lane as the overwhelming tragedian of the "Romantic" period. Coming to London (1814) from the drudgery of a strolling player, he startled his audience with the full-scale villainy of his Shylock***. We now think of Kean (who held the devotion of the day's leading drama critic, Hazlitt) in such parts as Richard III***, Othello*** and Macbeth. His life was wild, and some critics reasonably suspect that in his playing there were passages of impenetrable darkness between the "flashes of lightning" that astonished ▷Coleridge. He remains a cometary legend.

Keene, Laura (d.1873) English-born actress and the first woman theatre manager in the United States. There is a variation of sixteen years in several dates proposed for her birth (1830 or 1836 are most likely), and her real name is unknown. In 1855 she settled in New York, opened her own theatre in 1857 (until 1863) and played Rosalind there efficiently. She was well known on tour.

Kemble, Charles (1775–1854) Youngest brother of ▷Sarah Siddons and ▷John Philip Kemble and father of ▷Fanny Kemble, he was primarily a comedian. Also celebrated as, successively Romeo*** (1803 onwards) and Mercutio. Ended his career as Examiner of Plays.

Kemble, Fanny (Frances Anne) (1809–93) ▷Charles Kemble's daughter, she saved her father's Covent Garden venture from collapse by her unexpected triumph as an actress, beginning with a Juliet (1829), radiant in aspect as in performance. She also played Beatrice and Portia. Leaving the stage in 1834, after comparable American success, she married, unhappily, Pierce Butler, a plantation owner of Philadelphia, whom she ultimately divorced. Returning to the stage, she toured the English provinces and acted (1848) with ▷Macready in London, experiences described in her *Records of Later Life* (1882).

Kemble, John Philip (1757–1823) "His was the spell o'er hearts/That only Acting lends", wrote Thomas Campbell in an ode on Kemble's retirement, 1817. A stately, handsome actor in the grand style, who in his time managed both Drury Lane and Covent Garden (at each of which he appeared with his sister, ▷Sarah Siddons). Among his prized Shakespearian parts were Coriolanus***, Wolsey, and what Hazlitt honoured as a "sensible, lonely Hamlet".

Kempe, William (d.after 1603) Broad comedian who, from 1594 to 1599, acted with Shakespeare in the Lord Chamberlain's Men and probably created Dogberry. ▷Robert Armin, an altogether different type, followed him in the company. For a bet Kempe morris-danced from London to Norwich in a month during the spring of 1600 and wrote a book about it.

Kendal, Madge (1848–1935) Twenty-second child of a provincial manager, William Robertson, and sister of T.W. Robertson, the dramatist, she was an intimidating woman but a praised actress, primarily a comedienne. She played Rosalind (St James's, 1885) and Mistress Ford (with ▷Tree and ▷Ellen Terry, His Majesty's, 1902). Married to a competent actor, W.H. Kendal (his real name was Grimston), with whom she appeared through most of her career. They retired in 1908, and he died in 1917. DBE, 1926; GBE, 1927.

Kittredge, George Lyman (1861–1941) Famous Shakespearian scholar and editor, who taught at Harvard for nearly fifty years, and whom innumerable undergraduates knew as "Kitty".

Knox, Alexander (b.1907) Ontario-born, he has appeared often in London where he was stalwart and resourceful at the Old Vic,

1937–8. In 1940 he was the Friar (*Romeo and Juliet*) for ▷Laurence Olivier in New York; he returned to the Vic (1953) as Wolsey. He has worked a great deal in Hollywood and written effective novels.

Kohler, Estelle (b.1940) South African actress of clarity and emotional truth, who has played Ophelia (1966), Juliet (1967, 1973) and Isabella (1970) at Stratford.

Komisarjevsky, Theodore (1882–1954) Of Russian birth, he was recognized for twenty years – between the two world wars – as the most individual, sometimes bizarre, director in Britain. An invaluable Chekhovian, he was less at ease with fantasticated Shakespeare, though he directed much, especially at Stratford in the 1930s: in particular, the "aluminium" *Macbeth* (1933) set in scrolled aluminium screens, and the "staircase" *King Lear* (1936), a repetition, with a professional cast, of his Oxford revival (1927) on an arrangement of variously levelled narrow steps. For a time he was married to ▷Peggy Ashcroft.

Kynaston, Edward (*c.*1640–1706) In the Restoration period among the last boy players of women, he was what Pepys called "the loveliest lady that ever I saw". In maturity, a splendid Mark Antony and Henry IV.

Lacey, Catherine (1904–79) Small in physique, but never a miniaturist in interpretation, she gave some exquisite performances at Stratford (1935, 1967) and the Old Vic (1962–3). During each of her Stratford seasons she acted the Countess in *All's Well That Ends Well*, and she was Helena in the wartime revival of the same play at the Vaudeville (1940).

Lamb, Charles (1775–1834) Endearing critic and essayist, who with his sister Mary wrote the *Tales from Shakespeare* (1807), usually spoken of as "Lamb's Tales".

Lang, Matheson (1879–1948) ▷Benson-trained, he was later a popular actor-manager who rarely had the full critical consideration he deserved. Played Romeo (Lyceum, 1908) and Hotspur (for ▷Tree, His Majesty's, 1914); and as a manager (New, 1920), an Othello*** regarded by sound judges as the best of its period, though he never revived it after a matinée season.

Langtry, Lillie (1853–1929) Less regarded as an actress than as a fashionable, amorous beauty ("the Jersey Lily"), she appeared in London as Rosalind (1882, 1890) and Cleopatra (1890).

Laughton, Charles (1899–1961) Yorkshire-born and later an American citizen, he was an uncanny character actor, principally in films, though too seldom on terms with Shakespeare. As a young man, large, flabby and dominating (Vic/Wells, 1933–4), he had one triumph, Angelo***, a shivering glance at a cankered mind ("the right snow-broth for blood," said ▷Ivor Brown in the *Observer*), but he failed as Prospero, for him a kind of sinister Father Christmas, and in much of Macbeth. He returned to Shakespeare at Stratford-upon-Avon (1959) as Bottom, and as a Lear with a quick, gravelly voice, lacking the ultimate emotional drive. Married to Elsa Lanchester, who was a magical Old Vic Ariel*** (1933).

Laurie, John (1897–1980) A Scottish actor, as protean and spirited a Shakespearian as any of his generation (Old Vic, 1922–5, 1928–9; Stratford, 1925, 1927, 1939; Open Air, 1933–5, and much else). Hamlet on several occasions (first at Stratford, 1927). At Stratford (1939) he was a Malvolio consumed by a wintry ambition and by gout.

Le Gallienne, Eva (b.1899) Daughter of the English poet, Richard le Gallienne, she did not reach Shakespeare during her dedicated and fruitful American career as actress and manager until she played Viola at her own Civic Repertory Theatre, New

York (1927); she would also appear there as Juliet. When she disbanded her theatre after seven years she continued primarily as an intellectual player and returned sometimes to Shakespeare (Queen Katharine, 1946, with ▷Walter Hampden, for the short-lived American Repertory Theatre she founded with ▷Margaret Webster). At Stratford, Connecticut (1970) she was the Countess in *All's Well That Ends Well*.

Leigh, Andrew (1887–1957) A calm, relaxed actor and a resourceful Shakespearian clown. Trained with ▷Benson, and (1914) was a member of the first Shakespeare company at the Old Vic, where he directed (1925–9). Played at Stratford (particularly 1937–41) and the Open Air Theatre.

Leigh, Vivien (1913–67) Second wife of ▷Laurence Olivier. Played Ophelia to his Hamlet at Elsinore (1937). A delicately beautiful actress, whose small-scale Cleopatra (St James's, 1951, during Olivier's management) and Lady Macbeth (Stratford, 1955) were insufficiently acknowledged at the time; they had an intelligence that can be recollected in tranquility.

Leighton, Margaret (1922–76) One of ▷Barry Jackson's Birmingham Repertory discoveries. Tall and glowingly fair, she acted with the Old Vic company (at the New, 1944–7, as Regan to Olivier's Lear), and at Stratford (1952) as a Rosalind of irresistible raillery, and an Ariel*** described by a critic as a silver arrow. Enid Bagnold, the dramatist, called her "an extraordinary and shining woman, astonished at success". Her second husband was the actor Laurence Harvey, and her third the actor Michael Wilding.

Lunt, Alfred (1892–1977) With his wife, ▷Lynn Fontanne, he shared in one of the most-loved partnerships of the American theatre ("the Lunts"). They did one Shakespeare revival, *The Taming of the Shrew* (1935; Lunt as Petruchio***), remembered as the most high-spirited of its period.

McCarthy, Lillah (1875–1960) ▷Granville Barker's first wife, she acted Hermione, Viola and Helena (*A Midsummer Night's Dream*) for him at the Savoy, 1912–14. Sonorous and statuesque in later years, when she married and became Lady Keeble.

McCowen, Alec (b.1925) An actor of swiftly developing talent and range: a waspish Malvolio (Old Vic, 1960), the Fool in ▷Brook's revival of *King Lear* (Stratford, 1962), Antipholus of Syracuse** in *The Comedy of Errors* (Stratford, 1962), Hamlet at Birmingham Repertory (1970).

McCullough, John E. (1832–85) An Irish-born immigrant to the United States, aged fifteen, McCullough trained himself to act, became ▷Edwin Forrest's second lead, ran the California Theatre at San Francisco, and toured until illness obliged him to retire (1884). Physically dominating, powerfully melodramatic in style, and honoured for his goodwill, he acted such parts on tour as Lear (also New York, 1877), Coriolanus (New York, 1878) and Othello.

McEwan, Geraldine (b.1932) A witty, fragile actress, whose Olivia** in one of her three Stratford seasons (1958) cooed divertingly through *Twelfth Night*.

McKellen, Ian (b.1939) A practised Shakespearian, who can be magnetically true when he sheds his mannerisms (as in *Richard II*** for the Prospect company, London, 1969–70). He has played Hamlet (Cambridge Theatre, London, 1971) and a contentious RSC Macbeth (Stratford/London, 1976–8). Was Sir Thomas More in the second known professional revival (Nottingham, 1964) of the anonymous play to which Shakespeare may have contributed. CBE, 1979.

Macklin, Charles (*c.*1700–97) Irish actor and dramatist, turbulent and generous offstage. His fame rests on Shylock*** ("This is the Jew that Shakespeare drew," exclaimed the poet Pope), in which at Drury Lane (1741) he lifted the part from crude comedy to a tragic dignity.

MacLiammóir, Micheál (1899–1978) Romantic Irish actor, usually with the Dublin Gate company. His melodious, theatrical Hamlet was at the Westminster in 1935.

McMaster, Anew (1894–1962) An egocentric Irish actor who, in aspect, could have walked from a Florentine canvas of the High Renaissance. Though as a rule he was touring a company round the "smalls" of Ireland, playing most leading parts, he also went to Australia. In 1933 he was a dominating Coriolanus*** at Stratford and a far less persuasive Hamlet.

Macready, William Charles (1793–1873) Son of an actor-manager and an actress, and among the few great English tragedians. Five feet ten in height, he had a flat, high-cheekboned face, burning blue eyes, and a violoncello-voice of astounding range. Two of his great roles were Macbeth*** (between 1820 and 1851) and Lear*** (1838), a production in which he restored the Fool. He managed Covent Garden (1837–9) and Drury Lane (1841–3). Macready has been accused of despising his profession; but he was devoted to his art and had no time for "Bohemian" players who brought shame on their calling. Abnormally sensitive, he hid nothing from his journals.

Madden, Donald (b.1933) American actor whose vigorous, physical Hamlet was much talked of during an off-Broadway production (directed by ▷Stuart Vaughan) at the Phoenix, 1961. He was Richard II at Stratford, Connecticut (1968), Richard III for the New York Shakespeare Festival (1970) and Leontes at Stratford (1975).

Malleson, Miles (1888–1969) Actor-dramatist; an incomparable Shakespeare comedian, as in Sir Andrew Aguecheek (Court, 1918), Launcelot Gobbo (Court, 1919), Polonius*** (Haymarket, 1944), a Quince*** straight from any parish council (Haymarket, 1945), and – for the Old Vic company at the New, 1949 – Sir Nathaniel***, of which a critic wrote: "He has two kind anxious eyes in a sketch of a face that appears to be moulded from jelly."

Malone, Edmond (1741–1812) Irishman and acute Shakespearian scholar, who exposed the forgeries of ▷William Ireland.

Mansfield, Richard (1854–1907) American actor famed for several full-scale attacking performances, among them Richard III (in which he made a London début, 1889), Shylock, Henry V and Brutus.

Mantell, Robert (1854–1928) Scottish-born, he emigrated in 1878 to the United States, where he played most of the great tragic parts with a slow theatricality.

Marlowe, Christopher (1564–93) A cobbler's son from Canterbury, a graduate of Cambridge, born in the same year as Shakespeare, and a dramatist Shakespeare must have known and worked with (Marlowe was the "dead shepherd" of the As You Like It couplet (III.5), "Dead shepherd, now I find thy saw of might,/'Who ever lov'd that lov'd not at first sight?'" In Marlowe's hand the ten-syllabled iambic line, unrhymed, became a new and astonishing instrument. The poet of "high astounding terms", author of Tamburlaine the Great, Dr Faustus and Edward II, was killed in mysterious circumstances during a Deptford tavern brawl in May 1593.

Marlowe, Julia (1866–1950) (Real name, Sarah Frances Frost.) This extremely popular and able American actress (Juliet, Rosalind, Cleopatra) was the second wife of ▷E.H. Sothern, whom she partnered in the theatre for several years.

Martin-Harvey, John *see* **Harvey, John Martin**

Mason, Brewster (b.1922) An actor of size and assurance whose principal work since 1963 has been with the Royal Shakespeare Company in parts as various as Othello (1971–2) and the Falstaffs of *The Merry Wives of Windsor* (1968–9, 1975–6) and the two *Henry IV*s (1975–6).

Michell, Keith (b.1928) Australian-born, he has been with the RSC (notably Macduff*, 1955) and the Old Vic (Antony in *Antony and Cleopatra*, 1957). He directed the Chichester Festival, 1974–7, playing Iago, 1975.

Miles, Bernard (b.1907) His Iago***, a coarse and chilling fox, was highly praised in the Old Vic *Othello* (at New, 1942). Became actor-manager and founder of the Mermaid Theatre, Blackfriars. CBE, 1953; knighted, 1969; created life peer (Lord Miles), 1979. Married to the actress Josephine Wilson.

Miller, Jonathan (b.1934) After beginning as an eccentric comedian (both actor and author) in a revue, *Beyond the Fringe*, he divided his career between medicine and stage direction. Among his productions were unexpected views of *The Merchant of Venice* in late nineteenth-century settings (for National company at the Cambridge, London, 1970, with ▷Laurence Olivier), *The Tempest* (Mermaid, 1970), *Measure for Measure* and *All's Well That Ends Well* (Greenwich, 1974–5).

Milton, Ernest (1890–1974) An American-born actor, Old Vic-bred, and at his meridian during the 1920s and early 1930s, he was a hypnotic Shakespearian. He allowed his sibilant, mannered drawl to grow on him; but no one who saw his Hamlet***, which after an Old Vic appearance (1919) he acted in various productions, ever forgot the romantic sweep and Irvingesque passion. Some of his major performances, idiosyncratic and pictorial, were a racially proud Shylock (St James's, 1932), a genuinely fantastic Armado*** (Old Vic, 1936), and a marsh-lit King John*** (New, for Old Vic, 1941). Married to the novelist and dramatist, Naomi Royde-Smith. "Player of Shakespeare, root to crown," Walter de la Mare said of him in the prologue to Milton's own play, *Christopher Marlowe* (1924).

Mirren, Helen (b.1946) She acted Cleopatra, when nineteen, for the National Youth Theatre (Old Vic), did much for the RSC (including Cressida at Stratford and the Aldwych, 1968–9), and was an unflinching Isabella in the 1979 *Measure for Measure* at the Riverside Studios, Hammersmith.

Modjeska, Helena (1840–1909) Actress of Polish birth who was already distinguished in her own country when she emigrated to the United States (1876), learned English, and began a new career. Juliet, Rosalind and Cleopatra were three of her Shakespearian heroines.

Moiseiwitsch, Tanya (b.1914) Stage designer, daughter of the pianist Benno Moiseiwitsch, she did much for the Old Vic at the New Theatre in the 1940s and for Stratford-upon-Avon. Her artistic association with ▷Tyrone Guthrie was particularly fruitful. She worked for him, spaciously and imaginatively, on such productions as *Cyrano de Bergerac* (New, 1946), *Henry VIII* (Stratford, 1949), and a great deal at Stratford, Ontario. There she designed the Elizabethan "thrust" stage for the Festival Theatre, and over the years – before and after Guthrie's death – the décor for many productions. CBE, 1976.

Monck, Nugent (1877–1958) Influenced by ▷William Poel, he was a fastidious director – though given to cutting – who between 1921 and 1951 put on every Shakespeare play, with amateur and anonymous casts, on the Elizabethan stage of his Maddermarket Theatre, Norwich.

Montague, Charles Edward (1867–1928) *Manchester Guardian* drama critic, 1890–1925, one of the most scholarly and scrupulous practitioners of his time. He wrote the famous notice (1899) of ▷Benson's Richard II, "the capable and faithful artist in the same skin as the incapable and unfaithful king."

Moriarty, Michael (b.1941) American actor whose parts for the New York Shakespeare Festival have included Octavius (*Antony and Cleopatra*) and Florizel (both 1963) and Richard III in Mel Shapiro's production (1974).

Moss, Arnold (b.1910) A seasoned Shakespearian, he was a passionate, vigorous Prospero in ▷Margaret Webster's New York production (1945), and played the same part at the University of Kansas twenty years later. He toured the United States in 1959 as the Duke (*Measure for Measure*) and as Prospero, and has been an affecting King Lear at various universities.

Neilson, Adelaide (1848–80) Beautiful, dark-eyed, emotional, she rose from poverty, acted under various names, and earned in London and the USA a reputation as a tragedienne, especially as Juliet (Royalty, London, 1865). She was less assured in comedy.

Neilson, Julia (1868–1957) Wife of Fred Terry (▷Ellen's brother) with whom she acted for thirty years, wasting on romantic cardboard drama her talent for tragedy. Probably her best classical part was Constance (with ▷Tree, Her Majesty's, 1899). Neither her Rosalind with ▷Alexander (St James's, 1896), nor Oberon (with Tree, 1900) mattered much. Tall and gracious, she had long dark copper-coloured hair and a deep tragic contralto voice.

Neilson-Terry, Phyllis (1892–1977) Daughter of Fred Terry and ▷Julia Neilson. Nearly six feet tall, blonde and commandingly beautiful. Never the classical actress she might have been, she played Juliet (New, 1911, and for ▷Tree at His Majesty's, 1913), Olivia, Rosalind, Oberon, Hermione – all at the Open Air Theatre during the 1930s – and a Stratford Lady Macbeth (1938).

Nesbitt, Cathleen (b.1888) An actress of appealing integrity; an expert verse-speaker. She was Perdita** (for ▷Granville Barker, Savoy, 1912), Cleopatra (for the Oxford University Dramatic Society, 1920), and Katharina (for the Old Vic, 1935).

Neville, John (b.1925) Shakespearian whose principal triumphs were at the Old Vic. Grave and handsome, with a low baritone that could rise to splendour and modulate to tenderness, he had five years (1953–8) of striking success, particularly as Richard II***, Hotspur and Mark Antony (*Julius Caesar*), all in 1955, Othello and Iago (each of which he alternated with ▷Richard Burton) in 1956, and Hamlet*** and Angelo*** in 1957. In later years he directed the new Nottingham Playhouse and went during the 1970s to valuable theatre direction in Canada. OBE, 1965.

Ney, Marie (b.1895) She played eight testing parts (such as Ophelia, Beatrice, Lady Macbeth) for the Old Vic, 1924–5, and a profoundly felt Isabella (also Old Vic), 1937.

Nicoll, Allardyce (1894–1976) Formerly Professor of English Language and Literature at the University of Birmingham, he was the most prolific and erudite of stage historians and the founder of *Shakespeare Survey*.

Nunn, Trevor (b.1940) He followed ▷Peter Hall, another Cambridge man, in 1968 as artistic director of the Royal Shakespeare Company. His creative imagination in the theatre and out has fortified the work at Stratford and the Aldwych. Many productions, notably *Macbeth* (Stratford and Warehouse, London 1976–8). Married to ▷Janet Suzman.

O'Conor, Joseph (b.1916) Irish-born actor of vast Shakespearian experience since 1939. He was Hamlet (▷Wolfit's company, 1949), has played Othello, Lear and Macbeth on various stages, and at Greenwich he was persuasively relaxed as the Duke*** (*Measure for Measure*, 1974) and the King (*All's Well That Ends Well*, 1975) in productions by ▷Jonathan Miller.

Olivier, Laurence (b.1907) He and ▷John Gielgud, in their different ways, head the English classical theatre. Originally a Birmingham Repertory man (1926–8), Olivier, swift, lithe and galvanic, with a chameleon-gift of disguise and a voice like a searching blade, has given through half a century a series of famous performances. There were the Romeo*** and Mercutio*** he alternated with Gielgud (New, 1935), the Hamlet** (1937) and the first Coriolanus*** (1938) of the two Old Vic seasons, and the great run of 1944–6 (Old Vic company at the New) that covered Richard III***, villain of the blood royal from what he called "our aery ... in the cedar's top"; Hotspur***, Shakespeare's "light by which the chivalry of England moved"; Justice Shallow***, Lear. At Stratford (1955) he was the century's Macbeth*** and restored Titus Andronicus*** to the tragic stage. He directed the National Theatre company at the Old Vic, 1963–73, playing Othello*** (1964) and bringing from intolerable agony a wild and surging music. Shylock*** followed in 1970. He has directed much, and his three films, *Henry V, Hamlet* and *Richard III*, are frequently revived. Knighted, 1946; life peer (Lord Olivier of Brighton), 1970. Married to the actress ▷Joan Plowright, CBE, who was Portia to his Shylock (1970), and formerly to the actress ▷Vivien Leigh.

O'Neill, Eliza (1791–1872) A comet of the late Regency. Acted for only five distinguished years in London (1814–19), beginning in unaffected classical beauty with a Covent Garden Juliet***. ▷Hazlitt admired her; ▷Macready saw in her Juliet "the spirit of perfect innocence and purity". She retired to marry the later baronet, (Sir) William Becher.

O'Toole, Peter (b.1932) The National Theatre company's first Hamlet (inaugural production, Old Vic, 1963), a tormented spirit who did not always communicate his torment. An actor who, for all his potentiality and physique, has not wholly fulfilled himself in the theatre. Played Shylock and Petruchio (Stratford, 1960).

Palmer, John (1744–98) "A gentleman with a slight infusion of the footman," ▷Charles Lamb said of this actor. Whatever his outrageous behaviour offstage, Palmer could be highly competent in parts as dissimilar as Iago and Sir Toby Belch.

Papp, Joseph (b.1921) Public-spirited founder in the mid-1950s of the free New York Shakespeare Festival. After performances in several places (frequently out of doors), a permanent theatre, the Delacorte, was built in Central Park in 1962. Also directed the Festival at the Lincoln Center theatres, presenting a remarkable number of the plays, often contentiously, always with zest.

Pasco, Richard (b.1926) A cerebral and hauntingly voiced classical actor who was at Birmingham Repertory (1952–5) and played Henry V and Berowne (1964), Hamlet (1965–6) and Angelo (1966) for Bristol Old Vic. Between 1969 and 1975 he was with the Royal Shakespeare Company in a run that included Richard II*** and Bolingbroke*** (each alternated with ▷Ian Richardson, 1973–4), Jaques*** (1973) and the Bastard*** (1974). Played Timon for RSC, 1980. Married to the actress Barbara Leigh-Hunt.

Payne, Ben Iden (1881–1976) Innovator, idealist, teacher. Beginning as a young Bensonian actor, he later founded the English repertory movement, with the wealthy philanthropist Miss A.E.F. Horniman, in Manchester, 1907. In America he had an unmatched influence on the staging of Shakespeare in the Elizabethan manner. For eight years (1935–42) he directed at Stratford-upon-Avon in a theatre inimical to his methods. His daughter, the actress Rosalind Iden, became Lady Wolfit.

Petrie, D. Hay (1895–1948) First discovered at the Old Vic (1920–4), a young Scottish actor whose work as Puck, Costard, Touchstone, Launce and other parts was said to have the easy directness of the Elizabethan clown. But he lived unwisely, his acting memory faded, and with it his career.

Phelps, Samuel (1804–78) Respected actor-manager, who staged at Sadler's Wells (1844–62) all but six of Shakespeare's plays. He was a sound tragedian, and his productions were shrewd and unfussily pictorial.

Phillips, Robin (b.1942) Formerly an actor at Bristol Old Vic, he turned to direction. His Shakespearian work at Stratford, Ontario, of which he has been in artistic charge since 1974, has had a personal and potent style.

Pickup, Ronald (b.1941) A sensitive, poetic actor whose parts for the National Theatre company at the Old Vic included Rosalind in an all-male *As You Like It* (1967), Armado (1968), Richard II (1972).

Plowright, Joan (b.1929) For the National company this compact, sensitive actress played Rosaline (*LLL*) at the Old Vic (1968), and Portia (to the Shylock of her husband, Lord Olivier) at the Cambridge, London, 1970. CBE, 1970.

Plummer, Christopher (b.1927) Popular Canadian actor of power and presence who has had many leading roles at Stratford, Ontario (among them, Hamlet and Antony in *Antony and Cleopatra*) and for the RSC at Stratford (in 1961 he was Benedick* which he had acted in Ontario, 1958).

Poel, William (1852–1934) An ardent, lonely and concentrated fanatic, who believed – as ▷Robert Speaight said in a biography – that Shakespeare and the classics could be truly performed only by rediscovering, and as far as possible reproducing, the conditions of the Elizabethan stage, its unlocalized platform and its swift musical speech. This, with some strange vagaries, was his task through life. He found ▷Edith Evans as an amateur, and she was his Cressida (King's Hall, Covent Garden, 1912).

Porter, Eric (b.1928) Primarily from ▷Barry Jackson's Birmingham theatre, he grew into an exceedingly individual actor who enriched any production in which he played. He was, for example, the King in both *Henry IV*s, (Old Vic, 1955), a waddling, corpulent Duke** in *The Two Gentlemen of Verona* (Stratford, 1960), a Leontes*** (also 1960), a man in whom jealousy could flare without preparation – (he could have been a Celt) – Iachimo and Macbeth (1962), King Lear (1968) and Malvolio*** (Stratford, 1960, and St George's, Islington, 1976).

Pritchard, Hannah (1711–68) For many years with ▷Garrick, especially as Lady Macbeth, she was known for her extremely precise and lucid articulation.

Quartermaine, Leon (1876–1967) He was an elegantly vapid Sir Andrew for ▷Granville Barker (Savoy, 1912); his Mercutio (Lyric, 1919) shared the honours of a *Romeo and Juliet* with ▷Ellen Terry, who was the Nurse. In his later years, as a gracious actor with a tapestried voice, he was often exceptional in the ▷Gielgud company (John of Gaunt, Queen's, 1937) and at Stratford (Buckingham, 1949).

Quayle, Anthony (b.1913) He developed from a sturdy actor with Old Vic experience into the artistic controller (1948–56) of what was then the Memorial Theatre at Stratford. He directed various productions and acted with strength, in comedy as the

Falstaff of the historical cycle (1951), in tragedy as Aaron*** (1955; London, 1957). He returned to Shakespeare in England with Lear for the Prospect company (Old Vic, 1978). CBE, 1952.

Quiller-Couch, Arthur T. ("Q") (1863–1944) A loyal Cornishman, "Q" was many people – romantic novelist, essayist, poet and anthologist. Shakespearians think of him as King Edward VII Professor of English Literature at Cambridge, author of *Shakespeare's Workmanship* (1918), and joint editor with ▷Dover Wilson of the New Cambridge edition of the plays. His allusively convoluted style was impressive. Knighted, 1910.

Quin, James (1693–1766) Born in London, educated in Dublin, he acted many of the Shakespearian leads at Lincoln's Inn Fields, Drury Lane and Covent Garden. A lesser rival of ▷Garrick, he excelled as Falstaff (*Henry IV, Part 1*), a projection of his own rugged personality. Smollett, the novelist, called him "a man whose wit was apt to degenerate into extreme coarseness".

Redgrave, Michael (b.1908) A magnificent intellectual actor lacking, perhaps, the final intangible gift of personality, but honoured across the years. His Berowne*** (Old Vic at New, 1949) was sensitive to every cadence; ▷Ivor Brown described his Hamlet*** (New, 1950; Stratford, 1958) as "a less lyrical, less ethereal, more agonized, more actual figure than most". His Prospero*** (Stratford, 1951) added humanity to the grandeur of a major prophet; he was a leonine Antony*** in *Antony and Cleopatra* (Stratford and London, 1953); and Lear, Shylock, Benedick, Hotspur and Richard II were his other parts. CBE, 1952; knighted, 1959. Married to the actress Rachel Kempson.

Redgrave, Vanessa (b.1937) Elder daughter of ▷Sir Michael Redgrave. It was said of her Rosalind (Stratford, 1960) that she created the spring as she moved. Two seasons later she was Katharina and a lovely Imogen***, but she did not play in Shakespeare again for ten years, and neither her Viola (Shaw, 1972) nor Cleopatra (Bankside Globe, 1973) had her former spirit. CBE, 1967.

Redman, Joyce (b.1918) Irish actress, sympathetic and eager, who played Lady Anne (to ▷Olivier's Richard of Gloucester) for the Old Vic company at the New (1944), Doll Tearsheet to ▷Ralph Richardson's Falstaff (1945), and Cordelia to Olivier's Lear (1946). Was Helena (*All's Well That Ends Well*) and Mistress Ford at Stratford, 1955.

Rehan, Ada (1860–1916) Irish-born (her name was Crehan), she grew into one of America's most redoubtable players, as Rosalind, Katharina and Viola. Though ▷Shaw found her Rosalind (London, 1890 and 1897) "enchanting", he regretted that as yet she had "created nothing but Ada Rehan". Played Katharina, the Shrew***, at Stratford (1888); Eliot Gregory's portrait of her hangs there in the Royal Shakespeare Picture Gallery, a handsome fury with upflung head and folded arms.

Reinhardt, Max (1873–1943) Originally an actor, this Austrian man of the theatre became, in Berlin, an internationally renowned director, particularly in his treatment of crowds and lighting. Among his productions were *A Midsummer Night's Dream* (seen at Oxford, 1933, and in a contentious Hollywood film, 1935), *Julius Caesar* and *Macbeth*. He worked in America from 1933.

Reynolds, Frederick (1764–1841) Prolific hack dramatist who, in London between 1816 and 1824, turned several of Shakespeare's plays into what were loosely styled "operas". Violently adapting the texts, he borrowed the music from a variety of composers. The results were chaotic.

Richardson, Ian (b.1934) Scottish-born, he was at the Birmingham Repertory, 1958–9, acting a very young Hamlet able to suggest heartbreak in a single inflection. He appeared with the Royal Shakespeare Company (1960–70 and 1973–5), giving his glittering voice and intellect to such parts as Oberon***, Cassius, Ford, Berowne***, Pericles, Iachimo*** (Stratford/Aldwych, 1974), and – alternating them with ▷Richard Pasco, 1973–4 – Richard II*** and Bolingbroke***. Joined the Old Vic, 1979 (Mercutio***). Married to the actress Maroussia Frank.

Richardson, Ralph (b.1902) Began as a provincial Shakespearian in ▷Charles Doran's company; then won Old Vic and early Sadler's Wells audiences (1930–2) for his sharp definition and forthright manliness in such parts as Prince Hal, Enobarbus, Bottom***, the Bastard and Henry V. He was Mercutio in New York (1935); and as a joint director of the Old Vic in its New Theatre seasons (mid-1940s), a marvellously judged Falstaff*** (1945). At Stratford (1952), as Prospero and Macbeth, he gave curiously vague, unconcentrated performances; later, on various stages, he played Timon and Shylock. Falstaff aside, his fame rests on other theatre work. Though he has ample pathos, his first Shakespearian power has waned. Knighted, 1947.

Rigg, Diana (b.1938) Actress (for the RSC and National Theatre) of technique and physical beauty. She played Cordelia (first in 1962) and Viola (1966) at Stratford, and Lady Macbeth (1972) for the National company at the Old Vic.

Robertson, Toby (b.1928) Invigorating director, whose Prospect Theatre Company became at length the company of the Old Vic, assuming the famous name in 1979.

Robeson, Paul (1898–1976) Renowned Negro actor who appeared as Othello for almost 300 performances in New York, 1943–4. He had acted the part in London (Savoy, 1930) and returned to it (1959) at Stratford where, though his bass voice could be glorious, he seldom attained the glory of the verse.

Robey, George (1869–1954) A ripely expressive, broad comedian, whose Shakespearian experience was confined to his casting as Falstaff in *Henry IV, Part 1* (His Majesty's, 1935), a portrait – technically valiant – that was over-publicized. In ▷Olivier's *Henry V* film (1943) Robey had a few moments as the dying Falstaff. CBE, 1919; knighted, 1954.

Robson, Flora (b.1902) A superb emotional actress, at her meridian as Isabella (1933), and an ambitious, unimaginative and loving Lady Macbeth (1934), in the Old Vic/Sadler's Wells company. She was Paulina*** ("blazing like a wintry fire" said ▷Robert Speaight) in ▷Brook's revival (Phoenix, 1951). CBE, 1952; DBE, 1960.

Rogers, Paul (b.1917) Devon-born, he is a Shakespearian of powerful energy and attack. His Old Vic record in several seasons covered such parts as Iago and a Dartmoor-accented Bottom (1951), Shylock in Hebraic passion (1952), Henry VIII*** (1953), Macbeth (1954), at the last like a starved grey wolf, Falstaff*** (in both *Henry IV* and *The Merry Wives of Windsor*, 1955), Pandarus (1956) and Lear (1958). At Stratford (RSC) he was Apemantus (1965) and Falstaff (in the *Henry IV*s, 1966).

Rose, George (b.1910) A comfortable comedian, he was Dogberry, Snug and Pompey at Stratford during 1949–50, and acted Autolycus (1951) and again Dogberry (1952) with ▷John Gielgud in London productions at the Phoenix. He has been in America for many years.

Ryan, Robert (b.1913) Prominent actor of the American stage and cinema. Played Coriolanus in New York (1954) and Antony in *Antony and Cleopatra*, 1963.

Rylands, George (b.1902) Cambridge scholar, Fellow of King's College, who has had a pronounced influence on contemporary Shakespeare production. He was responsible for the fine recordings, by professional players and members of the Cambridge Marlowe Society, of the entire Shakespeare canon, uncut. He also directed ▷Gielgud's last *Hamlet* revival (Haymarket, 1944). CBE, 1961.

Sanderson, Mary (d.1712) ▷Thomas Betterton's wife, among the earliest actresses, and a Lady Macbeth approved by ▷Colley Cibber.

Saunders, Florence (1891–1926) Between 1916 and 1921, and in 1923–4, she was among the most adaptable and best loved leading actresses in Old Vic history. She died tragically young.

Schoenbaum, Samuel (b.1927) An American Shakespeare scholar who has taught at several universities (Northwestern, Chicago, Columbia and the Graduate School of the City University of New York). His books, *Shakespeare's Lives* (1970) and *William Shakespeare: A Documentary Life* (1975) are authoritative, astringent and entertaining. In 1971 he edited (with Kenneth Muir) *A New Companion to Shakespeare Studies*.

Scofield, Paul (b.1922) A man who can play Hamlet and Cloten, Armado and Timon, Mercutio, Lear and Prospero, is not to be labelled dogmatically. Scofield, in the English theatre, stands apart, an exploring actor, strangely exciting. He has a tense nobility of profile and what has been called "a mountain voice, rifted, chasmed, that can shine on the peak and fall, sombre, in the sudden crevasse". He was at Birmingham Repertory (1944–5) and established himself in three Stratford seasons (1946–8) that included Armado***, Mercutio***, Troilus*** and Hamlet*** (to which he returned in London, 1955). Later he was, for example, Coriolanus (Stratford, Ontario, 1961), a famous Lear*** (Stratford-upon-Avon, 1962), Timon*** (Stratford, 1965), Prospero*** (Leeds and Wyndham's, London, 1975–6) and Othello*** (National, 1980). Married to the actress Joy Parker. CBE, 1956.

Scott, Clement (1841–1904) Prolific London drama critic who was above all a descriptive and impressionist writer, and who disliked experiment. "The drama which asserts and argues will never be tolerated by him," said ▷Bernard Shaw.

Scott, George C. (b.1927) Richly experienced Virginia-born actor who had had more than 150 parts in stock companies before making his début for ▷Joseph Papp's New York Shakespeare Festival as Richard III (1957) and Jaques (1958). Later he appeared in New York as Antony (*Antony and Cleopatra*, 1959) and Shylock (1962), also for the New York Festival.

Scott, Margaretta (b.1912) With a gentle grace she played most of her Shakespeare (Viola, Olivia, Miranda, Hermia, Juliet, Rosalind) at the Open Air Theatre during the 1930s, and at Stratford (1941–2). There, with her work strengthened and deepened, she added Portia and Lady Macbeth to her parts at a time when, unfortunately, few drama critics were going to what was then the "Shakespeare Festival".

Seale, Douglas (b.1913) An actor at first, he made his reputation when he directed the complete trilogy of *Henry VI* at Birmingham Repertory and ultimately (1953) at the Old Vic. He has directed, faithfully and without extraneous parade, more than a dozen other Shakespeare plays at Stratford (*King John*, 1957), the Old Vic (between 1955 and 1959), and Stratford, Connecticut. Latterly he has worked in America.

Seyler, Athene (b.1889) Among the most expert English comediennes during well over half a century in the theatre. She was Rosalind (Lyric, Hammersmith, 1920), and her Old Lady*** (Old Vic/Sadler's Wells, 1933) was a perfect miniature. Married to the actor Nicholas Hannen. CBE, 1959.

Shaw, G. Bernard (1856–1950) ("Nothing exasperates me more than to be Georged in print.") The most provocative of English dramatists, and formerly a critic, he wrote often about Shakespeare, principally in performance. He could be extremely shrewd and also thoroughly off the mark, as in his view of the last act of *Cymbeline* as "a tedious string of unsurprising dénouements sugared with insincere sentimentality after a ludicrous stage battle". He sought to replace the act by his own thin version (acted at Embassy, London, 1937, with little response).

Shaw, Glen Byam (b.1904) Son of Byam Shaw, the artist, and formerly an actor, he ranks with ▷Bridges-Adams as one of the surest, most scholarly and least exhibitionist of Shakespeare directors. Co-directed at Stratford with ▷Anthony Quayle (1953–6) and continued alone until the end of 1959. His was the *Macbeth*** (1955) with ▷Olivier. He was married to the actress ▷Angela Baddeley. CBE, 1954.

Shaw, Sebastian (b.1905) A mature and engaging character actor. He played at Stratford in his youth, and in 1966 returned to what had become the Royal Shakespeare Company in a variety of parts. Two were the King of France (*All's Well That Ends Well*) in 1967–8, and the Duke (*Measure for Measure*) in 1970.

Siddons, Sarah (1755–1831) Sister of ▷John Philip Kemble, a great tragedienne. "Not less than a goddess, or than a prophetess inspired by the gods," wrote ▷Hazlitt. Though this may seem hyperbolical today, it is clear that Sarah Siddons (especially as Lady Macbeth*** – which she acted for the last time in 1812 – and as Constance***, Queen Katharine***, Isabella*** and Volumnia***) was, in her intense and sonorous fashion and her superb dignity, one of the rulers of the English stage.

Sinden, Donald (b.1923) First conspicuous when, as Arviragus at Stratford in 1946, he spoke the dirge "Fear no more the heat o' the sun" with ▷John Harrison (Guiderius). Between these points he had a long film contract and also became one of the most resilient comedians of his day. Added to technique, presence, authority and a responsive voice, his sheer love of acting has enabled him to move from his Stratford Malvolio*** of 1969, a glorious study in vanity, his Henry VIII*** (1969–70) and his Benedick*** (1976) to the tumults of Lear*** (1976) Othello (1979–80) and practically anything else asked of him. CBE, 1979.

Skinner, Otis (1858–1942) This renowned American actor worked with ▷Edwin Booth, whom he recalled with steady admiration, and later for ▷Augustin Daly (Romeo in London, 1890), and in Shakespeare repertory with ▷Ada Rehan (1904). In later years his Falstaff (*Henry IV, Part 1*), described as "a rotund old devil of the taverns", and a Shylock (with ▷Maude Adams, 1931) which failed to reach New York, were his most exacting parts.

Smith, Maggie (b.1934) An actress exceptional in looks and talent, principally as a comedienne with an exhilarating vocal range. Her parts for the National Theatre company at the Old Vic included Beatrice (1965); at Stratford, Ontario, Cleopatra (1976), Rosalind and a doubling of Titania and Hippolyta (1977). CBE, 1970.

Sothern, E.H. (Edward Hugh) (1859–1933) Respected, cultured Shakespearian, son of the actor, E.A. Sothern, and husband of ▷Julia Marlowe. Distinguished through many years for a style of acting that, impressive in its time, would become outmoded, as in the *Cymbeline* of 1923. But like his father, Sothern (who was

Macbeth, Hamlet, Shylock, Malvolio and much else) is still honoured for his integrity and skill when he headed the profession early in the century.

Speaight, Robert (1904–77) Both actor and eloquent scholar, Robert Speaight was a remarkable amateur Falstaff when he was an Oxford undergraduate. He joined the Old Vic/Sadler's Wells company (1931–2) as King John, Fluellen**, Cassius, Malvolio, Hamlet and much else, and spoke potently as Ulysses*** in the modern-dress *Troilus and Cressida* (Westminster, 1938). In later life, when writing occupied most of his time, he often directed university Shakespeare in the United States and Canada, though his main work for the plays was in drama criticism, lecturing, and his rich biography, *Shakespeare: The Man and His Achievement* (1977).

Sprague, Arthur Colby (b.1895) American scholar, Professor Emeritus at Bryn Mawr, the leading historical authority on the plays of Shakespeare in performance. Two of his wise, exact and absorbing books are *Shakespeare and the Actors: the Stage Business in His Plays* (1945) and *Shakespearian Players and Performances* (1954).

Spriggs, Elizabeth (b.1929) Uncommonly relaxed actress of great range, who played Cleopatra (Birmingham Repertory, 1961), and whose parts for the Royal Shakespeare Company and the National Theatre have included Hostess Quickly*** in both *Henry IVs*, and Juliet's Nurse*** (Stratford, 1966), Emilia*** and Beatrice (1971), and First Witch (National, 1978).

Spurgeon, Caroline (1869–1941) In her original and influential *Shakespeare's Imagery and What It Tells Us* (1935), this scholar examined in detail the dramatist's images which "unwittingly lay bare his own innermost likes and dislikes, observations and interests, associations of thoughts, attitudes of mind and beliefs".

Stewart, Patrick (b.1940) An actor who appeared first with the RSC in 1966, and whose calm certainty has been evident in such characters as Enobarbus (1972–3 and 1978–9) and Shylock (1978–9).

Stirling, Mrs (Mary Anne) (1815–95) Aged thirty, she was Cordelia to the Lears of both ▷Edwin Forrest and ▷Macready (Princess's, 1845). In 1882 (Lyceum) she was acting the Nurse in ▷Irving's revival of *Romeo and Juliet*, a performance of which ▷Ellen Terry wrote: "The only Nurse I have ever seen who did not play the part like a female pantaloon. . . . Her smile was the most irresistible thing imaginable."

Sullivan, Barry (1812–91) A stick-at-nothing tragedian who acted in Britain, the United States and Australia. ▷Bernard Shaw, remembering from youth, called him "the last of a race of heroic figures which had dominated the stage since the palmy Siddons–Kemble days". Away from tragedy, he was Benedick to the Beatrice of ▷Helen Faucit, in the first performance at the then Shakespeare Memorial Theatre at Stratford, April 23, 1879.

Suzman, Janet (b.1939) South African-born actress who as a member of the RSC has played nearly a score of Shakespearian parts with unblurred authority (Cleopatra, 1972–3). Married to the director ▷Trevor Nunn.

Swinley, Ion (1891–1937) Between the wars the might-have-been of the British classical theatre, who had brains, command, aspect (towards the end a settled melancholy), and a voice like James Elroy Flecker's "great bell swinging in a dome". Everything, indeed, except a secure memory; often it failed him during his Old Vic seasons (1923–4), when he played Hamlet***, Troilus**, Saturninus, Prospero*** and much else; and it did so more sadly still during his return (1935–6). ▷James Agate wrote of him in 1937: "Over a wide range of parts the finest

Shakespearian actor since the war. He regarded acting as a noble art, and pursued it to the uttermost of mind and spirit."

Tandy, Jessica (b.1909) Originally a leading ingénue of the London theatre, she was Ophelia to ▷Gielgud's second Hamlet (New, 1934), achieved the perilous double of Viola and Sebastian (Old Vic, 1937), and played Cordelia (Old Vic, 1940). She went to the United States, becoming a naturalized American citizen in 1954. First married to the British actor Jack Hawkins, later to the American actor ▷Hume Cronyn.

Tate, Nahum (1652–1715) Irish-born dramatist, Poet Laureate 1692–1715. Botched up three Shakespeare adaptations (of *Richard II, Coriolanus* and *King Lear*) of which *The History of King Lear* (1681), with its happy ending and its line, "Old Kent throws in his hearty wishes, too", was the most infamous. It lived in performance for a century and a half.

Tearle, Godfrey (1884–1953) Son of a Victorian actor, and through much of his life a Shakespearian. Though he acted so many parts (his Hamlet was at the Haymarket, 1931), he remained too unambitious to realize himself fully. Through the years his power ripened to an Antony (*Antony and Cleopatra*, with ▷Edith Evans, Piccadilly, London, 1946; with ▷Katharine Cornell, New York, 1947) in which he made the most of his majestic voice and bearing, and – more than anything else – to his final portrait of Othello (Stratford, 1948, his own production). All who heard him then would have consented readily to Cassio's "For he was great of heart". Knighted, 1951.

Terry, Ellen (1847–1928) From an acting family, she had her unmatchable period, in a career of sustained hard work, when she was ▷Irving's leading lady (Lyceum, 1878–1902, and eight visits to America). Serenely beautiful, and idolized by her profession and the public, her parts included Ophelia*** (1878), Portia***, Beatrice*** (1882), Cordelia*** (1892) and Imogen (1896). ▷Bernard Shaw said that "her name rang like a chime through the last quarter of the 19th century". ▷ Gordon Craig was her illegitimate son by E.W. Godwin. Her brother was the romantic actor, Fred Terry (1863–1933), ▷Julia Neilson's husband. DBE, 1925.

Thesiger, Ernest (1879–1961) Amusingly mannered London actor, who was Osric in the "all-star" *Hamlet* (Haymarket, 1930), the haughtiest of Malvolios (Open Air, 1944) and Polonius (Phoenix, 1955). CBE, 1960.

Thorndike, Sybil (1882–1976) She was the ▷Siddons of her century, with a range wider than Siddons had. As ▷Ivor Brown said of her: "The speech of modern use has become as moving on her lips as any poetry or rhetoric." During her early twenties she acted 112 parts in Shakespeare and Old Comedy for ▷Ben Greet's company in the United States. During four years at the Old Vic (1914–18) her parts – some, owing to wartime exigencies, masculine – were again astonishingly various. Later, to take only four triumphs from so many, she was Queen Katharine*** (Empire, 1925), Lady Macbeth*** (Princes, 1926), Volumnia*** (Old Vic, 1938), and Constance*** (Old Vic at New, 1941). Married to ▷Sir Lewis Casson. DBE, 1931. Her younger brother, Russell Thorndike (1885–1972) was a practised Shakespearian – also in most of the principal parts – joint director of the Old Vic (1919–20), and novelist.

Tree, Herbert Beerbohm (1853–1917) An extravagant English actor-manager, whose ability – most thorough and ingenious in "character" parts – has been clouded by criticism of his sumptuous productions, which have often sacrificed the text to needless pageantry. Between 1888 and 1914 he directed eighteen Shakespeare plays, the vast majority (from 1897) at Her/His Majesty's.

He appeared, for example, as Hamlet, Richard II, Falstaff, Macbeth, Shylock and Caliban. In 1904 he founded what became the Royal Academy of Dramatic Art. Knighted, 1909.

Trouncer, Cecil (1898–1953) An actor who had a kind of "Grinling Gibbons" voice that chiselled the phrases, shaping them into carved leaf and flower. Old Vic parts (1934–6) included Julius Caesar and Leonato; he was Menenius Agrippa in the first ▷Olivier *Coriolanus* (Old Vic, 1938).

Tutin, Dorothy (b.1930) A touching actress (Viola, Juliet and Ophelia at Stratford, 1958) who developed steadily in craft and enunciation to her Cressida*** (1960 and 1962), subtly the "daughter of the game", her second Juliet (1961), Rosalind (Stratford, 1967; and Los Angeles, 1968), and an uncanny Lady Macbeth (National Theatre, 1978). CBE, 1967.

Valk, Frederick (1895–1956) German actor, born in Hamburg, renowned for his classical parts at the German theatre in Prague, Czechoslovakia (he became a Czech citizen), Valk reached London in 1939. He acted a vigorously praised Othello (Old Vic at New Theatre, 1942), and with ▷Donald Wolfit's company, 1946 and 1947; also Shylock (Old Vic and New, 1943; Stratford, Ontario, 1955). His Othello, with its immensely high voltage and wounded-bull frenzies, had the power but little of the glory, texture or music of the verse.

Vanbrugh, Irene (1872–1949) One of two distinguished sisters, daughters of an Exeter clergyman. Irene, a superb comedienne and renowned also in Edwardian drawing-room drama, did relatively little Shakespeare, but played Queen Gertrude (Haymarket, 1930 and 1931) and Mistress Page, with her sister as Mistress Ford (Ring, Blackfriars, 1937). DBE, 1941.

Vanbrugh, Violet (1867–1942) The elder of the Vanbrugh sisters, Violet, tall and stately, was the more prominent as a classical actress. She was Anne Bullen with ▷Irving (Lyceum, 1892), Portia (with the Shylock of her husband, ▷Arthur Bourchier, a marriage that finally broke up) at the Garrick in 1905, Queen Katharine (1910), Mistress Ford and Lady Macbeth (1911) with ▷Tree at His Majesty's.

Vaughan, Stuart (b.1925) Beginning as an actor (and often returning to the stage in later years), he was the most prominent New York Shakespeare director during the late 1950s and early 1960s. He staged (1956) ▷Joseph Papp's first open-air Festival performances, *The Taming of the Shrew* and *Julius Caesar*, and did half a dozen other plays, 1957–9. He also directed *Hamlet* at the Phoenix, off-Broadway (1961), conducted repertory theatres in Seattle and New Orleans, and (again for the New York Festival) edited and directed *The Wars of the Roses* and *Richard III* (1970).

Vestris, Madame (Lucia Elizabetta or **Lucy Eliza)** (1797–1856) A good singer and black-curled comedienne, who acted a few Shakespeare parts, she later ran the Olympic Theatre for just over eight years (1831–9) as a disciplined and innovating manageress, and Covent Garden (with her husband, Charles Mathews, 1839–42). At Covent Garden she and Mathews staged *Love's Labour's Lost* (1839) and *A Midsummer Night's Dream* (1840).

Walkley, A.B. (Alfred Bingham) (1855–1926) Drama critic for *The Times* (1900–26), a careful judge and stylist, with a trick of French quotation.

Wallack, Lester (1820–88) One of the distinguished American acting family of English origin – his real name was John Johnstone Wallack – he made a New York début in the late 1840s, succeeded his father as manager of the first Wallack's Theatre and acted Benedick (1867–8) and Jaques (1880).

Waller, David (b.1920) An able Shakespearian who played numerous parts at the Old Vic, 1951–3 and 1957–8. Most of his work since 1964 has been with the RSC, notably as Pandarus (1968, 1976), Dogberry (1968), Bottom (1970).

Waller, Emma (1820–99) Actress who left London to be one of the principal players in New York and the United States. She had unusual dramatic power as Lady Macbeth; as Ophelia (1857) to her husband's Hamlet; and Queen Margaret in *Richard III* (Cibber's text). She even attempted Hamlet and Iago.

Waller, Lewis (1860–1915) Intensely virile, an actor for the strong, plain effect, and with a voice that rang like bell-metal, he was always (as Max Beerbohm put it) "frankly and sternly rooted in the prime of life". Famous for his Henry V (Lyceum, 1900, 1905, 1908, 1910) and Hotspur (1909).

Walter, Wilfrid (1882–1958) Formerly a painter and scenic artist, he made a stage début at the Old Vic (1919) when designing the sets, and rose to act most of the leading parts. He played Bottom at Drury Lane (1924) and from 1927 to 1930 gave his panache, presence and pictorial sense to the Stratford company; he acted Hotspur at the opening of the present theatre (1932). He reappeared as Othello, temperamentally true if vocally fretful, at the Westminster (1935) and was Claudius in a New York *Hamlet* (1936).

Ward, Genevieve (1838–1922) An American actress, at first an opera singer whose singing voice failed her through over-work, she spent most of her career in England. Known in classical theatre for the more alarming *grandes dame*, Cymbeline's Queen and Queen Margaret (in *Richard III*) (with ▷Irving at the Lyceum, 1896), and Volumnia***, mother of Coriolanus, which she played often with ▷Benson and at the Old Vic (1920), lamenting "in anger, Juno-like" and terrifying everyone within reach. DBE, 1921.

Warde, Frederick Barkham (1851–1935) American actor who played Shakespeare in New York with ▷John McCullough, ▷Edwin Booth and ▷Charlotte Cushman; but spent most of his stage career (which ended in 1919) heading his own company on tour, largely in Shakespeare. He was also a lecturer and author.

Warfield, David (1866–1951) For many years an extremely popular actor under the management of David Belasco, who took him out of burlesque and in the end (1922) staged *The Merchant of Venice* for him. Here Warfield played for pathos in a slow, elaborately scenic revival (with four intervals) which he held afterwards that Belasco had misconceived.

Warner, David (b.1941) A lonely, gentle Henry VI* in *The Wars of the Roses* (Stratford/Aldwych, 1963–4), he was less at ease with Richard II (Stratford, 1964). A critic described his Hamlet (Stratford/Aldwych, 1965–6) as anti-romantic and gauche.

Warren, William (1767–1832) An English actor who went to Philadelphia in 1796 and later managed the Chestnut Street Theatre (where ▷Edwin Forrest, as Young Norval, first appeared). Warren excelled in such characters as Falstaff and Sir Toby. He was married three times, and his six children all had theatrical associations.

Waterston, Sam (Samuel A.) (b.1940) During a full career he has appeared (for the New York Shakespeare Festival) as Prince Hal (both *Henry IV*s, 1968), a charming Benedick (1972), Prospero (1974), and an unpoetic Hamlet, directed by Michael Rudman (1975).

Watson, Douglas (b.1921) A conspicuous American actor who began (1946) in Chicago with the ungrateful part of Fenton. Since then, in other Shakespearian parts, well over twenty of them, he has had better luck: Romeo (to ▷Olivia de Havilland's Juliet, Broadhurst, New York, 1951), Henry V (Cambridge, Mass., 1956), Leontes (Stratford, Connecticut, 1960), a notable Edmund, with ▷Morris Carnovsky's Lear (Stratford, Conn., 1963), an unorthodox and less successful Richard III (Stratford, 1964), Othello (San Diego, 1967).

Webster, Margaret (1905–72) Born of stage parents, she was herself an actress (Lady Macbeth, Old Vic, 1930), and later had exciting achievement as a director (particularly Shakespearian) in New York, where she began with the Richard II of ▷Maurice Evans in 1937. *Othello* with ▷Robeson (1943) ran for a record-breaking 295 performances. Original and firm, she was never erratically experimental.

Weir, George R. (1853–1909) In ▷Frank Benson's company he was the principal comedian from 1883 until his death. A greatly loved Falstaff, and (said the *Manchester Guardian*) that "very rare thing, a comic artist with a sense of poetry".

Welles, Orson (b.1915) A "personality" actor of gigantic build, who played and directed much Shakespeare with intermittent effect and never without accompanying debate. His most arresting work as director was the modern-dress *Julius Caesar* (1937) which – in conjunction with John Houseman – he put on at the Mercury, New York. "Pure theatre," said the critic John Mason Brown, "vibrant and unashamed". Other work included his disappointing performance of Othello (St James's, London, 1951) and a King Lear (New York, 1956).

Whitby, Arthur (1869–1922) ▷Robert Speaight said that his Sir Toby** in ▷Granville Barker's *Twelfth Night* (Savoy, 1912) was "always a gentleman, with the beaming roundness of a full moon. The scenes with Aguecheek never degenerated into farce."

Wickwire, Nancy (1925–74) American actress often in classical parts: Rosalind (1958) for the New York Shakespeare Festival, Hermione at Stratford, Connecticut (1958); also at Stratford (1959), Titania, Mistress Ford and Helena (*All's Well That Ends Well*); and Queen Margaret (*Richard III*) at the Guthrie, Minneapolis (1965).

Wilks, Robert (c.1665–1732) A talented actor with an uncertain temper, he was primarily a comedian but could play Hamlet and move an audience as Macduff. Was joint-manager of Drury Lane.

Williams, Clifford (b.1926) An associate director of the RSC. Among his many productions are *The Comedy of Errors* (1962–3) and *Cymbeline* (1974); he directed an all-male *As You Like It* at the Old Vic (National company), 1967.

Williams, Emlyn (b.1905) Welsh actor and dramatist who, though he has done relatively little Shakespeare, used his measured vocal quality and faultless technique in such parts as Richard III (Old Vic, 1937), Angelo (Old Vic, 1937; Stratford, 1956), Shylock and Iago (Stratford, 1956). CBE, 1962.

Williams, E. Harcourt (1880–1957) "Billee" Williams, dark, stocky and earnest, was an affectionately considered actor, but especially, through four famous seasons, 1929–33, director at the Old Vic, where ▷John Gielgud played for him in 1929–31 and ▷Ralph Richardson in 1930–2. Much influenced by ▷Granville Barker, he insisted on speed and simplicity.

Williams, Michael (b.1935) An actor of concentrated intelligence, whose Shakespearian parts – more than a dozen of them – for the Royal Shakespeare Company, have moved between Puck (1963), a splendidly controlling Petruchio*** (1967), the Fool** in *King Lear* and Troilus (1968–9), Henry V (1971), and Dromio of Syracuse (1962–3 and 1976–7). Married to ▷Judi Dench.

Williamson, Nicol (b.1938) Scottish-born actor who has played, for the RSC, Coriolanus (Aldwych, 1973), Malvolio (Stratford/Aldwych, 1974–5) and Macbeth (1974–5) with a ruthless theatrical attack. He was an uncompromising and contentious Hamlet at the Round House, London, and in New York (1969).

Wilson, John Dover (1881–1969) An entirely dedicated Shakespearian scholar and critic, whose searching work in, for example, the New Cambridge edition of the plays, could sometimes be vitiated by too copious theorizing.

Woffington, Margaret (Peg) (c.1714–60) Irish actress from the slums of Dublin, who for sixteen years in London, from 1741, played most of Shakespeare's principal women. For a few years she lived with ▷Garrick. Her Rosalind, in spite of vocal harshness, could be captivating.

Wolfit, Donald (1902–68) Beginning in provincial Shakespeare (▷Charles Doran's company) he reached the Old Vic in 1929, and in 1936 animated the Stratford company, playing his first fervant Hamlet*. Turning actor-manager in 1937 with high ambition, unquenchable vigour and a moderate cast, he acted most of the great parts in the provinces, and had a Strand Theatre season during the London "blitz" of 1940–1. On the night his attack could startle, but he began to repeat his effects and to fray his strong, upward-thrusting voice. Praised vastly for Lear*** (especially at the Scala, 1944), for some he was more compelling as a Kent*** of "uncoined constancy" to ▷Ayrton's Stratford Lear (1936). His finest Shakespearian part (also 1936) was a nobly spoken Ulysses***, to which he never returned. Though he needed a director (his 1951 performance of Marlowe's *Tamburlaine* for ▷Tyrone Guthrie at the Old Vic was savagely exciting), he was usually too much of an individualist to accept one. Married to Rosalind Iden (▷Iden Payne's daughter) who for many years was his leading lady. CBE, 1950; knighted, 1957.

Wood, John A former president of the Oxford University Dramatic Society; began his professional career at the Old Vic, 1954–6. He has become a zestful actor of such Shakespearian extroverts as Saturninus** (Stratford/Aldwych, 1972–3) and Richard III* (National, 1979).

Worth, Irene (b.1916) American-born actress who has done most of her major work in England: Desdemona (1951) and Portia (1953) at the Old Vic, Lady Macbeth and Goneril (1962) at Stratford. She was Helena (in the Edwardian production of *All's Well That Ends Well*, 1953) and Rosalind (1959) at Stratford, Ontario.

Wymark, Patrick (1926–70) Relishing Shakespearian broad comedian recalled for his Stratford seasons (1955–8, 1960–2); an especially confident Sir Toby, Dogberry and Launce.

Wynyard, Diana (1906–64) Actress of glowing beauty, who at Stratford was Desdemona (1948), Lady Macbeth, Queen Katharine and Beatrice (1949). Gracefully and wittily, she was Beatrice*** to ▷Gielgud's Benedick (Phoenix, 1952), and she played Gertrude (Phoenix, 1955) to ▷Paul Scofield's Hamlet.

Young, Charles Mayne (1777–1856) Shakespearian (a tragedian principally) with a fine, melodious voice, who acted with ▷John Philip Kemble at Covent Garden and succeeded him in 1811. Among his parts were Hamlet, Macbeth, Brutus and Cassius.

Zeffirelli, Franco (b.1923) Italian director and designer whose lively work on various stages in England – *Romeo and Juliet* (Old Vic, 1960), *Othello* (Stratford, 1961), *Much Ado About Nothing* (National at Old Vic, 1965) – concentrated, often unwisely and superfluously, upon visual effect.

Characters that appear in biography section.

N.B. this list does not include characters whose names form either the whole or part of the title of a play (e.g. Hamlet, Juliet, or Lady Macbeth). (For abbreviations, see p. 171.)

Aaron TA
Abhorson MM
Angelo MM
Anne Bullen Hviii
Apemantus TofA
Ariel Tem.
Armado LLL
Arviragus Cym.
Autolycus WT

Bastard KJ
Banquo Mac.
Beatrice MA
Belch see Sir Toby B
Benedick MA
Berowne LLL
Bertram AW
Bolingbroke Rii,
 1Hiv, 2Hiv
Bottom MND
Brutus JC
Buckingham Riii,
 Hviii

Caliban Tem.
Cassio Oth.
Cassius JC
Claudius Ham.
Cloten Cym.
Constance KJ
Cordelia KL
Costard LLL
Countess AW

Desdemona Oth.
Dogberry MA
Doll Tearsheet 2Hiv
Duke MM
Duke TGV
Duke of Bedford Hv,
 1Hvi

Edward IV 2Hvi (as
 Edward
 Plantagenet), 3Hvi,
 Riii
Emilia Oth.
Enobarbus A&C
Falstaff 1Hiv, 2Hiv,
 Hv, MWW
Feste TN
First Gravedigger
 Ham.
First Witch Mac.
Fluellen Hv

Fool KL
Ford MWW

Gertrude see Queen G
Ghost Ham.
Gloucester KL
Guiderius Cym.·

Helen TC, Cym.
Helena AW
Helena MND
Hermia MND
Hermione WT
Hippolyta MND
Hostess Quickly
 1Hiv, 2Hiv, Hv
Hotspur Rii, 1Hiv

Iachimo Cym.
Iago Oth.
Imogen Cym.
Isabella MM

Jaques AYLI
John of Gaunt Rii
Justice Shallow 2Hiv,
 MWW

Katharina TS
Katharine see Queen
 Katherine
Kent KL
King of France AW

Lady Anne Riii
Lady Percy 1Hiv,
 2Hiv
Laertes Ham.
Launce TGV
Launcelot Gobbo
 MV
Lavache AW
Leonato MA
Leontes WT
Lucius TA

Macduff Mac.
Malvolio TN
Margaret of Anjou
 1Hvi, 2Hvi, 3Hvi,
 Riii
Marina Per.
Mark Antony JC,
 A&C
Menenius Agrippa
 Cor.

Mercutio R&J
Miranda Tem.
Mistress Ford MWW
Mistress Page MWW
Mistress Quickly
 MWW

Nurse R&J

Oberon MND
Old Lady Hviii
Olivia TN
Ophelia Ham.
Orlando AYLI
Osric Ham.

Pandarus T&C
Parolles AW
Paulina WT
Perdita WT
Petruchio TS
Polonius Ham.
Pompey MM
Portia MV
Prince Hal 1Hiv,
 2Hiv
Prospero Tem.
Puck MND
Queen Gertrude
 Ham.
Queen Katharine
 Hviii
Quince MND

Regan KL
Rosalind AYLI

Saturninus TA
Shallow see Justice S
Shylock MV
Sir Andrew
 Aguecheek TN
Sir Nathaniel LLL
Sir Toby Belch TN
Snug MND

Thaisa Per.
Theseus MND
Titania MND

Ulysses T&C

Viola TN
Volumnia Cor.

Wolsey Hviii

Abbreviations

A&C	*Antony and Cleopatra*	Mac.	*Macbeth*
AW	*All's Well That Ends Well*	MM	*Measure for Measure*
AYLI	*As You Like It*	MND	*A Midsummer Night's Dream*
CE	*The Comedy of Errors*	MV	*The Merchant of Venice*
Cor.	*Coriolanus*	MWW	*The Merry Wives of Windsor*
Cym.	*Cymbeline*	Oth.	*Othello*
1Hiv	*Henry IV, Part 1*	Per.	*Pericles*
2Hiv	*Henry IV, Part 2*	Rii	*Richard II*
Hv	*Henry V*	Riii	*Richard III*
1Hvi	*Henry VI, Part 1*	R&J	*Romeo and Juliet*
2Hvi	*Henry VI, Part 2*	T&C	*Troilus and Cressida*
3Hvi	*Henry VI, Part 3*	TofA	*Timon of Athens*
Hviii	*Henry VIII*	TA	*Titus Andronicus*
Ham.	*Hamlet*	Tem.	*The Tempest*
JC	*Julius Caesar*	TGV	*Two Gentlemen of Verona*
KJ	*King John*	TN	*Twelfth Night*
KL	*King Lear*	TNK	*The Two Noble Kinsmen*
LLL	*Love's Labour's Lost*	TS	*The Taming of the Shrew*
MA	*Much Ado About Nothing*	WT	*The Winter's Tale*

SHAKESPEARE THEATRES

Scholars go on debating about the exact appearance and theatrical use of Shakespeare's stage. It is generally agreed (see p. 6) that it was a wide platform, maybe 40 feet deep (and covered by a roof, or "heavens", supported by two pillars), which projected into an open courtyard. There the "groundlings", who had the cheapest seats, could stand close about the stage. Enclosing the theatre on three sides were seats in three galleried tiers. The only pictorial authority – and we do not know how authoritative it is – is a sketch (*c.*1596) of the Swan Theatre on Bankside, copies from one by a Dutch visitor, Johannes de Witt. Many questions remain unanswered. There were presumably three acting areas: the main stage on which most of the action would take place, well forward; a small rear section (not indicated in the Swan drawing) that could perhaps be curtained off and used when needed for such a scene as the discovery of Miranda and Ferdinand at chess towards the end of *The Tempest*; and an upper gallery that might be Juliet's balcony or the battlements of Flint Castle (*Richard II*). The gallery was immediately above the two pairs of doors in the back wall which would admit to the tiring-house, or dressing-room, beneath the stage.

Actors' costumes were rich, though specific periods (in the Roman plays, for example) were merely suggested – Elizabethan dress with classical trimmings. (A charming note in an existing inventory is "a ghost's suit and bodice".) "Properties" were numerous. There would be plenty of colour. Scenes were probably localized by the use of a few portable accessories – a tree or a table – and in any event Shakespeare usually made it clear where the action occurred: "This castle hath a pleasant seat" (*Macbeth*, I.6), "This green plot shall be our stage, this hawthorn brake our tiring-house" (*A Midsummer Night's Dream*, III.1), "In fair Verona, where we lay our scene" (*Romeo and Juliet*, Prologue), and so on.

Fire destroyed the first Globe Theatre on Bankside in June 1613 during a performance of *Henry VIII*; a second, tiled instead of thatched, was opened exactly a year later and demolished in 1644; the Swan, by 1632, had "fallen to decay"; the Fortune, used by the company of the Admiral's Men (which existed, under other names, until 1625) was burned down in 1621. From 1642 a Puritan edict closed all theatres. This was withdrawn in 1660, when King Charles II came to the throne.

Shakespeare's text at the Restoration was frequently rewritten, edited, unblushingly popularized, but in one form and another persistently acted, as indeed the plays would be for the next three hundred years. During the Restoration period the stage came permanently indoors. In their new theatres, and under the light of wax candles or lanterns, the players still used a shortened oval form of the projecting Elizabethan "apron", but there was now a curtain – though not dropped once a performance had begun – a proscenium arch and a rear-stage with painted "flats" (as yet merely a background). The theatre had begun its gradual retreat towards the complete picture-frame and the segregation of players from audience.

More important at that time, actresses had arrived. The Desdemona on December 8, 1660, in Vere Street, Clare Market, could have been Margaret Hughes. It was certainly Thomas Killigrew's company in a free version of *Othello*. The line "Here comes the lady; let her witness it" ushered in not Desdemona alone but all the English actresses. It was the cue for Mrs Barry, Mrs Bracegirdle, Peg Woffington and Kitty Clive, Jordan and Siddons; for the senior Dames who lead the modern British stage; for future stars attending the Royal Academy of Dramatic Art or the Central School; and for the newest recruit in a provincial repertory cast.

A century and a half beyond the Restoration everything in the then-ruling London theatres (the Theatres Royal of Drury Lane and Covent Garden) had been sacrificed to sheer size. Stages were enormous; the auditorium rose, tier upon tier, to a distant gallery. It could seem a day's march to the back of the pit; players had to boom out into the candle-lit immensities, always lighted before the coming of gas in the second decade of the nineteenth century made it possible to dim the house. The successive high tragedians, Kemble, Edmund Kean and Macready, were accustomed to size and spectacle. At the time of that pedantic antiquarian, Charles Kean (in the Princess's Theatre of the 1850s) spectacular presentation grew almost preposterous. Herbert Beerbohm Tree, at His Majesty's early in the twentieth century, was a more controlled Kean (though also given to excessive realism). The trouble with scenic display, even when limited, was its waste of valuable time; plays had to be lopped. Granville Barker's resolution surprised audiences at the Savoy in 1912 (*The Winter's Tale; Twelfth Night*). In his apparent obsession with speed the texts were practically uncut.

During the last half-century Shakespeare directors have in general insisted more and more on pace. Full texts are familiar. So is the Elizabethan-type stage, fortified now by the vast range of modern theatre techniques. Peter Hall said at Stratford in 1963: "The whole thing – stage, setting, costumes, speaking, creative acting – is all in a state of finding; of not expecting final solutions, but keeping open.... We want to be in a world of experiment."

There certainly we are today, still in "a state of finding", in a conflict of style and theory, a world of eccentricities, fantasies, triumphs, but withal – and in spite of the not infrequent disaster – a Shakespearian world. Though the plays are acted everywhere, a few theatres rule the classical stage. We can look at the histories of the most celebrated, the Royal Shakespeare at Stratford (as well as the town's Shakespeare record over two hundred years), and London's Old Vic, which grew up in Waterloo Road under the firm discipline of Lilian Baylis.

Stratford-upon-Avon

For well over a century after Shakespeare's death Stratford knew very little of the players (who were banned there in his later life). On a September night in 1746 a touring company led by John Ward, grandfather of John Philip Kemble and Sarah Siddons, gave a performance of *Othello* in the old Town Hall and raised £17 towards the cost of "repairing and beautifying" the Shakespeare monument in Holy Trinity Church; age had eaten away the soft stone, and visitors had a trick of breaking off bits as souvenirs. No one worried about the bicentenary of Shakespeare's birth in 1764; but five years later, David Garrick, principal actor of the period, who had been made a freeman of the borough by a council hopeful of favours to come, resolved that besides presenting to Stratford a picture and a leaden bust of Shakespeare, he must do something more. He chose what one day he called "my foolish hobby-horse", a Shakespeare "Jubilee" in September 1769 and erected an octagonal Rotunda on the Avon's west bank.

Plans were elaborate. Scores of Garrick's admirers travelled from London, and the first day went well enough, to the pleasure of local innkeepers who charged Jubilee prices. Disaster struck on the second day. Rain poured without ceasing. In the Rotunda Garrick delivered his ode ("'Tis he, 'tis he – that demi-god") to the sound of a flood outside, a downpour even worse that evening when the swollen Avon had turned the meadow into a swamp and guests for a masquerade ball had to cross to the Rotunda on duck-boards. All night and the next day the rain continued, until the third evening when it was at last possible to use the postponed fireworks. The fated Jubilee contained neither a play by Shakespeare nor more than half a line that he had written. Samuel Foote, the waspish dramatist, mocked "an ode without poetry, music without melody, dinners without victuals, and lodgings without bed . . . fireworks extinguished as soon as lit, and a gingerbread amphitheatre which tumbled to pieces as soon as it was finished".

After this, Stratford had only a few minor celebrations in nearly a hundred years. The only important events were the birth of the still-flourishing Shakespeare Club (1824) and the opening (1827) of a theatre in Chapel Lane on part of the site of Shakespeare's Great Garden; this modest place passed much of its life as a nondescript public hall and was demolished in 1872. Eight years earlier (1864) there had been a gallant but ultimately tame fortnight's festival for the tercentenary of Shakespeare's birth, its centre a timber Grand Pavilion in a paddock behind Hall's Croft. There were at least four Shakespeare plays, but few players of note.

Still, the age of silence was passing. In 1874 Charles Edward Flower, son of a local brewer, Edward Fordham Flower (who had been mayor at the tercentenary), gave as a site for a Shakespeare theatre the two riverside acres where Garrick's Rotunda had stood in the September rain, and a Shakespeare Memorial Association was founded. London critics described this as "presumptuous", but on Shakespeare's birthday, April 23, 1879, a new theatre, towered, many-gabled and turreted, and in the brightest red brick ("a striped sugar-stick" someone said), waited for its official opening. It had cost £20,000, most of which Charles Flower had given himself. Londoners laughed at the choice of play, *Much Ado About Nothing*, and on the night of the première rain beat down as heavily as it had done during Garrick's Jubilee. No matter: the opening performance, with Barry Sullivan as Benedick and Helen Faucit (who came especially from retirement on this one night) as Beatrice, went happily, the beginning of both a brief festival of three plays and the opening of a century of work that would end with Stratford as the world's centre of Shakespeare production.

Everything was tranquil at first. Various minor companies provided the short annual season, usually a spring fortnight. Then, on Easter Monday 1886 the Shakespeare Memorial Theatre found the man who (with only a gap or two) would be at its heart for more than thirty years. He was Frank Robert Benson. Aged twenty-seven, son of a Hampshire squire and laurelled at Oxford as actor and athlete, he had played briefly with Irving and later in a provincial touring company. When the manager abandoned it during a Scottish weekend, Benson took it over, and the followship of the Bensonians was born; a company that over the years, steadily renewing itself, became a touring university of the theatre. Benson ("F.R.B." or "Pa") was handsome and tireless; though his own work could vary like a fever-chart, on his night he was a fine actor. He trained many players who would grow into leaders of the English stage. W. Bridges-Adams, his Stratford successor in 1919, said of him: "He would have made a great headmaster or a great bishop, but the theatre was not to be denied, and he elected to become a great manager."

With Frank Benson it seemed always to be four o'clock on a summer morning; his life had the freshness of daybreak. An irresistible, sometimes vague, idealist, he has been accused tediously of an obsession with sport. But he simply trained his cast in mind and body, believing that an actor should be physically fit. Shakespeare always came first, "played by a company dedicated to his service". In his time he staged practically the complete canon on the awkward stage of the Memorial Theatre. "Festivals", as they were then, grew in length until there was a month in the spring and another in the summer; once, there were eighteen plays in eighteen days. In 1910 Benson was made a freeman of Stratford; in 1916, after he had played Julius Caesar in the English theatre's Shakespeare tercentenary matinée at Drury Lane, King George V knighted him in the room behind the royal box. This was the first knighting of an actor within the walls of a theatre. Benson, romantic from youth, could have wished no other setting. A pageant followed the play: a set of eight Shakespeare tableaux marshalled upon a black and gold staircase, an immense structure the width of the stage, that reached from the flies until it disappeared under the orchestra. The last tableau but one was *Coriolanus*, with Benson, his wife as Virgilia, and Geneviève Ward as Volumnia. As Sir Frank Benson descended the steps, Drury Lane rose at him in a tumultuous shout, renewed at the end when, led on by Sir George Alexander, he could barely utter his thanks: the words would not form, and standing, a sculptured Roman before an audience on its feet, crying "Benson! Bravo!", he could only bow his gratitude.

The First World War altered many things. From the summer of 1919, London's Shakespeare Memorial National Theatre Committee helped the local governors to maintain for the next three years the support a war-shaken Stratford needed. W. Bridges-Adams, a young ardent Shakespearian (nicknamed "Unabridges" because of his fidelity to the text) took over the direction from Benson and preserved the dignity of the festival, keeping it from being only an adjunct to a Shakespeare tourist-show in the new Petrol Age. After 1922 the governors became responsible for both the company and the theatre. In 1925 the Memorial received the honour of a royal charter.

It was during the next spring that a relentless fire – its cause remains a mystery to this day – destroyed the old building on the gusty afternoon of March 6, 1926. The theatre was burned to a hollow shell, only the library and picture gallery remaining. Bridges-Adams preserved the festivals' continuity by converting the shallow stage of the local cinema. Besides six remarkable seasons there (the acting of George Hayes in 1928–30 is sharply remembered), the Festival Company made three North American tours. Finally, the Americans gave two-thirds of the sum raised for the new building and its endowment.

The Prince of Wales opened the present theatre on April 23, 1932 (*Henry IV, Part 1* in the afternoon; *Part 2* at night). A few weeks later Frank Benson played Shylock in an all-star matinée of *The Merchant of Venice*. Built in red and smoke-grey bricks to the design of Elisabeth Scott, the second Memorial Theatre was much criticized, but fifty years later it is so weathered and familiar that early doubts are forgotten. In its first season 115,000 people visited a festival that lasted from Easter to Michaelmas; by 1939 the number had risen to 200,000. Strangely, during those eight financially triumphant years there was little for historical comment, except the fantastications of the Russian guest-director, Theodore Komisarjevsky (his *King Lear*, for example, in 1936). Bridges-Adams resigned after 1934 – a friendly parting, but he feared that with its newly acquired tourist support the theatre might slip into complacent parochialism. The scholarly Ben Iden Payne came next, a director with experience in the United States and Britain, whose Elizabethan-style productions, helpful sometimes, could be perilously dull. Moreover, projection in the new theatre was difficult: playing on its stage, said Baliol Holloway glumly, was like addressing Boulogne from Folkestone. The gulf between actor and audience had begun to nag at the mind like a misprint in a fine edition.

War did not stop the festivals; the principal visitors then were members of the Allied forces. After Payne left, two directors came and went, Milton Rosmer (1943) and Robert Atkins (1944–5). At length, in 1946, Sir Barry Jackson, coming across from the Birmingham Repertory to administer both the theatre and the festival, controlled the first of three famous seasons. He refused to crush the premières into one early week or ten days, and introduced to Stratford such people – among others who would be redoubtable names later on – as Peter Brook and Paul Scofield. Surprisingly his contract was not renewed after 1948; though he had shown his belief in youth, the governors looked for a younger man. Anthony Quayle, the actor, who was thirty four, succeeded him. Within the next eleven years – first under Quayle, then jointly (from 1952) under Quayle and Glen Byam Shaw, and from 1956 under Shaw alone – the Memorial Theatre was the home, season by season, of a constellation of classical players: John Gielgud, Peggy Ashcroft, Michael Redgrave, Laurence Olivier, Edith Evans, Charles Laughton, and many others. It was during this period, in 1955, that with Peter Brook's uncanny production of *Titus Andronicus* (Olivier as Titus) Stratford at last completed the full Shakespeare canon. The interior of the theatre had been remodelled in 1951 and the chasm between actors and audience disappeared.

Peter Hall, who followed Shaw in 1960, was a Cambridge graduate, aged twenty-nine. In the spring of 1961 the Memorial was rechristened the Royal Shakespeare, a name less backward-looking; and from the winter of 1960 the company had also a London home, the Aldwych Theatre – hitherto an all-purpose West End house – for non-Shakespearian classics, revivals and new plays: this was in keeping with the aim "to build a strong bridge between the classical theatre and the truly popular theatre of our time". Long-debated productions of the 1960s included Peter Brook's *King Lear* (1962) and a sequence entitled *The Wars of the Roses* (1963–4) which was John Barton's two-part conflation and adaptation of the *Henry VI* chronicles, followed by *Richard III*. "We want to live in a world of experiment", said Peter Hall at a time (1963) when the RSC was recognized everywhere as the leading Shakespeare repertory company. It has gone forward without break under Trevor Nunn – just twenty-eight when in 1968 he succeeded Hall – with annual audiences of over a million and with an exhilarating intellectual diversity. True, more than once the apparent compulsion to do something fresh with a play has muffled Shakespeare's intention. One splendid break with traditional method was Peter Brook's revival of *A Midsummer Night's Dream* in 1970. We had to look at the play, set in a white-walled bevelled cube – an empty space fit for the rigours of the game – as though it had never been acted. Brook employed daring circus techniques. Every sense was sharpened: the verse, so often clouded by familiarity, reached us as new. Nothing of the play's gaiety or ultimate healing gentleness was lost. The Mechanicals were neither over-strained nor mocked. In the ebb of the night, after Puck had spoken "Give me your hands, if we be friends," he jumped into the house and caught the nearest member of the audience by the hand while the company followed him closely. It was a world of "sweet peace," the end of a festival, certainly the end of a production (here, after a long gap, Brook was taking over from Granville Barker) quite alien to the 19th century method e.g. Augustin Daly's (Daly's, London, 1895), when – Shaw said – Oberon was a woman, Puck behaved "like a page-boy earnestly training himself for the post of footman," and the fairies were fitted up with "portable batteries and incandescent lights which they switch on and off from time to time, like children with a new toy."

With Dame Peggy Ashcroft and John Barton, Brook is one of the directors of the Royal Shakespeare Company. Its artistic cirectors are now Trevor Nunn and Terry Hands; Sir Peter Hall is there as consultant. The RSC is formed round a core of associate artists (actors, directors, designers) who seek, by working together for a long period with shared ideas, to achieve a distinctive style. Frank Benson would have recognised the aim.

Nowadays a Stratford season lasts for nearly an entire year. A subsidiary intimate studio-theatre, called The Other Place, is matched in London by the Warehouse at the foot of a street in Seven Dials. The studios do not keep to Shakespeare alone. Their programmes have moved between John Ford (*Perkin Warbeck*) and Beaumont and Fletcher (*The Maid's Tragedy*), O'Neill, Chekhov, Brecht, and a number of modern plays varying in quality. But Shakespeare is the RSC's dramatist; devotees from every part of the world come to what in Benson's time was still a quiet market-town. We can wonder what Daniel Baker, the puritan High Bailiff who banned the players while Shakespeare was still alive, would have said about this "sufferance" of plays "againste the example of other well-gooverned citties and burrowes."

The Old Vic

One of the best-loved theatres in Britain, the Old Vic, at the junction of Waterloo Road and The Cut, south of the Thames, was built in 1818 as the Royal Coburg, devoted to melodrama. Renamed the Royal Victoria, it had a turbulent early history (a "licensed pit of darkness"), but after various vagaries, and under the guidance of Emma Cons (1838–1912), it modulated in 1880 to the Royal Victoria Hall and Coffee Tavern. This developed into a kind of South London Mission, with variety shows, ballad concerts and lantern lectures – wholesome entertainment for working-class Lambeth.

Miss Cons's niece, the twenty-three-year-old Lilian Baylis, arriving in 1898 to help Aunt Emmie, gave her obstinate determination to the cause. In full charge, she chose during 1914 to present Shakespeare – as well as popular opera – in her cavernous theatre with its gaslit stage, ancient stock scenery and hutches for dressing-rooms.

Robert Atkins described the Vic as it was when he went there as an actor in the middle of the First World War: "The stage was knotty; ancient "grooves" that threatened to break away from the walls, supported the flats. Front curtain and some scenic cloths rose and fell on heavy tumblers that often dropped with a bump during the performance. The footlights were incandescent burners; number one and two battens [rows of lights fixed together] were naked gas flames caged with wire. In the prompt corner the six brass handles that controlled this gas supply were badly worn, and often, when "dimming" during a performance, both footlights and battens would pop-pop ominously and go out."

The adventure went so well under such directors ("producers" then) as Ben Greet (1915–18) and Robert Atkins (1921–5) that by the autumn of 1923, the tercentenary year of the First Folio, every play in the canon had been performed; the last was *Troilus and Cressida*. Lilian Baylis was a woman of single-hearted resolution, an intimidating want of tact, and great faith. Tyrone Guthrie said after her death: "No one with any sensibility could fail to be moved with reverence and respect for her faith; and no one but a fool could under-estimate its formidable power."

Sybil Thorndike had been a pillar of Old Vic acting during the First World War. Now, in the 1920s, many other distinguished players (Ion Swinley for one) were persuaded to come to the Vic – Edith Evans and Baliol Holloway starred during 1925–6 – and the theatre had long mobilized a loyal audience, as articulate as any in the country. From 1929 a new director, Harcourt Williams, had the young John Gielgud as leading man (Romeo, Richard II, Macbeth, Hamlet, Lear) during two renowned seasons; for the second (1930–1) Ralph Richardson joined the cast, and he remained in 1931–2.

At the New Year of 1931 the Vic also took over the disused Sadler's Wells in North London, glorified in 1843–62 by Samuel Phelps, who said of himself: "I have produced worthily 34 of Shakespeare's plays which no individual manager ever did before. They were acted in my theatre 4,000 times." This may have been true; but, as rebuilt, the new Wells proved to be inconvenient for modern classical use. After a few years the Shakespeare company, ceasing to move between Waterloo Road and Islington, remained at the Vic and left the Wells free for opera and ballet. During the 1930s the twin theatres, still at first under Harcourt Williams, had the serene presence of Peggy Ashcroft (1932–3); under Guthrie (1933–4) a company that included Charles Laughton and Flora Robson; and under Henry Cass (1934–6), Maurice Evans – lost to

America from the autumn of 1935 – and Vivienne Bennett. Guthrie returned; and presently (1937) Laurence Olivier's Hamlet and Henry V announced the rise of another major Shakespearian. Lilian Baylis died in November 1937; she had seen the Vic become, in effect, the English National Theatre, and its reputation would stand the ensuing changes and chances.

There were many. In the spring of 1940 Gielgud acted King Lear and Prospero; in 1941 the theatre was bombed. When it reopened in 1950 after nearly a decade, the name of the Vic meant more than ever; its company's West End work at the New (today the Albery) between 1944 and the spring of 1950 had moved ineffaceably into the records. For much of the time Olivier, Richardson and the director John Burrell (b.1910) administered the company. These were the years of a famous *Richard III* (1944), with Olivier moving across the play like a sable cloud; the two *Henry IV* chronicles (1945), with Richardson's Falstaff (still unmatched in total accomplishment) and Olivier's Hotspur and Shallow; and in 1946 Olivier's own production of *King Lear*. Hugh Hunt came up in 1949 from another Old Vic company at the ancient and beautiful Theatre Royal in Bristol, which had been honoured for its classical revivals, and he directed Michael Redgrave in such parts as Berowne and Hamlet.

Ultimately, and now under Hunt, the Waterloo Road theatre reopened on November 14, 1950. Edith Evans, at the première of *Twelfth Night*, spoke Christopher Hassall's prologue "London, be glad! your Shakespeare's home again", with its line: "Illyria next stop after Waterloo". Settling down was not easy. The demanding and temperamental Donald Wolfit stayed briefly in two non-Shakespearian revivals by Guthrie, one of them Marlowe's *Tamburlaine*. From 1953 Michael Benthall, a sensitive pictorial director, controlled the Vic during a period that within five years covered every Folio play: a feat later undervalued (especially by writers who were not there). Here such players as Barbara Jefford, John Neville and Paul Rogers came to flower. Finally, years of more humdrum achievement ended in June 1963 before the new National Theatre company, under Sir Laurence Olivier and as yet without a building of its own, took over the Vic and opened – rightly with *Hamlet* – on October 22. Internally, the Vic was still the theatre of what the writer Alan Pryce-Jones had called "gas-bracket rococo and plaster lace".

During the National's twelve years Shakespeare had to take his turn among other dramatists, though two occasions at least were redoubtable: the *Othello* of 1964 and (at the Cambridge Theatre during a West End season in 1970) a *Merchant of Venice*, in each of which Olivier was dominating. At the end of 1975 the National company left for its new theatre on the South Bank (much attacked, just as the Shakespeare Memorial had been at Stratford almost half a century before); and at the Vic, after transient trivialities, the Prospect Theatre company, already reputed in and out of London, appeared under Toby Robertson's guidance. This seemed to be the theatre's natural tenant. In 1979, after a few years' admirable work, Prospect became known officially as the Old Vic Company. That summer its *Hamlet*, with Derek Jacobi (who had been prominent in the National years of the 1960s), arrived at Elsinore in Denmark during a long international tour. Lilian Baylis, who had seen Olivier acting for the Vic on the Elsinore stage back in 1937, must have been happy in her own corner of Elysium. The theatre's present artistic director is Timothy West.

Meantime, since the National company moved to its building

on the South Bank of the Thames, under Sir Peter Hall, there have been full-scale performances of *Hamlet* (1976), *Macbeth* (1978), *As You Like It* and *Richard III* (1979), and *Othello* (1980), the first on the proscenium stage of the Lyttelton Theatre and the others on the open stage of the Olivier Theatre.

Stratford, Ontario

The mere coincidence of names first suggested to a local journalist, Tom Patterson, the possibility of an annual Shakespeare Festival in the Canadian Stratford, a small Ontario town by the Canadian Avon. Tyrone Guthrie, always tempted by unexpected ideas, agreed immediately to come from England to direct on an Elizabethan "thrust" stage evolved by Tanya Moiseiwitsch, so often his designer. Originally the festivals were held in a large tent where during the summer of 1953 Alec Guinness acted Richard III, and Irene Worth was Helena in *All's Well That Ends Well*, one of Guthrie's favourite plays. It was the beginning of an enterprise that through a quarter of a century, and since 1957 in a permanent theatre, has been the main North American home of acted Shakespeare, under a variety of administrators – successively Tyrone Guthrie, Michael Langham, Jean Gascon and Robin Phillips.

The stage, in spite of alterations, remains basically the Moiseiwitsch–Guthrie creation. Stratford, during its twenty-seven years, has worked through the Shakespeare Folio with consistent accomplishment by such visiting players as Irene Worth, James Mason, Paul Scofield, Douglas Campbell, Siobhan McKenna, Maggie Smith, Pauline Jameson, Brian Bedford and Margaret Tyzack; and by a powerful group of Canadians for whom Stratford is, in effect, a National Theatre. Among them are Christopher Plummer, William Hutt, Douglas Rain, Frances Hyland, Pat Galloway, John Colicos, William Needles, Kate Reid and Martha Henry. The summer festival, which has given international fame to its inconspicuous town, is directed by Robin Phillips, who went to Canada in 1974.

SHAKESPEARE FESTIVALS IN THE UNITED STATES

By the mid-1970s at least twenty-six Shakespeare festivals existed in the United States. The plays are done mostly during the summer at indoor theatres: some of these, Ashland (Oregon) for one, use the "Elizabethan" manner. The quality of production varies between the highly sophisticated and professional and the amateurish. Among the principal festivals are these:

New York

Conceived and nursed by Joseph Papp, the New York Shakespeare Festival derived from his small but intensive Shakespeare Workshop of 1953. By 1956 he had engaged Stuart Vaughan to direct *Julius Caesar* and *The Taming of the Shrew* (with Colleen Dewhurst) at the East River Amphitheatre. In 1957 Papp had presented a mobile *Romeo and Juliet, Two Gentlemen of Verona* and *Macbeth*, the last two settling in Central Park; also *Richard III* and

As You Like It which Vaughan directed at the Hecksher. Over the years there have been other indoor productions – at the Public Theatre in downtown New York and at the Newhouse, Lincoln Center – but the festival is most regarded for its free outdoor Shakespeare in the summer at the huge and recently reconstructed Delacorte in Central Park. There are several Delacorte productions each summer, a list that now includes *The Taming of the Shrew*, *The Tempest*, both parts of *Henry IV*, *The Comedy of Errors*, *Twelfth Night*, *King Lear*, *Much Ado About Nothing*, *Othello*, *Henry V*, *Pericles*, *The Merry Wives of Windsor*, *Titus Adronicus* and *Timon of Athens*. Among the leading players have been Colleen Dewhurst, James Earl Jones, Sam Waterston, Barbara Baxley and Stacy Keach; Stuart Vaughan, Gerald Freedman, Michael Kahn and Papp himself have directed.

Stratford, Connecticut

The festival (on a vast indoor stage and known since 1974 as the American Shakespeare Festival) began here in 1955 when the English director Denis Carey staged *Julius Caesar* and *The Tempest* (Raymond Massey as Prospero). During 1956–9 the artistic co-directors were John Houseman and Jack Landau, then Landau alone; he was followed in the early 1960s by Allen Fletcher. Later Michael Kahn took over, and between the late 1960s and 1976 staged such plays as *Henry V*, *Othello*, *All's Well That Ends Well*, *The Merry Wives of Windsor*, *Julius Caesar*, *Anthony and Cleopatra*, *Richard II*, *Love's Labour's Lost*, *Macbeth*, *Romeo and Juliet*, *The Winter's Tale* and *As You Like It*. Companies over the years have included Raymond Massey, Morris Carnovsky, Donald Madden, Jessica Tandy, Eva Le Gallienne, Fritz Weaver, Roddy McDowell, Alfred Drake, Katharine Hepburn, Tovah Feldshuh, Moses Gunn and Christopher Plummer. They have worked, with varying degrees of success, under such directors as Denis Carey, John Houseman, Jack Landau, William Ball, Michael Kahn, Allen Fletcher, Steven Porter, Edward Payson Call, Edwin Sherin, Ward Baker and Douglas Seale.

Ashland, Oregon

Founded in 1935 by Professor Angus L. Bowmer. The Oregon Shakespeare Festival, in continuity probably the oldest in America, now employs two theatres, the indoor Angus Bowmer and the Elizabethan Outdoor: much of the Shakespeare canon has been staged with both professional and amateur players, and by 1973 the festival was giving as many as 164 performances between mid-June and early September. The original "Fortune" contract was used in constructing the Elizabethan theatre. Angus Bowmer and the designer, Richard Hay, have sustained a long association with Ashland; and among the directors have been Ben Iden Payne, who brought to America the methods of William Poel.

San Diego, California

Here, too we find the influence of B. Iden Payne. The festival rose from his fifty-minute summarized Shakespeare productions as part of the California Pacific International Exposition in 1935. There was work at San Diego before the closure in the Second World War; later the reconstructed Old Globe in Balboa Park was in regular use for the National Shakespeare Festival that reached its twenty-fifth anniversary in 1974.

SELECT GLOSSARY OF SHAKESPEARE'S ENGLISH

abram auburn
abruption abrupt cessation
aby pay the penalty for
accite to summon
accomplish to arm completely
adamant loadstone, magnet
admiral flagship
affections inclinations, desires
affeer confirm
affined bound, related
aglet-baby lace-tag, sometimes shaped as small figure
agnize acknowledge
alderliefest dearest of all
alms-drink drink finished by another
amerce to fine
ames-ace two aces: the lowest throw at dice
amort dejected
anchor hermit
ancient ensign, standard-bearer
antic grotesque, odd
antre cave
apish affected
appliance remedy
apron-men artisans
arbitrement combat, settlement
argentine silver-shining
armipotent strong in arms
aroint begone
artificer artisan
astringer keeper of goshawks
atomies motes, dust-specks in sunbeam
atone unite
attentive observant
attorneyed performed by proxy
avouch make good
awful striking awe

baccare go back
bacons fat men
backsword man single-stick fencer
back-trick steps taken backward in galliard
baffle to punish a perjured knight
ballow a cudgel

ban curse
bared shorn
barful difficult, full of barriers
barm yeast
basilisk fabled cockatrice able to kill with a look
bastard (can mean) sweet Spanish wine
bavin brushwood
bawbling worthless
beam balance
beck bow
beetle to overhang
belike probably
be-mete thrash
bend glance
beray foul, defile
bergomask rustic dance
beteem allow
biggen nightcap
bilboes stocks used on board ship
bird-bolt blunted arrow for shooting birds
bisson blinding
bitumed caulked with pitch
boggler person selfishly unstable
bolt short, blunt-headed arrow
bolters cloths for sifting flour
bombard big leather wine bottle
bombast cotton-wool stuffing
bona-roba whore
bottom core of the skein upon which the weaver wound his wool; dell, valley
bounds pasturage
brabble brawl
brace armour for the arms
brach hound bitch
brake thicket
brave noble; to taunt
breese gadfly
Brownist one of a puritan sect
bruit a rumour; to make known
buck-basket basket for laundry
bucking washing
Bucklersbury herbalists' street off Cheapside, London
buckram coarse stiffened linen
budget leather wallet or pouch

bum-baily bailiff
by-drinking drinking between meals

cacodemon malign spirit
caddises worsted tapes for garters
cade herring barrel
Cain-coloured reddish
caliver musket
Candy Candia (Crete)
canker-blossom worm that destroys the bud
cansticks candlesticks
cantle segment cut out
canzonet short song
carcanet necklace
carlot churl, peasant
carpet consideration unmilitary services
Cataian Chinaman
cataplasm poultice
cater-cousins intimates
catling lute-string
cautelous deceitful
chaces points in game of tennis
chambers short cannon
champain unwooded plains
changeling fickle person
chapman salesman
chaps jaws
cheater escheater, an official of the Exchequer
cheveril flexible leather
chopine high-soled shoe
christom newly christened
chuff miser
cicactrice scar
cinquepace lively dance
circumstantial indirect
clack-dish beggar's dish
clapper-claw thrash
clew ball of thread or yarn
climatures regions
clinquant glittering
cloistress nun in enclosed order
cockle-hat hat with pilgrim's sign, a cockle-shell
codling unripe apple
coffin pie-crust
cog wheedle, cheat
cognizance token
collied grimed, murky
coloquintida drug from bitter-apple (colocynth)
colour excuse
commodity consignment
composition the sum agreed upon
con memorize, learn

conceit thought, fancy, image
concupiscible lustful
confiners inhabitants
conflux flowing together
confound stun with dismay
conster construe
constringed drawn together
contagious pestilential
converted summoned
convertite penitent
cony-catch to cheat
copatain high-crowned hat
coranto quick dance
corky withered
corporal bodily (corporeal)
corrigible docile
costard a large apple
coulter plough-blade
counterfeit portrait; to pretend
Counter-gate gate of debtors' prison in London
coystrill knave
cozier cobbler
crabbed harsh
crack small boy
cracker boaster
cranks winding paths
crants garlands
crescive increasing
crisped closely and stiffly curled
cross-row alphabet
crotchets whims
crow-keeper scarecrow-boy
crown imperial the cultivated fritillary
cullionly rascally
culverin type of cannon
cunning skill; (as adjective) informed, clever
curious careful
curtal dog dog with a docked tail
curtle-axe short sword
customer common woman, prostitute
cuttle cutpurse
cypress crape

daff put off, thrust aside
damask blush-colour
darnel a weedy grass
darraign prepare
date span of life
daubery pretence
debile feeble
debonair gentle
defunctive funereal
deliver disclose
denier small copper coin

denunciation formal announcement
deracinate weed out
dern dark
derogate debased
derogately disparagingly
digest assimilate, amalgamate
dimensions bodily parts
discandy melt
disguise drunken state
disponge drip
distressful earned by toil
disvouched contradicted
dog-apes baboons
dole lamentation
dotage infatuation
dout extinguish
dowlas coarse linen
dowle feather
down-gyved fallen to the ankle
draff swill
drawer tapster
drench medicinal drink
drift scheme, meaning
drumble to move slowly, loiter
dry-beat cudgel fiercely
dudgeon dagger handle
duello duelling code
dump slow mournful song
dup to open

eager sharp, biting, desiring deeply
eale evil
ean to give birth
eftest quickest
eisel vinegar
elder-gun toy gun for child
elf tangle
emboss swollen, foaming at the mouth
empiries quacks
emulous seeking glory, covetous of praise
encumbered folded
engage pledge
engine weapon of war, plot
enseamed greasy
ensign standard *or* standard-bearer
enskied dwelling in heaven
entertain take into service
eruption unnatural calamity
escoted maintained
estate to bequeath, settle
estridge goshawk, ostrich
evitate avoid
exigent crisis
exsufflicate puffed up

eyas young hawk

facinerous wicked
fadge turn out, succeed
fairing present (noun)
falchion curved sword
falling sickness, epilepsy
fan to winnow
fang to seize
fantasy imagination (adj. fantastical)
fap drunk
farced stuffed
fardel pack (on back)
fat hot, sweaty
fatigate exhausted
favour appearance, face
featly with agility, neatly
fedary confederate
feeder servant
fee-grief private woe
fere spouse
festinate speedy
fet derived from
fettle make ready
file list
fill-horse carthorse
firk beat
flaunts ostentatious, finery
fleer sneer, grimace
flewed having large chaps
flote sea
flux secretion
foin thrust
foison harvest
foppery folly
forfended forbidden
forgetive shaping, inventive
forthrights straight paths
frampold unpleasant
frank sty
frantic mad
freestone-coloured brownish-yellow
freshes freshwater springs
frieze coarse cloth
frippery old-clothes shop
frontlet headband; a frown
frush to batter
fulsome rank
furtherance aid

gaberdine a cloak
gad sharp metal point
gage pledge
gallimaufry a wild mixture
gaskins wide loose breeches
gaudy night feast
gear business
geck butt, dupe

183

gennet (or jennet) small Spanish horse
german blood relation
germen seed
gib tomcat
gig whipping-top
giglots harlots
glaze glare
gleek gibe, jest
gloze use flattering but specious words
gnarling snarling
goodman husband
goose tailor's iron; prostitute
gorget throat armour
grange lonely country house
grate vex, annoy
gravelled perplexed
great morning broad daylight
green sickness a form of anaemia among young girls
groat four pence
guard trimming on a garment
guerdon recompense
guidon pennant
gurnet fish with large head
gust taste
guttered jagged

hackney prostitute; horse for hire
haggard wild hawk
hale drag
handfast marriage contract
handsaw dialect form of "heronshaw" (heron)
hardiment valour
heady impetuous
heaviness drowsiness
hectic fever
heft hearing
hempseed gallows-bird
herb of grace rue
hilding good-for-nothing
hive straw hat
hoboys oboes
holland fine quality linen first made in Holland
hood jealous, a jealous woman
hoodman blind blindman's buff
horn beasts cuckolds
horn-mad mad as an angry bull
horologe clock
hoxes hamstrings
hoy small coasting vessel
hugger-mugger secretly
hull to lie at anchor
hurricano hurricane

hysterica passio hysteria, choking

imbar lay bare
imbrue shed blood
immoment unimportant, trivial
immures walled confine
impawned staked
implorator one who begs
imposthume swelling, abscess
imprese device, crest
incarnadine redden
inch small island
incony fine
indifferency reasonable size
indigest shapeless
indign unworthy
indue endow
inkle tape, thread
inland cultured, civilized
inly inwardly
insculped engraved
intendment intention
intenible unretentive
intituled displayed
intrenchant invulnerable
intrinsicate intricate
Iris goddess of rainbow, Juno's messenger
iwis assuredly

jack-dog mongrel
jade inferior horse; treat with contempt
jar discord; tick of clock
jaunce going back and forth
jesses straps on a hawk's legs
jet strut
journal daily
juggler buffoon

kam nonsense; crooked
kecksies weeds (like hemlock)
keech roll of fat
keel to skim; cool
kennel gutter
kern light-armed Irish soldier
kersey plain woollen fabric
key-cold cold as metal
kibe chilblain
kindness natural instinct
knapped knocked sharply; gnaw, nibble
knot flower-bed laid out in patterns
knot-grass plant thought to check growth of animals
knotty gnarled

lade to empty by ladling

landrakers thieves
lank to shrink
lapse arrest, delay
lark's-heels larkspur
latten a brass-like alloy
laund clearing in forest
lavolt high-leaping dance
lazar leper
league friendship
leaguer camp
leasing lying
leather-coat russet apple
leiger ambassador
leman sweetheart
leviathan whale
libbard leopard
liberal gross
light wanton
limbeck alembic for distilling
limber flabby, limp
linsey-woolsey cloth made of linen and wool; hence mixture or medley
lisp with foreign accent
lockram cheap linen fabric
loggats game in which small logs of wood are thrown at stake
long purples kind of orchid
loof luff, sail away
looped full of holes
love-in-idleness pansy
lozel rascal
lubber clumsy, stupid fellow
luce pike, freshwater fish
lugged baited (of bears of bulls)
lumpish low-spirited
lurch deprive, bear off the prize
luxurious salacious
lym bloodhound

machine body
maculation impurity
maiden strewment flowers scattered on grave of unmarried girl
maim punishment
malapert impudent
malkin slut
mallard a wild drake
maltworms ale drinkers
mammet doll
mammock pull in pieces
mandragora opiate made of the mandrake root
mandrake narcotic plant with forked root
manikin puppet
mansionry abode

march-chick precocious youngster
marchpane sweetmeat, like marzipan
martlet house-martin
marybuds marigolds
maugre in spite of
mazard head
meacock cowardly, spiritless
mell become involved with
meridian highest point
metaphysical supernatural
mew cage up
miching stealthy
milch moist
mince make light of
minikin dainty
minion darling
misgraffed wrongly matched
mobled with head muffled
module image
moldwarp mole
mome blockhead
montant (fencing) upward thrust
moonish fickle
mop grimace
morisco morris-dancer
mountant lifted up
mousing mauling
mowing pulling faces
muddy-mettled dull-spirited
multipotent all-powerful
mumble-news gossip
mure wall
murrain plague
muss a scramble
mystery profession, craft

napless threadbare
natural idiot
nave hub of wheel
nayward denial
nayword password, byword
neaf fist
Nereides sea-nymphs
nervy sinewy
nether-stocks stockings
nightgown dressing-gown
nimble-pinion'd swift-winged
nole head
nook-shotten with many corners and angles
nuncio messenger
nut-hook beadle

ob a halfpenny
obsequiously with proper duty; as a mourner
occulted hidden

185

odds superiority, advantage
oeillades amorous glances
oes circles
operant active
opposing displaying
oppugnancy discord
orchard garden
ordinant provident; controlling
ordinary meal
orgillous proud
orifex opening
ort scrap
othergates otherwise, in a very different way
ouches ornaments
ounce lynx
over-peering looking with evil eye
over-topping over-ambitious
owe possess
oxlip the great cowslip

packhorse drudge
packing plotting
paddock toad
pain toil
painted specious
palliament robe of candidature
pantler pantry servant
parcel part, portion
parcel-gilt silver ornamented with gilt
partialize to be partial
partisan long-handled spear with double blade
partlet hen
passing exceeding
patch fool
peak droop, mope
pelting paltry
pennyworth bargain
perdurable lasting
peremptory presumptuous
perpend attend, ponder
phantasime fantastic fellow
phraseless beyond description
pia mater brain (lit. membrane covering brain)
picked finical
pickers thieves
pickthank toady, talebearer
pigeon-livered spiritless
pinch worry
pioner sapper, soldier of the lowest rank
pismire ant
pitch highest point of falcon's flight
pith strength

plausive plausible
pleasant jocular, facetious
point-devise precise in all particulars
points laces to hold up breeches
policy craftiness
politic cunning, scheming
pomander scent-ball
pomewater kind of apple
pomgarnet pomegranate
pompous ceremonious
portage porthole
possessed informed
posset (as a verb) to curdle
postmaster master of the post-horses
posy inscription inside a ring
pottle tankard; half a gallon
pouncet-box small perfume box with perforated lid
practice plot, treason
pranked up bedecked
pressure impression
prig thief
prime youth
primero card game
princox pert young fellow
probation examination
prodigy ominous phenomenon
prolixious superfluous
propugnation defence
proscription condemning to death without trial
proud-pied with many fine colours
psaltery stringed instrument resembling zither
puddled muddied
pudency modesty
puling whimpering
punk whore
punto (fencing) direct thrust
purblind totally or partly blind
purgation acquittal
purlieu land bordering forest
purveyor officer who goes ahead to make arrangements
puttock kite
puzzel drab, harlot

quaintly artfully
qualify to moderate
quantity scrap
quat pimple
quean hussy
quell slaughter
questant seeker, candidate
quietus settling debt, release from trials of life

quillets quibbles
quite requite
quittance discharge from debt
quoif close-fitting cap
quoted noted
quotidian a continuous fever or ague

rack cloud wisp
rackers distorters
rampired fortified
rancours irritants
ravin gulp
reave rob by force
rebate make blunt
receipt prescription
recheat horn-call that summons back hounds
recordation remembrance
rector ruler
rede advice
red lattice windows of alehouse
re-edify rebuild
regiment government
rehearse narrate
reins loins
repugnancy resistance
repured purified again
rere-mice bats
reverend dignified
revolve ponder upon
rhapsody meaningless verbiage
rheumy dank
ribaudred lewd
riggish wanton
rigol ring, crown
rivage shore
rivelled wrinkled
road roadstead
roarers violent waves
romage upheaval
ronyon scabby creature
ropery roguery
rother ox
roundel dance in a circle
rowel spur-point
roynish rude, uncouth
rubious ruby coloured
rudesby rude, boisterous fellow
runagate deserter

sack sweet white wine
Sackerson famous bear kept near Bankside theatres
sacring bell rung during Mass
salamander fabled lizard that lived in fire

sallet salad; *also* close-fitting helmet
samphire herb used in pickling
sanctuarize shelter
sarcenet flimsy silk
saucy importunate
saving no offence to
scaffoldage boards of the stage
scald mean, scurvy
scathe harm
scope full authority
scorch to cut
scotch a gash
scrimer fencer
scrip pouch
scrivener notary
scruple an apothecary's weight; a minute portion
scut tail of a deer
sea-coal mineral coal as opposed to charcoal
seconds coarse flour
septentrion north
sere withered state
serpigo skin disease
setter spy for thieves
sewer butler
shard wing-case
shark up gather up
shearman cutter of cloth
shent blamed
shive slice
shoal shallow
shoulder-shotten with a dislocated shoulder
shrewdly grievously
shrift confessional
shrine image
shuffling evasion
sicle shekel
simple (unmixed as in "simple of itself")
simples herbs
singular expert
sirrah form of address to inferior
skillet kitchen pot
skipping flighty
skirr scour
slab sticky
sleave skein of silk
sleeve-band wristband
sleided untwisted
slips leashes
slops wide breeches
slubber to scamp, do carelessly
smatch smudge
smoke smell out, suspect
smooth flatter

sneap snub
snow-broth melted snow
soft not so fast
sonance sound
sonties saints
soothing flattery
Sophy Shah of Persia
sortance agreement
soured pickled in salt
souse swoop down on
spanieled to follow like a spaniel
spaniel-fawning toadying
specialties special terms or documents
spilth spilling
spinster spinning woman
splenetive impetuous
spongy sodden with drink
sprag quick
sprat contemptible creature
springe snare
spruce affected
square quarrel
squash unripe pea-pod
squier foot-rule
staggers giddiness
staniel kind of hawk
staple fibre
state canopy
statist statesman
stigmatic marked with deformity
stint to stop, check
stithy smithy
stock-fish dried cod
stout bold
stover winter fodder for cattle
strangeness aloofness
strappado form of torture
subscription obedience
sumpter packhorse
sur-reined over-ridden
sways level keeps steady
swinge thrash
syllogism logical argument

table tablet for memoranda
tabourine soldier's side-drum
taffeta shot-silk
tag-rag common
target shield
tarre urge (dogs to fight)
tassel-gentler male falcon
tawdry-lace country necklace
teen sorrow, trouble
tendering caring for
tercel male goshawk
terrene terrestrial
tertian recurring every other day

testril sixpence
tetter scurf, eczema, impetigo
thrasonical boastful
three-pile rich velvet
threne dirge
thriftless unprofitable
thrilling piercing
thronged crushed
thrummed made of coarse yarn
thwart perverse
time-pleaser time-server
tisick cough
tithe tenth
tithe-pig given as tithe to parson
tofore formerly
tomboy harlot
tortive twisted
tosspot drunkard
toy trifling affair
trammel up catch in a net
translate transform
tray-trip game of dice in which three was the vital throw
treatise story, discourse
tremor cordis palpitation of the heart
trey throw of three in dice
tribunal dais
tropically metaphorically
trot old woman
troth fidelity
truepenny honest fellow
trunk sleeve wide sleeve
tuck rapier
tucket trumpet-call
tun-dish funnel
Turk merciless person; infidel
tushes tusks
twiggen wicker-covered, made of wicker
twilled woven
twire twinkle
twit sneer at

umber kind of ochre, earthy-brown
umbrage shadow
unaccommodated natural
unadvised unconsidered
unaneled without receiving last rites
unattained impartial
unbated unblunted
uncoined genuine
unconfirmed inexperienced
unction ointment
under-skinker tapster
unhandled not broken in
unhatched unused

unhouseled without taking the sacrament
union pearl
unkennel disclose
unrest indisposition
unthrift spendthrift
upcast a term in bowls
urchin hedgehog, hobgoblin
usance lender's interest
utensils furnishings

vagabond unlicensed traveller
vail to let fall; setting of sun
vails dues
validity value
varletry mob
vastidity immensity
vaultage cavern
vaunt-couriers forerunners
vaward in the vanguard
velure velvet
veneys bouts
ventages holes
vex afflict, torment
vigil eve of a feast-day
vindicative vengeful
virginalling as if playing on the virginals
vouch testimony
vulgarly publicly

waftage passage
wafture motion of the hand
wappened worn out
warden pear
warder ceremonial baton
warranty permission
warren game preserve
wasp-stung irritable
watering drinking

water-work water-colours
weal state
web fabric
weet to know
welkin sky
wen tumour
wezand windpipe
whelk pimple
whey-face pale
whiffler official clearing way before procession
whiles until
whist hushed
whiting-time bleaching time
whitster bleacher
whittle small knife
wimpled veiled
winnowed select
wise woman witch
wittol complacent cuckold
wood mad
woodbine honeysuckle
woollen rough blankets
worm asp, small snake
wrangler opponent
writhled wrinkled
wroth misfortune
wry askew, to swerve

yard measuring tape
yarely deftly
yaw steer unsteadily
yeast foam
yellowing yelling
yellowness jealousy
yerk stab, lash out at
younker novice; another name for the Prodigal Son

zounds! by God's wounds!

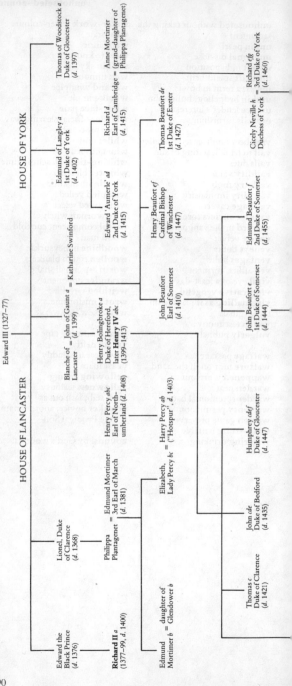

HOUSE OF LANCASTER   HOUSE OF YORK

Edward III (1327–77)

Edward the Black Prince (d. 1376)

Lionel, Duke of Clarence (d. 1368)

Philippa Plantagenet = Edmund Mortimer 3rd Earl of March (d. 1381)

Richard II a (1377–99, d. 1400)

Edmund Mortimer b = daughter of Glendower b

Elizabeth, = Harry Percy bc ("Hotspur', d. 1403)

Thomas c Duke of Clarence (d. 1421)

John de Duke of Bedford (d. 1435)

Humphrey def Duke of Gloucester (d. 1447)

Blanche of = John of Gaunt a = Katharine Swinford Lancaster (d. 1399)

Henry Bolingbroke a Duke of Hereford, later **Henry IV** abc (1399–1413)

Henry Percy abc Earl of Northumberland (d. 1408)

John Beaufort Earl of Somerset (d. 1410)

Henry Beaufort ef Cardinal Bishop of Winchester (d. 1447)

John Beaufort e 1st Duke of Somerset (d. 1444)

Edmund Beaufort f 2nd Duke of Somerset (d. 1455)

Edmund of Langley a 1st Duke of York (d. 1402)

Thomas of Woodstock a Duke of Gloucester (d. 1397)

Richard a Earl of Cambridge (d. 1415)

Anne Mortimer = (grand-daughter of Philippa Plantagenet)

Edward 'Aumerle' ad 2nd Duke of York (d. 1415)

Thomas Beaufort de 1st Duke of Exeter (d. 1427)

Cicely Neville h Duchess of York

Richard efg 3rd Duke of York (d. 1460)

190

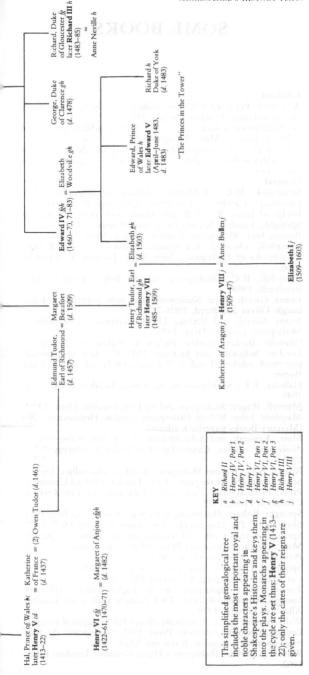

Hal, Prince of Wales *kc*
later **Henry V** *d*
(1413–22)

Katherine
of France = (2) Owen Tudor (*d.* 1461)
(*d.* 1437)

Henry VI *efg*
(1422–61, 1470–71) = Margaret of Anjou *efgh*
(*d.* 1482)

Edmund Tudor,
Earl of Richmond
(*d.* 1457)

Margaret
= Beaufort
(*d.* 1509)

Henry Tudor, Earl
of Richmond *gh*
later **Henry VII**
(1485–1509)

Katherine of Aragon *j* = **Henry VIII** *j*
(1509–47)

George, Duke
of Clarence *gh*
(*d.* 1478)

Richard, Duke
of Gloucester *fg*
later **Richard III** *h*
(1483–85)
=
Anne Neville *h*

Edward IV *fgh*
(1460–70, 71–83) = Elizabeth
Woodvil *hj*

Elizabeth *gh*
(*d.* 1503)

Elizabeth *gh*
(*d.* 1503) = Henry Tudor...

Edward, Prince
of Wales *h*
later **Edward V**
(April–June 1483,
d. 1483)

Richard *h*
Duke of York
(*d.* 1483)

"The Princes in the Tower"

Elizabeth I *j*
(1509–1603)

KEY

a	*Richard II*
b	*Henry IV, Part 1*
c	*Henry IV, Part 2*
d	*Henry V*
e	*Henry VI, Part 1*
f	*Henry VI, Part 2*
g	*Henry VI, Part 3*
h	*Richard III*
j	*Henry VIII*

This simplified genealogical tree
includes the most important royal and
noble characters appearing in
Shakespeare's Histories and keys them
into the plays. Monarchs appearing in
the cycle are set thus: **Henry V** (1413–
22); only the dates of their reigns are
given.